The International after 150 Years

The International Workingmen's Association was the prototype of all organizations of the Labor movement and the 150th anniversary of its birth (1864–2014) offers an important opportunity to rediscover its history and learn from its legacy.

The International helped workers to grasp that the emancipation of labor could not be won in a single country but was a global objective. It also spread an awareness in their ranks that they had to achieve the goal themselves, through their own capacity for organization, rather than by delegating it to some other force; and that it was essential to overcome the capitalist system itself, since improvements within it, though necessary to pursue, would not eliminate exploitation and social injustice.

This book reconsiders the main issues broached or advanced by the International – such as labor rights, critiques of capitalism, and the search for international solidarity – in light of present-day concerns. With the recent crisis of capitalism, that has sharpened more than before the division between capital and labor, the political legacy of the organization founded in London in 1864 has regained profound relevance, and its lessons are today more timely than ever.

This book was published as a special issue of *Socialism and Democracy*.

George C. Comninel has written books and articles on the French Revolution and Marxism. His next volume, *Marx's Conception of Alienation and Emancipation*, is forthcoming with Palgrave Macmillan (2015).

Marcello Musto teaches Sociological Theory at York University, Toronto. Among his edited and co-authored volumes are *Karl Marx's 'Grundrisse'* (Routledge 2008), *Marx for Today* (Routledge 2012), and *Workers Unite! The International 150 Years Later* (Bloomsbury 2014). www.marcellomusto.org

Victor Wallis is the Managing Editor of *Socialism and Democracy* and the author of several articles on Marxism and the Labor movement.

'*The International after 150 Years*, edited by Comninel, Musto, and Wallis, although marking an important anniversary, could not have come at a better time. A century and a half after its birth, the lessons of the International Working Men's Association are now once again directly relevant to the world in which we live. The global assault of capitalism on workers and popular movements everywhere demands the creation in response of a New International – one which, as Marcello Musto eloquently says in his chapter, "cannot evade that twin requirement" of the old International: "it must be plural and it must be anti-capitalist."'
John Bellamy Foster, editor of Monthly Review

'This fine volume brings together leading scholars and movement activists in commemorating a turning point in the history of workers' struggles. It strikes a fruitful balance between reflections on the labour movement's past, and critical analysis of the present global situation.'
Ellen Meiksins Wood, author of Democracy Against Capitalism

'As capital became more mobile and global in the late 20th century, labor was slow to catch up. Now, workers under siege throughout the world better understand the need for cross-border solidarity and coordinated action against common corporate adversaries. This timely collection examines the origins of socialist-inspired labor internationalism and some of the challenges facing union campaigners today in the global north and south. *The International after 150 Years* provides insights and inspiration for activists and academics alike.'
Steve Early, author of Save Our Unions:
Dispatches from a Movement in Distress

'This book is an especially timely and crucial reference now. Another global capitalist crisis deepening inequalities of wealth and income provokes again basic questions and challenges to capitalism. People need and increasingly want to learn (and build on) the critical lessons from the theories and practices of previous generations that sought to do better than capitalism. This book directly serves such needs and wants.'
Richard D. Wolff, Prof. of Economics Emeritus,
Univ. of Massachusetts,

The International after 150 Years

Labor vs capital, then and now

Edited by
George C. Comninel, Marcello Musto and Victor Wallis

Routledge
Taylor & Francis Group

LONDON AND NEW YORK

First published 2015
by Routledge
2 Park Square, Milton Park, Abingdon, Oxfordshire OX14 4RN

and by Routledge
711 Third Avenue, New York, NY 10017, USA

First issued in paperback 2017

Routledge is an imprint of the Taylor & Francis Group, an informa business

British Library Cataloguing in Publication Data
A catalogue record for this book is available from the British Library

ISBN 13: 978-1-138-06175-0 (pbk)
ISBN 13: 978-1-138-88984-2 (hbk)

Typeset in Palatino
by RefineCatch Limited, Bungay, Suffolk

Publisher's Note
The publisher accepts responsibility for any inconsistencies that may have arisen during the conversion of this book from journal articles to book chapters, namely the possible inclusion of journal terminology.

Disclaimer
Every effort has been made to contact copyright holders for their permission to reprint material in this book. The publishers would be grateful to hear from any copyright holder who is not here acknowledged and will undertake to rectify any errors or omissions in future editions of this book.

Contents

CONTENTS

Citation Information

The chapters in this book were originally published in *Socialism and Democracy*, volume 28, issue 2 (2014). When citing this material, please use the original page numbering for each article, as follows:

Chapter 1
Introduction
Victor Wallis
Socialism and Democracy, volume 28, issue 2 (2014) pp. 1–4

Chapter 2
Notes on the History of the International
Marcello Musto
Socialism and Democracy, volume 28, issue 2 (2014) pp. 5–38

Chapter 3
Documents from the International Workingmen's Association
Socialism and Democracy, volume 28, issue 2 (2014) pp. 39–58

Chapter 4
Marx and the Politics of the First International
George C. Comninel
Socialism and Democracy, volume 28, issue 2 (2014) pp. 59–82

Chapter 5
Capitalist Crisis, Cooperative Labor, and the Conquest of Political Power: Marx's 'Inaugural Address' (1864) and its Relevance in the Current Moment
Michael Joseph Roberto
Socialism and Democracy, volume 28, issue 2 (2014) pp. 83–106

CITATION INFORMATION

Chapter 6
A Common Banner: Marxists and Anarchists in the First International
Michael Löwy
Socialism and Democracy, volume 28, issue 2 (2014) pp. 107–114

Chapter 7
Race, Internationalism and Labor: Reflections upon the 150th Anniversary of the First International
Bill Fletcher Jr.
Socialism and Democracy, volume 28, issue 2 (2014) pp. 115–130

Chapter 8
The International Working Class in 1864 and Today
Ricardo Antunes
Socialism and Democracy, volume 28, issue 2 (2014) pp. 131–142

Chapter 9
The Strength of Our Collective Voice: Views of Labor Leaders from around the World
Babak Amini
Socialism and Democracy, volume 28, issue 2 (2014) pp. 143–165

Chapter 10
The German War on American Workers: Deutsche Telekom in the United States
Tony Daley
Socialism and Democracy, volume 28, issue 2 (2014) pp. 166–182

Chapter 11
Barriers and Openings to a New Socialist Internationalism: South African Histories, Strategies and Narratives
Patrick Bond
Socialism and Democracy, volume 28, issue 2 (2014) pp. 183–214

Chapter 12
Marcello Musto, ed., Workers Unite! The International 150 Years Later
Reviewed by George C. Comninel
Socialism and Democracy, volume 28, issue 2 (2014) pp. 215–220

Please direct any queries you may have about the citations to
clsuk.permissions@cengage.com

Notes on Contributors

Babak Amini is a sociology student at York University, Toronto. He immigrated to Canada from Iran at the age of 19, finished his Engineering degree at the University of British Columbia, and worked for a number of companies such as General Electric and TRIUMF before moving to Toronto. Having been brought up in a politically engaged family, he has always maintained his engagement with social and labor movements.

Ricardo Antunes is Professor of Sociology at the Institute of Philosophy and Human Sciences at UNICAMP (State University at Campinas, São Paulo). He was Visiting Research Fellow at the University of Sussex, UK, and is a Researcher at the CNPq (National Council for Scientific Research) in Brazil. His most recent book is *The Meanings of Work* (2013).

Patrick Bond was born in Northern Ireland, raised in Alabama, and educated at Swarthmore College, the Wharton School, and Johns Hopkins where his PhD on Zimbabwe's economic geography was supervised by David Harvey. His early anti-apartheid internationalism was developed by the late poet Dennis Brutus, Toronto-based scholar–activist John Saul, and former Durban marxist community organizer (now neoliberal South African finance minister) Pravin Gordhan. Since 1989 he has lived in Harare, Johannesburg, and Durban, and he currently directs the Centre for Civil Society at the University of KwaZulu-Natal: http://ccs.ukzn.ac.za

George C. Comninel is Associate Professor of Political Science at York University, Toronto. He has written books and articles on the French Revolution, the transition from feudalism to capitalism, the relationship between history and Marxism, and the continuity between Marx's early writings on human emancipation and his mature

ix

critique of political economy. His next volume, *Marx's Conception of Alienation and Emancipation*, is forthcoming with Palgrave Macmillan (2015).

Tony Daley has been a Research Economist with the Communications Workers of America since 2001 and coordinator of the T-Mobile campaign since 2009. He has taught at Wesleyan University, Connecticut College, and the National Labor College. He is the author of *Steel, State, and Labor: Labor and Adjustment in France* (1996); co-author of *Brave New World of European Labor* (1999); and editor of *The Mitterrand Era* (1996) and of a special issue of *International Journal of Political Economy* (1992–93) on "Labor Unions, Left Parties, and the New Europe."

Bill Fletcher Jr. is a racial justice, labor, and international activist and writer. He is a Senior Scholar with the Institute for Policy Studies, former president of TransAfrica Forum, co-author (with Fernando Gapasin) of *Solidarity Divided*, and author of *"They're Bankrupting Us" – And Twenty Other Myths about Unions*. Follow him on Facebook and at www.billfletcherjr.com.

Michael Löwy is Research Director Emeritus at the CNRS (National Center for Scientific Research) in Paris. His books and articles have been translated into twenty-nine languages. Among his main publications are *Georg Lukács: From Romanticism to Bolshevism* (1981) and *Fire Alarm: Reading Walter Benjamin's 'On the Concept of History'* (2005).

Marcello Musto teaches Sociological Theory at York University, Toronto. Among his edited and co-authored volumes are *Karl Marx's 'Grundrisse'* (Routledge 2008), *Marx for Today* (Routledge 2012), and *Workers Unite! The International 150 Years Later* (Bloomsbury 2014). www.marcellomusto.org

Michael Joseph Roberto teaches Contemporary World History at North Carolina Agricultural and Technical State University in Greensboro, North Carolina, and is a longstanding participant in the political life of the city. His article on cooperative ownership in Greensboro appeared in *Monthly Review* (May 2014). He is currently working on a book about fascism in the US during the interwar period.

Victor Wallis, Managing Editor of *Socialism and Democracy*, teaches in the Liberal Arts department at the Berklee College of Music, Boston. His recent publications include "Workers' Control and Revolution," in *Ours to Master and to Own: Workers' Control from the Commune to the Present* (2011) and "Song and Vision in the US Labor Movement," in *Sounds of Resistance: The Role of Music in Multicultural Activism* (2013).

Introduction

Victor Wallis

As several authors in this collection observe, global conditions of the present have moved back into alignment with those of 1864, as a result of two quite recent historical developments. First came the collapse of first-epoch socialism, which brought the world back to its pre-1917 setting of unfettered capitalism. Second was the worldwide financial meltdown of 2008, which, along with continuing unconstrained social polarization (squeezing the poor to bloat the rich), subjected the working class to an immediate level of stress comparable to that described by Marx in his Inaugural Address to the First International.

This is not to deny the immense differences between the two periods, which can perhaps be grouped under two major headings: one having to do with the configuration of nationalities, and the other with the material conditions that would constitute the point of departure for any possible alternative social order.

In today's capitalist world, national boundaries are in some respects more porous than in that of 1864. Although imperial rivalries have not entirely vanished, they pale next to the unprecedented concentration of military might – and disposition to use it anywhere – in the hands of a single major power. Equally important have been the vast worldwide displacements of both capital and people. As a consequence of this, we now have complex patterns of cross-investment among the major powers (on top of their already existing financial stake in colonized regions), and we also find new modalities of migration, in which economic migrants come to constitute a permanent sub-proletariat – or join an already existing one, "racially" defined – in the countries to which they move (with or without legal authorization).

The world of 1864 has also been left far behind in material terms. This refers at once to numbers of people, sophistication of technology,

1

and depletion of resources.[1] Social transformation has become more difficult at the same time that threats to species-survival have made it more urgent. The increasingly problematic character of national borders reminds us in political terms of a truth that has long been acknowledged – if not sufficiently popularized – at the level of science, namely, that all life converges in a unitary global ecosphere. Non-human species – notably, those that migrate – do not recognize state boundaries; nor do viruses, greenhouse gases, airborne particulate matter, weather-patterns, or rising sea-levels. What is done to the resource-base within any single locality inescapably affects the conditions of life everywhere else.

This global interdependence has existed since life began, but the strains along some of its axes have now reached a new level. The margin for permissible use of resources has drastically tightened. This means that solidarity – which implies mutual understanding, sympathy, and (eventually) full collaboration – will have to encompass more dimensions of human life than ever before. Solidarity in the 19th century was grounded theoretically in the internationalism of the Communist Manifesto. Activists of the First International saw its potential usefulness above all in protecting workers against firms that might hire scab labor from abroad. But thanks in part to Marx's participation in the practical work of that body, notions of common class interest were raised above the kind of short-term calculus that still grips too many working-class organizations today (as for instance when they prioritize capitalist growth-objectives over environmental protection).[2] English textile workers thus rejected the superficially plausible notion that their interests lay with the plantation-owners of the US South, whose slave-labor exports supplied the raw material on which their jobs depended.

Now as then, solidarity – the guiding spirit of internationalism – must rest on a broadly conceived understanding of common interest. The US is currently the scene of massive protests among fast-food workers – with support-demonstrations in thirty other countries – calling for a living wage. The forces most resistant to that demand are the same ones that seek to obstruct basic public awareness

---

1. On the severity of resource-depletion, see Michael T. Klare, *The Race for What's Left: The Global Scramble for the World's Last Resources,* New York: Henry Holt, 2012.
2. On the environment as a class issue, see Victor Wallis, "The Search for a Mass Ecological Constituency," *International Critical Thought,* vol. 3, no. 4 (2013), 496–509, and Jeremy Brecher, "'Jobs vs. the Environment': How to Counter This Divisive Big Lie," http://www.labor4sustainability.org/articles/%E2%80%98jobs-vs-the-environment%E2%80%99-how-to-counter-this-divisive-big-lie/

about the environmental crisis – and, above all, about the massive reordering of priorities required in order to effectively address that crisis. The common core-interest of the ruling class (across issues) is clear to its protagonists, whereas that of the working class, i.e., of the popular majority, continues to be perceived by its subjects only in fragmentary fashion. The building blocks of 21st-century solidarity thus present themselves in a variety of distinct spheres – from the Social Forums that sparked worldwide protest in February 2003 against the impending US assault on Iraq, to the globally inspired environmental movement 350.org (referring to the commonly understood target-concentration for atmospheric carbon dioxide).

Within the labor movement as such, the steps toward a revived internationalism have so far been halting. Much manufacturing work has shifted to countries with massive reserve armies of the urban poor. New technologies, driven by corporate criteria of efficiency, have fostered the casualization of labor, further weakening workers' capacity to organize. But where there has been (as in South Africa) a strong tradition of organizing transcending strictly trade-unionist goals, new centers of solidarity emerge. Within the now partly deindustrialized countries of the global North, unionism tends to be stronger in the service sectors, and in some of these – such as security services – organizing tactics have shifted from job-actions to corporate campaigns, which have come to focus on issues of "governance" (in the sense of rules needing to be imposed on corporate conduct). In this respect, internationalism is now coming to take on the specific form of *transnationalism*. That is, solidarity has become a matter of linking workers across borders not just at certain climactic moments (e.g., during strikes), but as a routine part of their work-lives.[3] A noteworthy expression of this, documented below, is the practice – initiated among communications workers – of union-sponsored cross-national contacts for rank-and-file workers as well as for union officials.

Consistent with this latter development is a revival of interest in workers' self-management,[4] reminding us of an aspect of Marx's thought that, as also described in these pages, informed his organizational work in the International. Together with activation of the

---

3. Jamie K. McCallum, *Global Unions, Local Power: The New Spirit of Transnational Labor Organizing*, Ithaca: Cornell University Press, 2013. See also Kim Scipes, ed., *Global Labor Solidarity*, special issue of *Working USA: The Journal of Labor and Society*, vol. 17, no. 2 (June 2014).

4. See Immanuel Ness and Dario Azzellini, eds., *Ours to Master and to Own: Workers' Control from the Commune to the Present*, Chicago: Haymarket, 2011, and Richard D. Wolff, *Democracy at Work: A Cure for Capitalism*, Chicago: Haymarket, 2012.

rank-and-file, a renewed attention to cooperative principles of work-place organization restores a sense of workers as full citizens – actively shaping social production – and not just as repositories of a particular functional interest.

In this respect, it is worth noting a final sense in which the conditions of 1864 and today differ from those prevailing during much of the intervening period. Today, as in 1864, there is no hegemonic working-class political party. The prospect of developing such a party was implicit in the work of the First International, and the fact that a party had not yet materialized explains at once the limitations in what the Association could implement and, on the other hand, the range of positions that it could consider seriously in its debates. We now have the opportunity to learn from that experience.

On the History and Legacy of the International

Marcello Musto

Opening steps

On 28 September 1864, St Martin's Hall in the very heart of London was packed to overflowing with some two thousand workmen.[1] They had come to attend a meeting called by English trade union leaders and a small group of workers from the Continent. The preparatory *Address of English to French Workmen* stated:

> A fraternity of peoples is highly necessary for the cause of labour, for we find that whenever we attempt to better our social condition by reducing the hours of toil, or by raising the price of labour, our employers threaten us with bringing over Frenchmen, Germans, Belgians and others to do our work at a reduced rate of wages; and we are sorry to say that this has been done, though not from any desire on the part of our continental brethren to injure us, but through a want of regular and systematic communication between the industrial classes of all countries. Our aim is to bring up the wages of the ill-paid to as near a level as possible with that of those who are better remunerated, and not to allow our employers to play us off one against the other, and so drag us down to the lowest possible condition, suitable to their avaricious bargaining.[2]

The organizers of this initiative did not imagine – nor could they have foreseen – what it would lead to shortly afterwards. Their idea was to build an international forum where the main problems affecting workers could be examined and discussed, but this did not include the actual founding of an organization to coordinate the trade union and political action of the working class. In reality, it gave birth to the prototype of all organizations of the workers' movement, which

---

1. This article is based upon the "Introduction" to Marcello Musto (ed.), *Workers Unite!: The International 150 Years Later* (New York and London: Bloomsbury, 2014), an anthology of key documents of the International. Citations given here as GC and PI refer to multi-volume official Minutes published under the respective titles *General Council of the First International* and *Première Internationale*. See notes 1 and 4 to the Documents section in this issue.
2. David Ryazanov, "Zur Geschichte der Ersten Internationale," in *Marx–Engels Archiv*, vol. 1 (1925), 172.

both reformists and revolutionaries would subsequently take as their point of reference: the International Working Men's Association.[3]

It was soon arousing passions all over Europe. It made class solidarity a shared ideal and inspired large numbers of men and women to struggle for the most radical of goals: changing the world. Thus, on the occasion of the Third Congress of the International, held in Brussels in 1868, the leader writer of *The Times* accurately identified the scope of the project:

> It is not ... a mere improvement that is contemplated, but nothing less than a regeneration, and that not of one nation only, but of mankind. This is certainly the most extensive aim ever contemplated by any institution, with the exception, perhaps, of the Christian Church. To be brief, this is the programme of the International Workingmen's Association.[4]

Thanks to the International, the workers' movement was able to gain a clearer understanding of the mechanisms of the capitalist mode of production, to become more aware of its own strength, and to develop new and more advanced forms of struggle. The organization resonated far beyond the frontiers of Europe, among the artisans of Buenos Aires, the early workers' associations in Calcutta, and even the labour groups in Australia and New Zealand that applied to join it.

The right man in the right place

The workers' organizations that founded the International were a motley assemblage. The central driving force was British trade unionism, whose leaders were mainly interested in economic questions; they fought to improve the workers' conditions, but without calling capitalism into question. Hence they conceived of the International as an instrument that might prevent the import of manpower from abroad in the event of strikes.

Then there were the mutualists, long dominant in France but strong also in Belgium and French-speaking Switzerland. In keeping with the theories of Pierre-Joseph Proudhon, they were opposed to

---

3. Near the end of the life of the International when considering for approval the revised statutes of the organization, members of the General Council raised the question of whether "persons" should be substituted for "men." Friedrich Engels responded that "it was generally understood that men was a generic term including both sexes," making the point that the association was and had been open to women and men, GC, V, 256.

4. Quoted in G. M. Stekloff, *History of the First International* (New York: Russell & Russell, 1968 [1928]), ii.

any working-class involvement in politics and to the strike as a weapon of struggle, as well as holding conservative positions on women's emancipation. Advocating a cooperative system along federalist lines, they maintained that it was possible to change capitalism by means of equal access to credit. In the end, therefore, they may be said to have constituted the right wing of the International.

Alongside these two components, which comprised the majority, there were still others. Third in importance were the communists. Grouped around Karl Marx and active in small circles with limited influence, they were anticapitalist: opposing the existing system of production and espousing the necessity of political action to overthrow it.

At the time of its founding, the ranks of the International also included vaguely democratic elements that had nothing to do with the socialist tradition. The picture is further complicated by the fact that some workers who joined the International brought with them a variety of confused theories, some of a utopian inspiration; while the party led by followers of Ferdinand Lassalle, which never affiliated to the International but orbited around it – was hostile to trade unionism and conceived of political action in rigidly national terms.

To secure cohabitation of all these currents in the same organization, around a program so distant from the approaches with which each had started out, was Marx's great accomplishment. His political talents enabled him to reconcile the seemingly irreconcilable, ensuring that the International did not swiftly follow the many previous workers' associations down the path to oblivion.[5] It was Marx who gave a clear purpose to the International, and Marx too who achieved a non-exclusionary, yet firmly class-based, political program that won it a mass character beyond all sectarianism. The political soul of its General Council (GC) was always Marx: he drafted all its main resolutions and prepared most of its congress reports. He was "the right man in the right place," as the German workers' leader Johann Georg Eccarius once put it.[6]

Contrary to later fantasies that pictured Marx as the founder of the International, he was not even among the organizers of the meeting at St Martin's Hall, and was a non-speaking participant.[7] Yet he

---

5. Cf. Henry Collins and Chimen Abramsky, *Karl Marx and the British Labour Movement* (London: MacMillan, 1965), 34.

6. Johann George Eccarius to Karl Marx, 12 October 1864, in *Marx–Engels-Gesamtausgabe*, vol. III/13 (Berlin: Akademie, 2002), 10.

7. Marx to Engels, 4 November 1864, in Karl Marx - Friedrich Engels, *Collected Works*, 50 vol., 1975–2005 (Moscow: Progress Publishers [henceforth MECW]), vol. 42, 1987, 16.

immediately grasped the potential in the event and worked hard to ensure that the new organization successfully carried out its mission. Thanks to the prestige attaching to his name, at least in restricted circles, he was appointed to the standing committee,[8] where he soon gained sufficient trust to be given the task of writing the *Inaugural Address* and the *Provisional Statutes of the International*. In these fundamental texts, as in many others that followed, Marx drew on the best ideas of the various components of the International. He firmly linked economic and political struggle to each other, and made international thinking and international action an irreversible choice.

It was mainly thanks to Marx's capacities that the International developed its function of political synthesis, unifying the various national contexts in a project of common struggle. The maintenance of unity was gruelling at times, especially as Marx's anticapitalism was never the dominant political position within the organization. Over time, however, partly through his own tenacity, partly through occasional splits, Marx's thought became the hegemonic doctrine. The character of workers' mobilizations, the antisystemic challenge of the Paris Commune, the unprecedented task of holding together such a large and complex organization, the successive polemics with other tendencies in the workers' movement on various theoretical and political issues: all this impelled Marx beyond the limits of political economy alone, which had absorbed so much of his attention since the defeat of the 1848 revolution and the ebbing of the most progressive forces. He was also stimulated to develop and sometimes revise his ideas, to put old certainties up for discussion and ask himself new questions, and in particular to sharpen his critique of capitalism by drawing the broad outlines of a communist society. The orthodox Soviet view of Marx's role in the International, according to which he mechanically applied to the stage of history a political theory already forged in the confines of his study, is thus totally divorced from reality.

Membership and structure

During its lifetime, the International was depicted as a vast, powerful organization. The size of its membership was always overestimated. The public prosecutor who arraigned some of its French

---

8. At the founding meeting of the International, a Standing Committee was struck to organize the association. This became its Central Council, which subsequently became known as the General Council. Henceforth, these committees are referred to here simply as the General Council.

leaders in June 1870 stated that the organization had more than 800,000 members in Europe;[9] a year later, after the defeat of the Paris Commune, *The Times* put the total at two and a half million.[10] In reality, the membership figures were much lower. It has always been difficult to arrive at even approximate estimates, and that was true for its own leaders and those who studied it most closely. But the present state of research allows the hypothesis that, at its peak in 1871–72, the membership may been over 150,000, but not much higher.

In those times, when there was a dearth of effective working-class organizations apart from the English trade unions and the General Association of German Workers, that figure was still sizeable. It should also be borne in mind that, throughout its existence, the International was recognized as a legal organization only in Britain, Switzerland, Belgium and the United States. In other countries it was at best on the margins of legality, and its members were subject to persecution. On the other hand, the Association had a remarkable capacity to weld its components into a cohesive whole. Within a couple of years from its birth, it had succeeded in federating hundreds of workers' societies; after 1868 societies were added in Spain, and following the Paris Commune sections sprang up also in Italy, Holland, Denmark and Portugal. The development of the International was doubtless uneven, yet a strong sense of belonging prevailed among those who joined it. They retained the bonds of class solidarity and responded as best they could to the call for a rally, the words of a poster or the unfurling of the red flag of struggle, in the name of an organization that had sustained them in their hour of need.[11]

Members of the International, however, comprised only a small part of the total workforce. In Britain, with the sole exception of steelworkers, the International always had a sparse presence among the industrial proletariat.[12] The great majority of members there came from tailoring, clothing, shoemaking and cabinet-making – that is, from sectors of the working class that were then the best organized and the most class-conscious. Nowhere did factory workers ever form a majority, at least after the expansion of the organization in

---

9.   See Oscar Testut, *L'Association internationale des travailleurs*, Lyon: Aimé Vingtrinier, 1870, 310.
10.   *The Times*, 5 June 1871.
11.   See Julius Braunthal, *History of the International* (New York: Nelson, 1966 [1961]), 116.
12.   Collins and Abramsky, *Karl Marx and the British Labour Movement*, 70; Jacques D'Hondt, "Rapport de synthèse," in Colloque International sur la première Internationale, *La Première Internationale: l'institution, l'implantation, le rayonnement* (Paris: Editions du Centre national de la recherche scientifique, 1968), 475.

Southern Europe. The other great limitation was the failure to draw in unskilled labour,[13] despite efforts in that direction beginning with the run-up to the first congress. The *Instructions for Delegates of the Provisional General Council* are clear on this: "Considering themselves and acting as the champions and representatives of the whole working class [the unions] cannot fail to enlist the non-society men into their ranks."[14]

In one of the key political-organizational documents of the International, Marx summarized its functions as follows: "It is the business of the International Working Men's Association to combine and generalize the spontaneous movements of the working classes, but not to dictate or impose any doctrinary system whatever."[15] Still, despite the considerable autonomy granted to federations and local sections, the International always retained a locus of political leadership. Its GC was the body that worked out a unifying synthesis of the various tendencies and issued guidelines for the organization as a whole. From October 1864 until August 1872 it met with great regularity, as many as 385 times, and debated a wide range of issues: working conditions, the effects of new machinery, support for strikes, the role and importance of trade unions, the Irish question, various foreign policy matters, and, of course, how to build the society of the future, and drafted the documents of the International.[16]

The formation of the International

Britain was the first country where applications were made to join the International; the 4000-member Operative Society of Bricklayers affiliated in February 1865, soon to be followed by associations of construction workers and shoemakers. In the first year of its existence, the GC began serious activity to publicize the principles of the Association. This helped to broaden its horizon beyond purely economic questions, as we can see from the fact that it was among the organizations belonging to the (electoral) Reform League founded in February 1865.

---

13. Ibid., 289.
14. GC, I, 340–351.
15. Musto, *Workers Unite!*, Document 2; also, Karl Marx to Paul Lafargue, 19 April 1870, in MECW, vol. 43, 491: "The General Council was not the Pope, that we allowed every section to have its own theoretical views of the real movement, always supposed that nothing directly opposite to our Rules was put forward."
16. See Georges Haupt, *L'Internazionale socialista dalla Comune a Lenin*, Turin: Einaudi, 1978, 78.

In France, the International began to take shape in January 1865, when its first section was founded in Paris. But it remained very limited in strength, had little ideological influence, and was unable even to establish a national federation. Nevertheless, the French supporters of the International, who were mostly followers of Proudhon's mutualist theories, established themselves as the second largest group at the first conference of the organization.

In the following year, the International continued to expand in Europe and established its first important nuclei in Belgium and French-speaking Switzerland. The Prussian Combination Laws, however, meant that the International was unable to open sections in what was then the German Confederation. The 5000-member General Association of German Workers – the first workers' party in history – followed a line of ambivalent dialogue with Otto von Bismarck and showed little or no interest in the International during the early years of its existence. It was an indifference shared by Wilhelm Liebknecht, despite his political proximity to Marx.

The activity of the GC in London was decisive for the further strengthening of the International. In spring 1866, with its support for the strikers of the London Amalgamated Tailors, it played an active role for the first time in a workers' struggle, and following the success of the strike five societies of tailors, each numbering some 500 workers, decided to affiliate to the International. The International was the first association to succeed in the far from simple task of enlisting trade union organizations into its ranks.[17]

In September 1866, the city of Geneva hosted the first congress of the International, with 60 delegates from Britain, France, Germany and Switzerland. By then the Association could point to a very favourable balance-sheet of the two years since its foundation, having rallied to its banner more than one hundred trade unions and political organizations. Those taking part in the congress essentially divided into two blocs. The first, consisting of the British delegates, the few Germans and a majority of the Swiss, followed the GC directives drawn up by Marx (who was not present in Geneva). The second, comprising the French delegates and some of the French-speaking Swiss, was made up of the mutualists. At that time, in fact, moderate positions were prevalent in the International.

Basing themselves on resolutions prepared by Marx, the GC leaders succeeded in marginalizing the mutualists at the congress,

---

17. Collins and Abramsky, *Karl Marx and the British Labour Movement*, 65.

and obtained votes in favour of state intervention. On the latter issue, Marx had spelled things out clearly:

> In enforcing such laws [of social reform], the working class do not fortify governmental power. On the contrary, they transform that power, now used against them, into their own agency.[18]

Thus, far from strengthening bourgeois society (as Proudhon believed), these reformist demands were an indispensable starting point for the emancipation of the working class.

Furthermore, the "instructions" that Marx wrote for the Geneva congress underline the basic function of trade unions against which not only the mutualists but others had taken a stand:

> This activity of the Trades' Unions is not only legitimate, it is necessary. It cannot be dispensed with so long as the present system of production lasts. ... On the other hand, unconsciously to themselves, the Trades' Unions were forming *centres of organization* of the working class, as the mediaeval municipalities and communes did for the middle class. If the Trades' Unions are required for the guerrilla fights between capital and labour, they are still more important as *organized agencies for superseding the very system of wages labour and capital rule.*

In the same document, Marx did not spare the existing unions his criticism. For they were:

> ... too exclusively bent upon the local and immediate struggles with capital [and had] not yet fully understood their power of acting against the system of wages slavery itself. They therefore kept too much aloof from general social and political movements.[19]

Growing strength

From late 1866 on, strikes intensified in many European countries. Organized by broad masses of workers, they helped to generate an awareness of their condition and formed the core of a new and important wave of struggles.

Although some governments of the time blamed the International for the unrest, most of the workers in question did not even know of its existence; the root cause of their protests was the dire working and living conditions they were forced to endure. The mobilizations did, however, usher in a period of contact and coordination with the International, which supported them with declarations and calls for

---

18. Musto, *Workers Unite!*, Document 2.
19. Ibid.

solidarity, raised funds for strikers, and helped fight attempts by the bosses to weaken the workers' resistance.

It was because of its practical role in this period that workers began to recognize the International as an organization that defended their interests and, in some cases, asked to be affiliated to it.[20] Workers in other countries raised funds in support of the strikers and agreed not to accept work that would have turned them into industrial mercenaries, so that the bosses were forced to compromise on many of the strikers' demands. In the towns at the centre of the action, hundreds of new members were recruited to the International. As was later observed in a GC report: "It is not the International Working Men's Association that pushes people into strikes, but strikes that push workers into the arms of the International Working Men's Association."[21] Thus, for all the difficulties bound up with the diversity of nationalities, languages and political cultures, the International managed to demonstrate the absolute need for class solidarity and international cooperation, moving decisively beyond the partial character of the initial objectives and strategies.

From 1867 on, strengthened by success in achieving these goals, by increased membership and by a more efficient organization, the International made advances all over Continental Europe. It was its breakthrough year in France in particular, where the bronze workers' strike had the same knock-on effect that the London tailors' strike had produced in England. The International now had 25 sections in Geneva alone.

But Britain was still the country where the International had its greatest presence. In the course of 1867, the affiliation of another dozen organizations took the membership to a good 50,000.[22] Nowhere else did the membership of the International ever reach that level. In contrast to 1864–67 period, however, the subsequent years in Britain were marked by a kind of stagnation. There were several reasons for this, but the main one was that the International did not manage to break through into factory industry or unskilled labour.

The growing institutionalization of the labour movement further contributed to this slowdown in the life of the International. The

---

20. Jacques Freymond, "Introduction," in PI, I, xi.
21. Various Authors, "Report of the [French] General Council," 1 September 1869, in PI, II, 24.
22. Henri Collins, "The International and the British Labour Movement: Origin of the International in England" in Colloque International, *La Première Internationale*, 34.

Reform Act, resulting from the battle first joined by the Reform League, expanded the franchise to more than a million British workers. The subsequent legalization of trade unions, which ended the risk of persecution and repression, allowed the fourth estate to become a real presence in society, with the result that the pragmatic rulers of the country continued along the path of reform, and the labouring classes, so unlike their French counterparts, felt a growing sense of belonging as they pinned more of their hopes for the future on peaceful change.[23]

The situation on the Continent was very different indeed. In the German Confederation, collective wage-bargaining was still virtually non-existent. In Belgium, strikes were repressed by the government almost as if they were acts of war, while in Switzerland they were still an anomaly that the established order found it difficult to tolerate. In France, striking was legalized in 1864, but the first labour unions still operated under severe restrictions.

This was the backdrop to the congress of 1867, where the International assembled with a new strength based on expanded membership. Marx was busy working on the proofs of *Capital* and was absent from the GC when preparatory documents were drafted as well as from the congress itself.[24] The effects were certainly felt, as is evident in the congress's focus on bare reports of organizational growth in various countries and on Proudhonian themes dear to the strongly represented mutualists.

Also discussed there was the question of war and militarism, in which the delegate from Brussels, César De Paepe, formulated what later became the classical position of the workers' movement: "so long as there exists what we call the principle of nationalities ... so long as there are distinct classes, there will be war ... the true cause of war is the interests of some capitalists."[25] In addition there was a discussion of women's emancipation,[26] and finally the congress voted in favour of a report stating that "the efforts of nations should tend toward state ownership of the means of transport and circulation."[27] This was the first collectivist declaration approved at a congress of the International.

---

23. Collins and Abramsky, *Karl Marx and the British Labour Movement*, 290–291.
24. Marx in fact continued not to attend congresses, with the exception of the crucial Hague Congress (1872).
25. Musto, *Workers Unite!*, Document 49.
26. Ibid., Document 6.
27. Ibid., Document 32.

Defeat of the mutualists

From the earliest days of the International, Proudhon's ideas were hegemonic in much of French-speaking Europe. For four years the mutualists were the most moderate wing of the International. The British trade unions, which constituted the majority, did not share Marx's anticapitalism, but nor did they have the same pull on the policies of the organization that the followers of Proudhon were able to exercise.

Marx undoubtedly played a key role in the long struggle to reduce Proudhon's influence in the International. His ideas were fundamental to the theoretical development of its leaders, and he showed a remarkable capacity to assert them by winning every major conflict inside the organization. The workers themselves, however, were already sidelining Proudhonian doctrines; it was above all the proliferation of strikes that convinced the mutualists of the error of their conceptions. And it was the workers' movement itself that demonstrated, in opposition to Proudhon, that it was impossible to separate the social-economic question from the political question.[28]

The Brussels Congress of 1868 finally clipped the wings of the mutualists. The high point came when the assembly approved De Paepe's proposal on the socialization of the means of production – a decisive step forward in defining the economic basis of socialism, no longer simply in the writings of particular intellectuals but in the program of a great transnational organization. As regards agriculture, mines and transport, the congress declared the necessity of converting land into "the common property of society," even observing the destructive environmental effect of private ownership of forests.[29] This marked an important victory for the GC and the first appearance of socialist principles in the political program of a major workers' organization.

If the collectivist turn of the International began at the Brussels Congress, it was the Basel Congress held the next year that consolidated it and eradicated Proudhonism even in its French homeland. Eleven of the French delegates even approved a new text which declared "that society has the right to abolish individual ownership of the land and to make it part of the community."[30] The 78 delegates were drawn not only from France, Switzerland, Germany, Britain and Belgium, but also from Spain, Italy and Austria, plus the National

---

28. Freymond, "Introduction," in PI, I, xiv.
29. Musto, *Workers Unite!*, Document 3.
30. PI, II, 74.

Labor Union of the United States. The constituency of the association was visibly enlarged, and the record of the proceedings as well as general reports on the activity of the congress transmitted the enthusiasm of the workers gathered there.

The Basel Congress was also of interest because Mikhail Bakunin took part in the proceedings as a delegate. When his International Alliance for Socialist Democracy had applied to join the International, the GC initially turned down the request, on the grounds that it continued to be affiliated to another, parallel transnational structure, and that one of its objectives – "the equalization of classes"[31] – was radically different from a central pillar of the International, the abolition of classes. Shortly afterwards, however, the Alliance modified its program and agreed to wind up its network of sections; its 104-member Geneva section was accordingly admitted to the International.

Marx knew Bakunin well enough, but underestimated the consequences of this step. The influence of the famous Russian revolutionary rapidly increased in a number of Swiss, Spanish and French sections (as it did in Italian ones after the Paris Commune), and already at the Basel Congress he managed to affect the outcome of deliberations. The vote on the right of inheritance, for example, was the first occasion on which the delegates rejected a proposal of the GC. Having finally defeated the mutualists and laid the spectre of Proudhon to rest, Marx now had to confront a much tougher rival, who formed a new tendency – collectivist anarchism – and sought to win control of the organization.

Before the Paris Commune

The late sixties and early seventies were a period rich in social conflicts. Many workers who took part in protest actions decided to make contact with the International. When 8000 silk dyers and ribbon weavers in Basel asked for its support, the GC could not send them more than four pounds from its own funds, but it issued a circular that resulted in the collection of another £300 from workers' groups in various countries. Even more significant was the struggle of Newcastle engineering workers to reduce the working day to nine hours,

---

31. Mikhail Bakunin, "Programme of the Alliance [International Alliance of Socialist Democracy]," in Arthur Lehning (ed.), *Michael Bakunin: Selected Writings* (London: Jonathan Cape, 1973), 174. The translation provided in this book is inaccurate and misleading. In *Fictitious Splits in the International* (GC, V, 356–409), Engels and Marx quoted directly from Bakunin's original document ("l'égalisation politique, économique et sociale des classes").

when two emissaries of the GC played a key role in stymying the bosses' attempt to introduce strikebreakers from the Continent. The success of this strike, a nationwide *cause célèbre*, served as a warning for the English capitalists, who from that time on gave up recruiting workers from across the Channel.[32]

The year 1869 witnessed significant expansion of the International all over Europe. Britain was an exception in this respect, however. While the union leaders fully backed Marx against the mutualists, they had little time for theoretical issues[33] and did not exactly glow with revolutionary ardour. This was the reason why Marx for a long time opposed the founding of a British federation of the International independent of the GC.

In every European country where the International was reasonably strong, its members gave birth to new organizations completely autonomous from those already in existence. In Britain, however, the unions that made up the main force of the International naturally did not disband their own structures. The London-based GC therefore fulfilled two functions at once: as world headquarters and as the leadership for Britain, where trade union affiliations kept some 50,000 workers in its orbit of influence.

In France, the repressive policies of the Second Empire made 1868 a year of serious crisis for the International. The following year, however, saw a revival of the organization, and new leaders who had abandoned mutualist positions came to the fore. The peak of expansion for the International came in 1870, but despite its considerable growth, the organization never took root in 38 of the 90 *départements*. The national total has been put somewhere between 30,000 and 40,000.[34] Thus, although the International did not become a true mass organization in France, it certainly grew to a respectable size and aroused widespread interest.

In Belgium, membership peaked in the early 1870s at several tens of thousands, probably exceeding the number in the whole of France. It was here that the International achieved both its highest numerical density in the general population and its greatest influence in society. The positive evolution during this period was also apparent in Switzerland. In 1870, however, Bakunin's activity divided the

---

32. Braunthal, *History of the International*, 173.
33. Freymond, "Introduction," in PI, I, xix.
34. Jacques Rougerie, in "Les sections françaises de l'Association Internationale des Travailleurs," in *Colloque International sur la premieère Internationale*, 111, spoke of "some tens of thousands."

organization into two groups of equal size, which confronted each other at the congress of the Romande Federation precisely on the question of whether his International Alliance for Socialist Democracy should be admitted to the Federation.[35] When it proved impossible to reconcile their positions, the proceedings continued in two parallel congresses, and a truce was agreed only after an intervention by the GC. The group aligned with London was slightly smaller, yet retained the name Romande Federation, whereas the one linked to Bakunin had to adopt the name Jura Federation, even though its affiliation to the International was again recognized.

During this period, Bakunin's ideas began to spread, but the country where they took hold most rapidly was Spain. In fact, the International first developed in the Iberian peninsula through the activity of the Neapolitan anarchist Giuseppe Fanelli, who, at Bakunin's request, travelled to Barcelona and Madrid to help found both sections of the International and groups of the Alliance for Socialist Democracy. His trip achieved its purpose. But his distribution of documents of both international organizations, often to the same people, was a prime example of the Bakuninite confusion and theoretical eclecticism of the time; the Spanish workers founded the International with the principles of the Alliance for Socialist Democracy.

In the North German Confederation, despite the existence of two political organizations of the workers' movement – the Lassallean General Association of German Workers and the Marxist Social Democratic Workers' Party of Germany – there was little enthusiasm for the International and few requests to affiliate to it. During its first three years, German militants virtually ignored its existence, fearing persecution at the hands of the authorities. The picture changed somewhat after 1868, as the fame and successes of the International multiplied across Europe, and both rival parties aspired to represent its German wing. The weak internationalism of the Germans ultimately weighed more heavily than any legal aspects, however, and declined still further when the movement became more preoccupied with internal matters.[36]

Against this general background, marked by evident contradictions and uneven development between countries, the International made provisions for its fifth congress. The outbreak of the Franco-Prussian war, however, left no choice but to call off the congress. The conflict at the heart of Europe meant that the top priority now was to

---

35. Jacques Freymond (ed.), *Études et documents sur la Première Internationale en Suisse* (Geneva: Droz, 1964), 295.
36. Ibid., x.

help the workers' movement express an independent position, far from the nationalist rhetoric of the time. In his *First Address on the Franco-Prussian War*, Marx called upon the French workers to drive out Louis Bonaparte and to obliterate the empire he had established 18 years earlier. The German workers, for their part, were supposed to prevent the defeat of Bonaparte from turning into an attack on the French people:

> ... in contrast to old society, with its economical miseries and its political delirium, a new society is springing up, whose international rule will be *Peace*, because its national ruler will be everywhere the same – Labour. The pioneer of that new society is the International Working Men's Association.[37]

The leaders of the Social Democratic Workers' Party, Wilhelm Liebknecht and August Bebel, were the only two members of parliament in the North German Confederation who refused to vote for the special war budget, and sections of the International in France also sent messages of friendship and solidarity to the German workers. Yet the French defeat sealed the birth of a new and more potent age of nation-states in Europe, with all its accompanying chauvinism.

The International and the Paris Commune

After the German victory at Sedan and the capture of Bonaparte, the Third Republic was proclaimed in France on 4 September 1870. In January of the following year, a four-month siege of Paris ended in the French acceptance of Bismarck's conditions; an ensuing armistice allowed the holding of elections and the appointment of Adolphe Thiers as President of the Republic. In the capital, however, Progressive-Republican forces swept the board and there was widespread popular discontent. Faced with the prospect of a government that wanted to disarm the city and withhold any social reform, the Parisians turned against Thiers and on 18 March initiated the first great political event in the life of the workers' movement: the Paris Commune.

Although Bakunin had urged the workers to turn patriotic war into revolutionary war,[38] the GC in London initially opted for silence. It assigned Marx the task of writing a text in the name of the

37. Musto, *Workers Unite!*, Document 54.
38. Arthur Lehning, "Introduction," in Idem. (ed.), *Bakunin – Archiv*, vol. VI: *Michel Bakounine sur la Guerre Franco-Allemande et la Révolution Sociale en France (1870–1871)* (Leiden: Brill, 1977), xvi.

International, but he delayed its publication for complicated, deeply held reasons. Well aware of the real relationship of forces on the ground as well as the weaknesses of the Commune, he knew that it was doomed to defeat. He had even tried to warn the French working class in his *Second Address on the Franco-Prussian War*: "Any attempt at upsetting the new government in the present crisis, when the enemy is almost knocking at the doors of Paris, would be a desperate folly. The French workmen ... must not allow themselves to be swayed by national memories of 1792."[39] A fervid declaration hailing the Commune would have risked creating false expectations among workers throughout Europe, eventually becoming a source of demoralization and distrust. His grim forebodings soon proved all too well founded, and on 28 May the Paris Commune was drowned in blood. Two days later, he reappeared at the GC with a manuscript entitled *The Civil War in France*; it was read and unanimously approved, then published over the names of all the Council members. The document had a huge impact over the next few weeks, greater than any other document of the workers' movement in the nineteenth century.

Despite Marx's passionate defence, and despite the claims both of reactionary opponents and of dogmatic Marxists eager to glorify the International,[40] the GC played no part in pushing for the Parisian insurrection. Prominent figures in the organization did play a role, but the leadership of the Commune was in the hands of its radical-republican Jacobin wing. Marx himself pointed out that "the majority of the Commune was in no sense socialist, nor could it have been."[41]

Marx had to spend whole days answering press slanders about the International and himself: "at this moment," he wrote, [he was] "the best calumniated and the most menaced man of London."[42] Meanwhile, governments all over Europe sharpened their instruments of repression, fearing that other uprisings might follow the one in Paris. Criticism of the Commune even spread to sections of the workers' movement. Following the publication of *The Civil War in France*, both the trade union leader George Odger and the old Chartist Benjamin Lucraft resigned from the International, bending under the pressure of the hostile press campaign. However, no trade union withdrew its support for the organization – which suggests once again that the

---

39. Musto, *Workers Unite!*, Document 57.
40. Georges Haupt, *Aspects of International Socialism 1871–1914* (Cambridge: Cambridge University Press, 1986), 25, warns against "the reshaping of the reality of the Commune in order to make it conform to an image transfigured by ideology."
41. Karl Marx to Domela Nieuwenhuis, 22 February 1881, MECW, vol. 46, 66.
42. Karl Marx to Ludwig Kugelmann, 18 June 1871, in MECW, vol. 44, 157.

failure of the International to grow in Britain was due mainly to political apathy in the working class.[43]

Despite the bloody denouement in Paris and the wave of calumny and government repression elsewhere in Europe, the International grew stronger and more widely known in the wake of the Commune. For the capitalists and the middle classes it represented a threat to the established order, but for the workers it fuelled hopes in a world without exploitation and injustice.[44] Insurrectionary Paris fortified the workers' movement, impelling it to adopt more radical positions. The experience showed that revolution was possible, that the goal could and should be to build a society utterly different from the capitalist order, but also that, in order to achieve this, the workers would have to create durable and well-organized forms of political association.[45]

This enormous vitality was apparent everywhere. Attendance at GC meetings doubled, while newspapers linked to the International increased in both number and overall sales. Finally, and most significantly, the International continued to expand in Belgium and Spain – where the level of workers' involvement had already been considerable before the Paris Commune – and experienced a real breakthrough in Italy. Although Giuseppe Garibaldi had only a vague idea of the Association,[46] the "hero of the two worlds" decided to throw his weight behind it and wrote a membership application that contained the famous sentence: "The International is the sun of the future."[47] Printed in dozens of workers' newssheets and papers, the letter was instrumental in persuading many waverers to join the organization.

The International opened a new section in Portugal in October 1871. In Denmark, in the same month, it began to link up most of the newly born trade unions in Copenhagen and Jutland. Another important development was the founding of Irish workers' sections in Britain; their leader John MacDonnell was appointed the GC's corresponding secretary for Ireland. Unexpected requests for affiliation came from various other parts of the world: some English workers in Calcutta, labour groups in Victoria, Australia and Christchurch, New Zealand, and a number of artisans in Buenos Aires.

---

43. Collins and Abramsky, *Karl Marx and the British Labour Movement*, 222.
44. See Haupt, *L'internazionale socialista dalla Comune a Lenin*, 28.
45. Ibid., 93–95.
46. Nello Rosselli, *Mazzini e Bakunin*, Turin: Einaudi, 1927, 323–324.
47. Giuseppe Garibaldi to Giorgio Pallavicino, 14 November 1871, in Enrico Emilio Ximenes, *Epistolario di Giuseppe Garibaldi*, vol. I, Milan: Brigola 1885, 350.

The London Conference of 1871

Two years had passed since the last congress of the International, but a new one could not be held under the prevailing circumstances. The GC therefore decided to organize a conference in London. Despite efforts to make the event as representative as possible, it was in fact more like an enlarged GC meeting. Marx had announced beforehand that the conference would be devoted "exclusively to questions of organization and policy,"[48] with theoretical discussions left to one side. He spelled this out at its first session:

> The General Council has convened a conference to agree with delegates from various countries [on] measures that need to be taken against the dangers facing the Association in a large number of countries, and to move towards a new organization corresponding to the needs of the situation. In the second place, to work out a response to the governments that are ceaselessly working to destroy the Association with every means at their disposal. And lastly to settle the Swiss dispute once and for all.[49]

Marx summoned all his energies for these priorities: to reorganize the International, to defend it from hostile forces, and to check Bakunin's growing influence. By far the most active delegate at the conference, Marx took the floor as many as 102 times, blocked proposals that did not fit in with his plans, and won over those not yet convinced.[50] The gathering in London confirmed his stature within the organization, not only as the brains shaping its political line, but also as one of its most combative and capable militants.

The most important decision taken at the conference, for which it would be remembered later, was the approval of Édouard Vaillant's Resolution IX. The leader of the Blanquists – whose residual forces had joined the International after the end of the Commune – proposed that the organization should be transformed into a centralized, disciplined party, under the leadership of the GC. Despite some differences, particularly over the Blanquist position that a tightly organized nucleus of militants was sufficient for the revolution, Marx did not hesitate to form an alliance with Vaillant's group: not only to strengthen the opposition to Bakuninite anarchism within the International, but above all to create a broader consensus for the changes deemed necessary in the new phase of the class struggle. The resolution passed in London therefore stated:

---

48. Karl Marx, 15 August 1871, in GC, IV, 259.
49. Karl Marx, 17 September 1871, in PI, II, 152.
50. Miklós Molnár, *Le déclin de la première internationale*, Geneva: Droz, 1963, 127.

... that against this collective power of the propertied classes the working class cannot act, as a class, except by constituting itself into a political party, distinct from, and opposed to, all old parties formed by the propertied classes; that this constitution of the working class into a political party is indispensable in order to ensure the triumph of the social revolution and its ultimate end – the abolition of classes; and that the combination of forces which the working class has already effected by its economic struggles ought at the same time to serve as a lever for its struggles against the political power of landlords and capitalists.

The conclusion was clear: "the economic movement [of the working class] and its political action are indissolubly united."[51]

Whereas the Geneva Congress of 1866 established the importance of trade unions, the London Conference of 1871 shifted the focus to the other key instrument of the modern workers' movement: the political party. It should be stressed, however, that the understanding of this was much broader than that which developed in the twentieth century.[52] Marx's conception should therefore be differentiated both from the Blanquists' – the two would openly clash later on – and from Lenin's, as adopted by Communist organizations after the October Revolution.

Only four delegates opposed Resolution IX at the London Conference, but Marx's victory soon proved to be ephemeral. For the call to establish what amounted to political parties in every country and to confer broader powers on the GC had grave repercussions in the internal life of the International; it was not ready to move so rapidly from a flexible to a politically uniform model of organization.[53]

Marx was convinced that virtually all the main federations and local sections would back the resolutions of the Conference, but he soon had to think again. On 12 November, the Jura Federation called a congress of its own in the small commune of Sonvilier, and, although Bakunin was unable to attend, it officially launched the opposition within the International. Bakunin's close ally James Guillaume and

---

51. Musto, *Workers Unite!*, Document 74.
52. In the early 1870s the working-class movement was organized as a political party only in Germany. Usage of the word party, whether by followers of Marx or of Bakunin, was therefore very confused. Even Marx used the term more as synonymous with class. Debate in the International between 1871 and 1872 did not focus on the construction of a political party (an expression uttered only twice at the London Conference and five times at the Congress of The Hague), but rather on the "use ... of the adjective 'political'" (Haupt, *L'Internazionale socialista dalla Comune a Lenin*, 84).
53. Jacques Freymond and Miklós Molnár, "The Rise and Fall of the First International," in Milorad M. Drachkovitch, *The Revolutionary Internationals, 1864–1943* (Stanford, CA: Stanford University Press, 1966), 27.

the other participants accused the GC of having introduced the "authority principle" into the International and transformed its original structure into "a hierarchical organization directed and governed by a committee." The Swiss declared themselves "against all directing authority, even should that authority be elected and endorsed by the workers," and insisted on "retention of the principle of autonomy of the Sections," so that the GC would become "a simple correspondence and statistical bureau."[54]

Although the position of the Jura Federation was not unexpected, Marx was probably surprised when signs of restlessness and even rebellion against the GC's political line began to appear elsewhere. In a number of countries, the decisions taken in London were judged an unacceptable encroachment on local political autonomy. Even the Belgian Federation, which at the conference had aimed at mediation between the different sides, began to adopt a much more critical stance towards London, and the Dutch too later took their distance. In Southern Europe, where the reaction was even stronger, the opposition soon won considerable support. Indeed, the great majority of Iberian Internationalists came out against the GC and endorsed Bakunin's ideas. In Italy too, the results of the London Conference were seen in a negative light. In fact, the founding congress of the Italian Federation of the International took the most radical position against the GC: they would not participate in the forthcoming congress of the International but proposed to hold an "anti-authoritarian general congress"[55] in Neuchâtel, Switzerland. This would prove to be the first act of the impending split.

Feuding across the Atlantic also harmed relations among members in London. The relations of two allies with Marx took a turn for the worse, and in Britain too the first internal conflicts began to emerge. Support for the GC also came from the majority of the Swiss, from the French (now mostly Blanquists), the weak German forces, the recently constituted sections in Denmark, Ireland and Portugal, and the East European groups in Hungary and Bohemia. But they added up to much less than Marx had expected at the end of the London Conference.

The opposition to the GC was varied in character and sometimes had mainly personal motives. Still, beyond the fascination with

---

54. Various Authors, "Circulaire du Congrès de Sonvilier," in PI, II, 264–265.
55. Various Authors, *Risoluzione, programma e regolamento della federazione italiana dell'Associazione Internazionale dei Lavoratori*, in Gian Mario Bravo, *La Prima Internazionale*, Rome: Editori Riuniti, 1978, 787.

Bakunin's theories in certain countries and Guillaume's capacity to unify the various oppositionists, the main factor militating against the resolution on "Working-Class Political Action" was an environment unwilling to accept the qualitative step forward proposed by Marx. Not only the group linked to Bakunin but most of the federations and local sections regarded the principle of autonomy and respect for the diverse realities as a cornerstone of the International. Marx's miscalculation on this score accelerated the crisis of the organization.[56]

The end of the International

The final battle came towards the end of summer 1872. After the terrible events of the previous three years – the Franco-Prussian war, the wave of repression following the Paris Commune, the numerous internal skirmishes – the International could at last meet again in congress. In the countries where it had recently taken root, it was expanding through the enthusiastic efforts of union leaders and worker-activists suddenly fired by its slogans. Yet most of the membership remained unaware of the gravity of the conflicts that raged on within its leading group.[57]

The Fifth Congress of the International took place in The Hague in September, attended by 65 delegates from a total of 14 countries. The crucial importance of the event impelled Marx to attend in person,[58] accompanied by Engels. In fact, it was the only congress of the organization in which he took part. Neither De Paepe nor Bakunin made it to the Dutch capital, but the "autonomist" contingent, a total of 25 in all, was present in strength.

By an irony of fate, the congress unfolded in Concordia Hall, though all the sessions were marked by irreducible antagonism between the two camps, resulting in debates that were far poorer than at the two previous congresses. This hostility was exacerbated by three days of wrangling over credentials. The representation of delegates was indeed skewed, not reflecting the true relationship of forces within the organization. French sections had been driven underground, and their mandates were highly debatable, yet the largest group of delegates was French; Germany had no sections of the

---

56. See Freymond and Molnár, "Rise and Fall of the First International" (note 53), 27–28.
57. Haupt, *L'Internazionale socialista dalla Comune a Lenin*, 88.
58. See Karl Marx to Ludwig Kugelmann, 29 July 1872, in MECW, vol. 44, 413, where he noted that this congress would be "a matter of life and death for the International; and before I resign I want at least to protect it from disintegrating elements."

International, yet nearly one-quarter of the delegates. Other representatives had been delegated as members of the GC and did not express the will of any section.

Approval of the Hague Congress resolutions was possible only because of its distorted composition. The most important decision taken at The Hague was to incorporate Resolution IX of the 1871 London Conference into the statutes of the Association, as a new article 7a. Political struggle was now the necessary instrument for the transformation of society since: "the lords of land and the lords of capital will always use their political privileges for the defence and perpetuation of their economic monopolies, and for the enslavement of labour. The conquest of political power has therefore become the great duty of the working class."[59]

The International was now very different from how it had been at the time of its foundation: the radical-democratic components had walked out after being increasingly marginalized; the mutualists had been defeated and many converted; reformists no longer constituted the bulk of the organization (except in Britain); and anticapitalism had become the political line of the whole Association, as well as of recently formed tendencies such as the anarcho-collectivists. Moreover, although the years of the International had witnessed a degree of economic prosperity that in some cases made conditions less parlous, the workers understood that real change would come not through such palliatives but only through the end of human exploitation. They were also basing their struggles more and more on their own material needs, rather than the initiatives of particular groups to which they belonged.

The wider picture, too, was radically different. The unification of Germany in 1871 confirmed the onset of a new age in which the nation-state would be the central form of political, legal and territorial identity; this placed a question mark over any supranational body that financed itself from membership dues in each individual country and required its members to surrender a sizeable share of their political leadership. At the same time, the growing differences between national movements and organizations made it extremely difficult for the GC to produce a political synthesis capable of satisfying the demands of all.

It is true that, right from the beginning, the International had been an agglomeration of trade unions and political associations far from easy to reconcile with one another, and that these had represented

---

59. Musto, *Workers Unite!*, Document 65.

sensibilities and political tendencies more than organizations properly so called. By 1872, however, the various components of the Association – and workers' struggles, more generally – had become much more clearly defined and structured. The legalization of the British trade unions had officially made them part of national political life; the Belgian Federation of the International was a ramified organization, with a central leadership capable of making significant, and autonomous, contributions to theory; Germany had two workers' parties, the Social Democratic Workers' Party of Germany and the General Association of German Workers, each with representation in parliament; the French workers, from Lyon to Paris, had already tried "storming the heavens"; and the Spanish Federation had expanded to the point where it was on the verge of becoming a mass organization. Similar changes had occurred in other countries.

The initial configuration of the International had thus become outmoded, just as its original mission had come to an end. The task was no longer to prepare for and organize Europe-wide support for strikes, nor to call congresses on the usefulness of trade unions or the need to socialize the land and the means of production. Such themes were now part of the collective heritage of the organization as a whole. After the Paris Commune, the real challenge for the workers' movement was a revolutionary one: how to organize in such a way as to end the capitalist mode of production and to overthrow the institutions of the bourgeois world. It was no longer a question of how to reform the existing society, but how to build a new one.[60] For this new advance in the class struggle, Marx thought it indispensable to build working-class political parties in each country. The document *To the Federal Council of the Spanish Region of the International Working Men's Association*, written by Engels in February 1871, was the most explicit statement of the GC on this matter:

> Experience has shown everywhere that the best way to emancipate the workers from this domination of the old parties is to form in each country a proletarian party with a policy of its own, a policy which is manifestly different from that of the other parties, because it must express the conditions necessary for the emancipation of the working class. This policy may vary in details according to the specific circumstances of each country; but as the fundamental relations between labour and capital are the same everywhere and the political domination of the possessing classes over the exploited classes is an existing fact everywhere, the principles and aims of proletarian policy will be identical, at least in all Western countries. ... To give up fighting our adversaries in the political

---

60. Freymond, "Introduction," in PI, I, x.

field would mean to abandon one of the most powerful weapons, particularly in the sphere of organization and propaganda.[61]

From this point on, therefore, the party was considered essential for the struggle of the proletariat: it had to be independent of all existing political forces and to be built, both programmatically and organizationally, in accordance with the national context. At the GC session of 23 July 1872, Marx criticized not only the abstentionists (opposed to any political engagement by the working class) but the equally dangerous position of "the working classes of England and America," "who let the middle classes use them for political purposes."[62] On the second point, he had already declared at the London Conference that "politics must be adapted to the conditions of all countries,"[63] and the following year, in a speech in Amsterdam immediately after the Hague Congress, he stressed:

> Someday the worker must seize political power in order to build up the new organization of labour; he must overthrow the old politics which sustain the old institutions, if he is not to lose Heaven on Earth, like the old Christians who neglected and despised politics. But we have not asserted that the ways to achieve that goal are everywhere the same. ... We do not deny that there are countries ... where the workers can attain their goal by peaceful means. This being the case, we must also recognize the fact that in most countries on the Continent the lever of our revolution must be force; it is force to which we must some day appeal in order to erect the rule of labour.[64]

Thus, although the workers' parties emerged in different forms in different countries, they should not subordinate themselves to national interests.[65] The struggle for socialism could not be confined in that way, and especially in the new historical context internationalism must continue to be the guiding beacon for the proletariat, as well as its vaccine against the deadly embrace of the state and the capitalist system.

During the Hague Congress, harsh polemics preceded a series of votes. Following the adoption of article 7a, the goal of winning political power was inscribed in the statutes, and there was also an indication that a workers' party was the essential instrument for this. The subsequent decision to confer broader powers on the GC – with 32 votes in favour, 6 against and 12 abstentions – made the situation

---

61. Musto, *Workers Unite!*, Document 69.
62. Karl Marx, 23 July 1872, in GC, V, 263.
63. Karl Marx, 20 September 1871, in PI, II, 195.
64. Musto, *Workers Unite!*, Document 56.
65. See Haupt, *L'Internazionale socialista dalla Comune a Lenin*, 100.

even more intolerable for the minority, since the Council now had the task of ensuring "rigid observation of the principles and statutes and general rules of the International," and "the right to suspend branches, sections, councils or federal committees and federations of the International until the next congress."[66]

For the first time in the history of the International, a congress approved the GC's decision to expel an organization: namely, the New York Section 12. Its motivation was that "The International Working Men's Association is based on the principle of the abolition of classes and cannot admit any bourgeois section."[67] The expulsions of Bakunin and Guillaume also caused quite a stir, having been proposed by a commission of enquiry that described the Alliance for Socialist Democracy as "a secret organization with statutes completely opposite to those of the International."[68] The call to expel Adhemar Schitzguébel, on the other hand, one of the founders and most active members of the Jura Federation, was rejected.[69] Finally, the congress authorized publication of a long report, *The Alliance for Socialist Democracy and the International Working Men's Association*, which traced the history of the organization led by Bakunin and analysed its public and secret activity country by country. Written by Engels, Lafargue and Marx, the document was published in French in July 1873.

The opposition at the congress was not uniform in its response to these attacks. On the final day, however, a joint declaration read out by the worker Victor Dave (1845–1922) from the Hague section stated:

1. We ... supporters of the autonomy and federation of groups of working men shall continue our administrative relations with the General Council ...
2. The federations which we represent will establish direct and permanent relations between themselves and all regular branches of the Association [...]
4. We call on all the federations and sections to prepare between now and the next general congress for the triumph within the International of the principles of federative autonomy as the basis of the organization of labour.[70]

This statement was more a tactical ploy – designed to avoid responsibility for a split that by then seemed inevitable – than a serious political undertaking to relaunch the organization. In this sense, it was similar

---

66. PI, II, 374.
67. Ibid., 376.
68. Ibid., 377.
69. Ibid., 378.
70. Various Authors, ["Statement of the Minority"], in Institute of Marxism-Leninism of the CC, C.P.S.U. (ed.) *The Hague Congress of the First International, vol. 1: Minutes and Documents*, Moscow: Progress, 1976, 199–200.

to the proposals of the "centralists" to augment the powers of the GC, at a time when they were already planning a far more drastic alternative.

For what took place in the morning session on 6 September – the most dramatic of the congress – was the final act of the International as it had been conceived and constructed over the years. Engels stood up to speak and, to the astonishment of those present, proposed that "the seat of the General Council [should] be transferred to New York for the year 1872–1873, and that it should be formed by members of the American federal council."[71] Thus, Marx and other "founders" of the International would no longer be part of its central body, which would consist of people whose very names were unknown. The delegate Maltman Barry, a GC member who supported Marx's positions, described better than anyone the reaction from the floor:

> Consternation and discomfiture stood plainly written on the faces of the party of dissension as [Engels] uttered the last words. . . . It was some time before anyone rose to speak. It was a *coup d'état*, and each looked to his neighbour to break the spell.[72]

Engels argued that "inter-group conflicts in London had reached such a pitch that [the GC] had to be transferred elsewhere,"[73] and that New York was the best choice in times of repression. But the Blanquists were violently opposed to the move, on the grounds that "the International should first of all be the permanent insurrectionary organization of the proletariat"[74] and that "when a party unites for struggle . . . its action is all the greater, the more its leadership committee is active, well armed and powerful." Vaillant and other followers of Blanqui present at The Hague thus felt betrayed when they saw "the head" being shipped "to the other side of the Atlantic [while] the armed body was fighting in [Europe]."[75] Based on the assumption that "the International had had an initiating role of economic struggle,"

---

71. Friedrich Engels, 5 September 1872, in PI, II, 355.
72. Maltman Barry, "Report of the Fifth Annual General Congress of the International Working Men's Association, Held at The Hague, Holland, September 2–9, 1872," in Hans Gerth, *The First International: Minutes of The Hague Congress of 1872,* Madison, WI: University of Wisconsin Press, 1958, 279–280. This report does not appear in *The Hague Congress, vol. 1.*
73. Friedrich Engels, 5 September 1872, in PI, II, 356.
74. Édouard Vaillant, *Internationale et Révolution. A propos du Congrès de La Haye,* in PI, III, 140.
75. Ibid., 142.

they wanted it to play "a similar role with respect to political struggle" and its transformation into an "international workers' revolutionary party."[76] Realizing that it would no longer be possible to exercise control over the GC, they left the congress and shortly afterwards the International.

Many even in the ranks of the majority voted against the move to New York as tantamount to the end of the International as an operational structure. The decision, approved by a margin of only three votes (26 for, 23 against), eventually depended on nine abstentions and the fact that some members of the minority were happy to see the GC relocated far from their own centres of activity. Another factor in the move was certainly Marx's view that it was better to give up the International than to see it end up as a sectarian organization in the hands of his opponents. The demise of the International, which would certainly follow the transfer of the GC to New York, was infinitely preferable to a long and wasteful succession of fratricidal struggles.

Still, it is not convincing to argue – as many have done[77] – that the key reason for the decline of the International was the conflict between its two currents, or even between two men, Marx and Bakunin, however great their stature. Rather, it was the changes taking place in the world around it that rendered the International obsolete. The growth and transformation of the organizations of the workers' movement, the strengthening of the nation-state as a result of Italian and German unification, the expansion of the International in countries like Spain and Italy (where the economic and social conditions were very different from those in Britain or France), the drift towards even greater moderation in the British trade union movement, the repression following the Paris Commune: all these factors together made the original configuration of the International inappropriate to the new times.

Against this backdrop, with its prevalence of centrifugal trends, developments in the life of the International and its main protagonists naturally also played a role. The London Conference, for instance, was far from the saving event that Marx had hoped it would be; indeed, its rigid conduct significantly aggravated the internal crisis, by failing to take account of the prevailing moods or to display the foresight needed to avoid the strengthening of Bakunin and his

---

76. Ibid., 144.
77. Miklós Molnár, "Quelques remarques à propos de la crise de l'Internationale en 1872," in Colloque International, *La Première Internationale*, 439.

group.[78] It proved a Pyrrhic victory for Marx – one which, in attempting to resolve internal conflicts, ended up accentuating them. It remains the case, however, that the decisions taken in London only speeded up a process that was already under way and impossible to reverse.

In addition to all these historical and organizational considerations, there were others of no lesser weight regarding the chief protagonist. As Marx had reminded delegates at a session of the London Conference in 1871, "the work of the Council had become immense, obliged as it was to tackle both general questions and national questions."[79] It was no longer the tiny organization of 1864 walking on an English and a French leg; it was now present in all European countries, each with its particular problems and characteristics. Not only was the organization everywhere wracked by internal conflicts, but the arrival of the Communard exiles in London, with new preoccupations and a variegated baggage of ideas, made it still more arduous for the GC to perform its task of political synthesis.

Marx was sorely tried after eight years of intense activity for the International. Aware that the workers' forces were on the retreat following the defeat of the Paris Commune – the most important fact of the moment for him – he therefore resolved to devote the years ahead to the attempt to complete *Capital*. When he crossed the North Sea to the Netherlands, he must have felt that the battle awaiting him would be his last major one as a direct protagonist.

From the mute figure he had cut at that first meeting in St Martin's Hall in 1864, he had become recognized as the leader of the International not only by congress delegates and the GC but also by the wider public. Thus, although the International certainly owed a very great deal to Marx, it had also done much to change his life. Before its foundation, he had been known only in small circles of political activists. Later, and above all after the Paris Commune – as well as the publication of his magnum opus in 1867, of course – his fame spread among revolutionaries in many European countries, to the point where the press referred to him as the "red terror doctor." The responsibility deriving from his role in the International – which allowed him to experience up close so many economic and political struggles – was a further stimulus for his reflections on communism and profoundly enriched the whole of his anticapitalist theory.

---

78. Molnár, *Le Déclin de la Première Internationale*, 144.
79. Karl Marx, 22 September 1872, in PI, II, 217.

Marx versus Bakunin

The battle between the two camps raged in the months following the Hague Congress, but only in a few cases did it centre on their existing theoretical and ideological differences. Marx often chose to caricature Bakunin's positions, painting him as an advocate of "class equalization" (based on the principles of the 1869 programme of the Alliance for Socialist Democracy) or of political abstentionism *tout court*. The Russian anarchist, for his part, who lacked the theoretical capacities of his adversary, preferred the terrain of personal accusations and insults. The only exception that set forth his positive ideas was the incomplete *Letter to La Liberté* (a Brussels paper) of early October 1872 – a text which, never sent, lay forgotten and was of no use to Bakunin's supporters in the constant round of skirmishes. The political position of the "autonomists" emerges from it clearly enough:

> There is only one law binding all the members ... sections and federations of the International. ... It is the international solidarity of workers in all jobs and all countries in their economic struggle against the exploiters of labour. It is the real organisation of that solidarity through the spontaneous action of the working classes, and the absolutely free federation ... which constitutes the real, living unity of the International. Who can doubt that it is out of this increasingly widespread organisation of the militant solidarity of the proletariat against bourgeois exploitation that the political struggle of the proletariat against the bourgeoisie must rise and grow? The Marxists and ourselves are unanimous on this point. But now comes the question that divides us so deeply from the Marxists. We think that the policy of the proletariat must necessarily be a revolutionary one, aimed directly and solely at the destruction of States. We do not see how it is possible to talk about international solidarity and yet to intend preserving States ... because by its very nature the State is a breach of that solidarity and therefore a permanent cause of war. Nor can we conceive how it is possible to talk about the liberty of the proletariat or the real deliverance of the masses within and by means of the State. State means dominion, and all dominion involves the subjugation of the masses and consequently their exploitation for the sake of some ruling minority. We do not accept, even in the process of revolutionary transition, either constituent assemblies, provincial government or so called revolutionary dictatorships; because we are convinced that revolution is only sincere, honest and real in the hand of the masses, and that when it is concentrated into those of a few ruling individuals it inevitably and immediately becomes reaction.[80]

Thus, although Bakunin had in common with Proudhon an intransigent opposition to any form of political authority, especially in the direct form of the state, it would be quite wrong to tar him with the

---

80. Mikhail Bakunin, "A Letter to the Editorial Board of *La Liberté*," in Lehning (ed.), *Michael Bakunin: Selected Writings*, 236–237.

same brush as the mutualists. Whereas the latter had in effect abstained from all political activity, the autonomists – as Guillaume stressed in one of his last interventions at the Hague Congress – fought for "a politics of social revolution, the destruction of bourgeois politics and the state."[81] It should be recognized that they were among the revolutionary components of the International, and that they offered an interesting critical contribution on the questions of political power, the State and bureaucracy.

How, then, did the "negative politics" that the autonomists saw as the only possible form of action differ from the "positive politics" advocated by the centralists? In the resolutions of the International Congress of Saint-Imier, held 15–16 September 1872 on the proposal of the Italian Federation and attended by other delegates returning from The Hague, it is stated that "all political organization can be nothing other than the organization of domination, to the benefit of one class and the detriment of the masses, and that if the proletariat aimed to seize power, it would itself become a dominant and exploiting class." Consequently, "the destruction of all political power is the first task of the proletariat," and "any organization of so-called provisional and revolutionary political power to bring about such destruction can only be a further deception, and would be as dangerous to the proletariat as all governments existing today."[82] As Bakunin stressed in "The International and Karl Marx" (another incomplete text), the task of the International was to lead the proletariat "outside the politics of the State and of the bourgeois world"; the true basis of its program should be "quite simple and moderate: the organization of solidarity in the economic struggle of labour against capitalism."[83] In fact, while taking various changes into account, this declaration of principles was close to the original aims of the organization and pointed in a direction very different from the one taken by Marx and the GC after the London Conference of 1871.[84]

This profound opposition of principles and objectives shaped the climate in The Hague. Whereas the majority looked to the "positive" conquest of political power,[85] the autonomists painted the political

---

81. Musto, *Workers Unite!*, Document 76.
82. Ibid., Document 78.
83. Mikhail Bakunin, "The International and Karl Marx," in Sam Dolgoff (ed.), *Bakunin on Anarchy* (New York: Alfred A. Knopf, 1971), 303.
84. On Bakunin's rejection of the conquest of the State by the working class organized in a political party, see Lehning, "Introduction" (note 38), cvii.
85. See James Guillaume, *L'Internationale, Documents et Souvenirs (1864–1878)*, vol. II, New York: Burt Franklin, 1969 [1907], 342.

party as an instrument necessarily subordinate to bourgeois institutions and grotesquely likened Marx's conception of communism to
the Lassallean *Volksstaat* that he had always tirelessly combated.
However, in the few moments when the antagonism left some space
for reason, Bakunin and Guillaume recognized that the two sides
shared the same aspirations. In *The Alleged Splits in the International*,
which he wrote together with Engels, Marx had explained that one
of the preconditions of socialist society was the elimination of the
power of the state:

> All socialists see anarchy as the following program: Once the aim of the prole-
> tarian movement – i.e., abolition of classes – is attained, the power of the state,
> which serves to keep the great majority of producers in bondage to a very small
> exploiter minority, disappears, and the functions of government become
> simple administrative functions.

The irreconcilable difference stemmed from the autonomist insistence
that the aim must be realized immediately. Indeed, since they considered the International not as an instrument of political struggle
but as an ideal model for the society of the future in which no kind
of authority would exist, Bakunin and his supporters proclaim (in
Marx's description):

> ... anarchy in proletarian ranks as the most infallible means of breaking the
> powerful concentration of social and political forces in the hands of the exploi-
> ters. Under this pretext, [they ask] the International, at a time when the Old
> World is seeking a way of crushing it, to replace its organization with
> anarchy.[86]

Thus, despite their agreement about the need to abolish classes
and the political power of the state in socialist society, the two
sides differed radically over the fundamental issues of the path to
follow and the social forces required to bring about the change.
Whereas for Marx the revolutionary subject *par excellence* was a particular class, the factory proletariat, Bakunin turned to the "great
rabble of the people," the so-called "lumpenproletariat," which,
being "almost unpolluted by bourgeois civilization, carries in its
inner being and in its aspirations, in all the necessities and miseries
of its collective life, all the seeds of the socialism of the future."[87]
Marx the communist had learned that social transformation required
specific historical conditions, an effective organization and a long
process of the formation of class consciousness among the masses;

---

86. Musto, *Workers Unite!*, Document 75.
87. Bakunin, "The International and Karl Marx" (note 83), 294.

Bakunin the anarchist was convinced that the instincts of the common people, the so-called "rabble," were both "invincible as well as just," sufficient by themselves "to inaugurate and bring to triumph the Social Revolution."[88]

Another disagreement concerned the instruments for the achievement of socialism. Much of Bakunin's militant activity involved building (or fantasizing about building) small "secret societies," mostly of intellectuals: a "revolutionary general staff composed of dedicated, energetic, intelligent individuals, sincere friends of the people above all,"[89] who will prepare the insurrection and carry out the revolution. Marx, on the other hand, believed in the self-emancipation of the working class and was convinced that secret societies conflicted with "the development of the proletarian movement because, instead of instructing the workers, these societies subject them to authoritarian, mystical laws which cramp their independence and distort their powers of reason."[90] The Russian exile opposed all political action by the working class that did not directly promote the revolution, whereas the stateless person with a fixed residence in London did not disdain mobilizations for social reforms and partial objectives, while remaining absolutely convinced that these should strengthen the working-class struggle to overcome the capitalist mode of production rather than integrate it into the system.

The differences would not have diminished even after the revolution. For Bakunin, "abolition of the state [was] the precondition or necessary accompaniment of the economic emancipation of the proletariat",[91] for Marx, the state neither could nor should disappear from one day to the next. In his *Political Indifferentism*, which first appeared in *Almanacco Repubblicano* in December 1873, he challenged the hegemony of the anarchists in Italy's workers' movement by asserting that:

> ... if the political struggle of the working class assumes violent forms and if the workers replace the dictatorship of the bourgeois class with their own revolutionary dictatorship, then [according to Bakunin] they are guilty of the terrible crime of *lèse-principe*; for, in order to satisfy their miserable profane daily needs and to crush the resistance of the bourgeois class, they, instead of

---

88. Ibid., 294–295.
89. Mikhail Bakunin, "Programme and Purpose of the Revolutionary Organization of International Brothers," in Lehning (ed.), *Michael Bakunin: Selected Writings*, 155.
90. Karl Marx, "Record of Marx's speech on Secret Societies," in MECW, vol. 22, 621.
91. Mikhail Bakunin, "Aux compagnons de la Fédération des sections internationales du Jura," in Arthur Lehning et al. (eds.), *Bakunin – Archiv*, vol. II: *Michel Bakounine et les Conflits dans l'Internationale*, (Leiden: Brill, 1965), 75.

laying down their arms and abolishing the state, give to the state a revolutionary and transitory form.[92]

It should be recognized, however, that despite Bakunin's sometimes exasperating refusal to distinguish between bourgeois and proletarian power, he foresaw some of the dangers of the so-called "transitional period" between capitalism and socialism – particularly the danger of bureaucratic degeneration after the revolution. In his unfinished *The Knouto-Germanic Empire and the Social Revolution*, on which he worked between 1870 and 1871, he wrote:

> But in the People's State of Marx, there will be, we are told, no privileged class at all. All will be equal, not only from the juridical and political point of view, but from the economic point of view. . . . There will therefore be no longer any privileged class, but there will be a government, and, note this well, an extremely complex government, which will not content itself with governing and administering the masses politically, as all governments do today, but which will also administer them economically, concentrating in its own hands the production and the just division of wealth, the cultivation of land, the establishment and development of factories, the organization and direction of commerce, finally the application of capital to production by the only banker, the State. . . . It will be the reign of scientific intelligence, the most aristocratic, despotic, arrogant and contemptuous of all regimes. There will be a new class, a new hierarchy of real and pretended scientists and scholars, and the world will be divided into a minority ruling in the name of knowledge and an immense ignorant majority. . . . All states, even the most republican and most democratic states . . . are in their essence only machines governing the masses from above, through an intelligent and therefore privileged minority, allegedly knowing the genuine interests of the people better than the people themselves.[93]

Partly because of his scant knowledge of economics, the federalist path indicated by Bakunin offered no really useful guidance on how the question of the future socialist society should be approached. But his critical insights already point ahead to some of the dramas of the twentieth century.

Conclusion

The International would never be the same again. The great organization born in 1864, which had successfully supported strikes and struggles for eight years, and had adopted an anticapitalist program and established a presence in all European countries, finally imploded

---

92. Karl Marx, "Political Indifferentism," MECW, vol. 23, p. 393.
93. Mikhail Bakunin, *Marxism, Freedom and the State* (London: Freedom Press, 1950), 21 [translation edited].

at the Hague Congress. In later decades, however, the workers' movement adopted a socialist program, expanded throughout Europe and then the rest of the world, and built new structures of supranational coordination. Beyond the continuity of names (the Second International from 1889–1916, the Third International from 1919 to 1943), each of these structures constantly referred to the values and doctrines of the First International. Thus, its revolutionary message proved extraordinarily fertile, producing results over time still greater than those achieved during its existence.

The International helped workers to grasp that the emancipation of labour could not be won in a single country but was a global objective. It also spread an awareness in their ranks that they had to achieve the goal themselves, through their own capacity for organization, rather than by delegating it to some other force; and that – here Marx's theoretical contribution was fundamental – it was essential to overcome the capitalist mode of production and wage labour, since improvements within the existing system, though necessary to pursue, would not eliminate dependence on employers' oligarchies.

An abyss separates the hopes of those times from the mistrust so characteristic of our own, the antisystemic spirit and solidarity of the age of the International from the ideological subordination and individualism of a world reshaped by neoliberal competition and privatization. The passion for politics among the workers who gathered in London in 1864 contrasts sharply with the apathy and resignation prevalent today.

And yet, as the world of labour reverts now to conditions of exploitation similar to those of the nineteenth century, the project of the International has once again acquired an extraordinary topicality. Today's barbarism of the "world order," ecological disasters produced by the present mode of production, the growing gulf between the wealthy exploitative few and the huge impoverished majority, the oppression of women, and the blustery winds of war, racism and chauvinism, impose upon the contemporary workers' movement the urgent need to reorganize itself on the basis of two key characteristics of the International: the multiplicity of its structure and radicalism in objectives. The aims of the organization founded in London 150 years ago are today more vital than ever. To rise to the challenges of the present, however, the new International cannot evade that twin requirement: it must be plural and it must be anticapitalist.

Translated by Patrick Camiller

Documents from the International Workingmen's Association

[The first three of the following documents are excerpted from the *General Council of the First International*[1]. Documents 4–6 are excerpted from *Première Internationale*[2] and are translated here from the French. Selection and introductory notes are by Marcello Musto; translations are by Victor Wallis.]

1. Inaugural Address of the International Workingmen's Association

Karl Marx

[Written between October 21 and 27, 1864, the text was approved by the General Council of the International Workingmen's Association (IWA) in its session of November 1. It was published three days later in the London weekly *The Bee-Hive*, and was then re-issued in the same month, along with the statutes of the organization, in a booklet entitled *Address and Provisional Rules of the Working Men's International Association*. Karl Marx was the driving force behind the IWA. He wrote all its major resolutions and was a member of the General Council (GC) from its founding until 1872. He participated in the London preparatory conferences of 1865 and 1871 and in the Hague Congress of 1872. The complete text of the Address appears in GC, I,277–287.]

Workingmen:

[*In an extensive prelude, Marx documents at length the increasing misery in the United Kingdom during the enormous expansion, since the 1840s, of England's commerce.*]

We have dwelt so long upon these facts "so astonishing to be almost incredible" because England heads the Europe of commerce and industry. It will be remembered that some months ago one of the refugee sons of Louis Philippe publicly congratulated the English agricultural laborer on the superiority of his lot over that of his less florid comrade on the

---

1. *The General Council of the First International* (Moscow: Foreign Languages Publishing House, 1962–1968), edited by the Institute of Marxism-Leninism of the C.C., C.P.S.U., 5 voll., hereafter indicated as GC.
2. *La première Internationale* (Geneva: Droz, 1962), edited by Henri Burgelin, Knut Langfeldt and Miklós Molnár, 2 voll., hereafter indicated as PI.

other side of the Channel. Indeed, with local colours changed, and on a scale somewhat contracted, the English facts reproduce themselves in all the industrious and progressive countries of the Continent. In all of them there has taken place, since 1848, an unheard-of development of industry, and an unheard-of expansion of imports and exports. In all of them, as in England, a minority of the working classes got their real wages somewhat advanced; while in most cases the monetary rise of wages denoted no more a real access of comforts than the inmate of the metropolitan poorhouse or orphan asylum, for instance, was in the least benefited by his first necessaries costing £9 15 s. 8d. in 1861 against £7 7 s. 4d. in 1852. Everywhere the great mass of the working classes were sinking down to a lower depth, at the same rate at least that those above them were rising in the social scale. In all countries of Europe it has now become a truth demonstrable to every unprejudiced mind, and only decried by those whose interest it is to hedge other people in a fool's paradise, that no improvement of machinery, no appliance of science to production, no contrivances of communication, no new colonies, no emigration, no opening of markets, no free trade, not all these things put together, will do away with the miseries of the industrious masses; but that, on the present false base, every fresh development of the productive powers of labour must tend to deepen social contrasts and point social antagonisms. Death of starvation rose almost to the rank of an institution, during this intoxicating epoch of economical progress, in the metropolis of the British empire. That epoch is marked in the annals of the world by the quickened return, the widening compass, and the deadlier effects of the social pest called a commercial and industrial crisis.

After the failure of the revolutions of 1848, all party organizations and party journals of the working classes were, on the Continent, crushed by the iron hand of force, the most advanced sons of labour fled in despair to the transatlantic republic, and the short-lived dreams of emancipation vanished before an epoch of industrial fever, moral marasm, and political reaction. ... The discoveries of new goldlands led to an immense exodus, leaving an irreparable void in the ranks of the British proletariat. Others of its formerly active members were caught by the temporary bribe of greater work and wages, and turned into "political blacks." All the efforts made at keeping up, or remodeling, the Chartist movement failed signally; the press organs of the working class died one by one of the apathy of the masses, and in point of fact never before did the English working class seem so thoroughly reconciled to a state of political nullity. If, then, there had been no solidarity of action between the

British and the continental working classes, there was, at all events, a solidarity of defeat.

And yet the period passed since the revolutions of 1848 has not been without its compensating features. We shall here only point to two great facts.

After a 30 years' struggle, fought with most admirable perseverance, the English working classes [using to their advantage] a momentaneous split between the landlords and money lords, succeeded in carrying the Ten Hours Bill. The immense physical, moral, and intellectual benefits hence accruing to the factory operatives, half-yearly chronicled in the reports of the inspectors of factories, are now acknowledged on all sides. Most of the continental governments had to accept the English Factory Act in more or less modified forms, and the English Parliament itself is every year compelled to enlarge its sphere of action. But besides its practical import, there was something else to exalt the marvellous success of this working men's measure. Through their most notorious organs of science, such as Dr. Ure, Professor Senior, and other sages of that stamp, the middle class[3] had predicted, and to their heart's content proved, that any legal restriction of the hours of labour must sound the death knell of British industry, which, vampirelike, could but live by sucking blood, and children's blood, too. In olden times, child murder was a mysterious rite of the religion of Moloch, but it was practiced on some very solemn occassions only, once a year perhaps, and then Moloch had no exclusive bias for the children of the poor. This struggle about the legal restriction of the hours of labour raged the more fiercely since, apart from frightened avarice, it told indeed upon the great contest between the blind rule of the supply and demand laws which form the political economy of the middle class, and social production controlled by social foresight, which forms the political economy of the working class. Hence the Ten Hours Bill was not only a great practical success; it was the victory of a principle; it was the first time that in broad daylight the political economy of the middle class succumbed to the political economy of the working class.

But there was in store a still greater victory of the political economy of labour over the political economy of property. We speak of the

---

3. *Editor's note*: The Inaugural Address was written in English. The English term "middleclass" was normally used by Marx and Engels to translate "bourgeoisie" (see Florian Schmaltz, "Bourgeoisie," in *Historisch-Kritisches Wörterbuch des Marxismus*, vol.2 [Hamburg: Das Argument, 1995], 302–303), even though the bourgeoisie by the mid-nineteenth century was, as these very passages indicate, no longer a middle class but had already largely displaced the landed aristocracy as the ruling class.

cooperative movement, especially the cooperative factories raised by the unassisted efforts of a few bold "hands." The value of these great social experiments cannot be overrated. By deed instead of by argument, they have shown that production on a large scale, and in accord with the behests of modern science, may be carried on without the existence of a class of masters employing a class of hands; that to bear fruit, the means of labour need not be monopolized as a means of dominion over, and of extortion against, the labouring man himself; and that, like slave labour, like serf labour, hired labour is but a transitory and inferior form, destined to disappear before associated labour plying its toil with a willing hand, a ready mind, and a joyous heart. In England, the seeds of the co-operative system were sown by Robert Owen; the workingmen's experiments tried on the Continent were, in fact, the practical upshot of the theories, not invented, but loudly proclaimed, in 1848.

At the same time the experience of the period from 1848 to 1864 has proved beyond doubt that, however, excellent in principle and however useful in practice, cooperative labour, if kept within the narrow circle of the casual efforts of private workmen, will never be able to arrest the growth in geometrical progression of monopoly, to free the masses, nor even to perceptibly lighten the burden of their miseries. It is perhaps for this very reason that plausible noblemen, philanthropic middle-class spouters, and even keep political economists have all at once turned nauseously complimentary to the very cooperative labour system they had vainly tried to nip in the bud by deriding it as the utopia of the dreamer, or stigmatizing it as the sacrilege of the socialist. To save the industrious masses, cooperative labour ought to be developed to national dimensions, and, consequently, to be fostered by national means. Yet the lords of the land and the lords of capital will always use their political privileges for the defense and perpetuation of their economic monopolies. So far from promoting, they will continue to lay every possible impediment in the way of the emancipation of labour. Remember the sneer with which, last session, Lord Palmerston put down the advocated of the Irish Tenants' Right Bill. The House of Commons, cried he, is a house of landed proprietors.

To conquer political power has therefore become the great duty of the working classes. They seem to have comprehended this, for in England, Germany, Italy, and France, there have taken place simultaneous revivals, and simultaneous efforts are being made at the political reorganization of the working men's party.

One element of success they possess – numbers; but numbers weigh in the balance only if united by combination and led by knowledge. Past experience has shown how disregard of that bond of brotherhood which ought to exist between the workmen of different countries, and incite them to stand firmly by each other in all their struggles for emancipation, will be chastised by the common discomfiture of their incoherent efforts. This thought prompted the working men of different countries assembled on 28 September 1864, in public meeting at St. Martin's Hall, to found the International Association.

Another conviction swayed that meeting.

If the emancipation of the working classes requires their fraternal concurrence, how are they to fulfill that great mission with a foreign policy in pursuit of criminal designs, playing upon national prejudices, and squandering in piratical wars the people's blood and treasure? It was not the wisdom of the ruling classes, but the heroic resistance to their criminal folly by the working classes of England, that saved the west of Europe from plunging headlong into an infamous crusade for the perpetuation and propagation of slavery on the other side of the Atlantic. The shameless approval, mock sympathy, or idiotic indifference with which the upper classes of Europe have witnessed the mountain fortress of the Caucasus falling a prey to, and heroic Poland being assassinated by, Russia; the immense and unresisted encroachments of that barbarous power, whose head is at St. Petersburg, and whose hands are in every cabinet of Europe, have taught the working classes the duty to master themselves the mysteries of international politics; to watch the diplomatic acts of their respective governments; to counteract them, if necessary, by all means in their power; when unable to prevent, to combine in simultaneous denunciations, and to vindicate the simple laws of morals and justice, which ought to govern the relations of private individuals, as the rules paramount of the intercourse of nations.

The fight for such a foreign policy forms part of the general struggle for the emancipation of the working classes.

Proletarians of all countries, unite!

2. Instructions for Delegates of the Provisional General Council: The Different Questions

Karl Marx

[This selection is excerpted from a text written by Marx in August 1866. It was read at the Geneva Congress, during which the delegates approved all the parts here included except the one on "Direct and indirect taxation," which was sent back for further elaboration. The revised version was published between February and March 1867, in *The International Courier*, and appears also in GC, I: 340–351.]

[...]

Limitation of the working day

A preliminary condition, without which all further attempts at improvement and emancipation must prove abortive, is the *limitation of the working day*.

It is needed to restore the health and physical energies of the working class, that is, the great body of every nation, as well as to secure them the possibility of intellectual development, sociable intercourse, social and political action.

We propose 8 *hours work* as the *legal limit* of the working day. This limitation being generally claimed by the workmen of the United States of America, the vote of the Congress will raise it to the common platform of the working classes all over the world.

For the information of continental members, whose experience of factory law is comparatively short-dated, we add that all legal restrictions will fail and be broken through by Capital if the *period of the day* during which the 8 working hours must be taken, be not fixed. The length of that period ought to be determined by the 8 working hours and the additional pauses for meals. For instance, if the different interruptions for meals amount to *one hour*, the legal period of the day ought to embrace 9 hours, say from 7a.m. to 4p.m., or from 8a.m. to 5p.m., etc. Nightwork to be but exceptionally permitted, in trades or branches of trades specified by law. The tendency must be to suppress all nightwork [...].

Juvenile and children's labour (both sexes)

We consider the tendency of modern industry to make children and juvenile persons of both sexes co-operate in the great work of social production, as a progressive, sound and legitimate tendency, although under capital it was distorted into an abomination [...].

It may be desirable to begin elementary school instruction before the age of 9 years; but we deal here only with the most indispensable antidotes against the tendencies of a social system which degrades the working man into a mere instrument for the accumulation of capital, and transforms parents by their necessities into slave-holders, sellers of their own children. The *right* of children and juvenile persons must be vindicated. They are unable to act for themselves. It is, therefore, the duty of society to act on their behalf.

If the middle and higher classes neglect their duties toward their offspring, it is their own fault. Sharing the privileges of these classes, the child is condemned to suffer from their prejudices.

The case of the working class stands quite different.[4] The working man is no free agent. In too many cases, he is even too ignorant to understand the true interest of his child, or the normal conditions of human development. However, the more enlightened part of the working class fully understands that the future of its class, and, therefore, of mankind, altogether depends upon the formation of the rising working generation. They know that, before everything else, the children and juvenile workers must be saved from the crushing effects of the present system. This can only be effected by converting *social reason* into *social force*, and, under given circumstances, there exists no other method of doing so, than through *general laws*, enforced by the power of the state. In enforcing such laws, the working class do not fortify governmental power. On the contrary, they transform that power, now used against them, into their own agency. They effect by a general act what they would vainly attempt by a multitude of isolated individual efforts.

Proceeding from this standpoint, we say that no parent and no employer ought to be allowed to use juvenile labour, except when combined with education.

Co-operative labour

It is the business of the International Working Men's Association to combine and generalise the *spontaneous movements* of the working classes, but not to dictate or impose any doctrinary system whatever. The Congress should, therefore, proclaim no *special system* of co-operation, but limit itself to the enunciation of a few general principles.

(a) We acknowledge the co-operative movement as one of the transforming forces of the present society based upon class antagonism. Its

---

4. *Note from International Publishers*: Instead of this sentence, the French and German texts have two sentences ending the preceding paragraph and beginning a new one: "However, for the present, we have only to deal with the children and young persons belonging to the working class.// We deem it necessary, basing on physiology, to divide children and young persons of both sexes," and then as in the English text.

great merit is to practically show, that the present pauperising and despotic system of the *subordination of labour* to capital can be superseded by the republican and beneficent system of *the association of free and equal producers.*

(b) Restricted, however, to the dwarfish forms into which individual wages slaves can elaborate it by their private efforts, the co-operative system will never transform capitalist society. to convert social production into one large and harmonious system of free and co-operative labour, *general social changes* are wanted, *changes of the general conditions of society,* never to be realised save by the transfer of the organised forces of society, viz., the state power, from capitalists and landlords to the producers themselves.

(c) We recommend to the working men to embark in *co-operative production* rather than in *co-operative stores*. The latter touch but the surface of the present economical system, the former attacks its groundwork.

(d) We recommend to all co-operative societies to convert one part of their joint income into a fund for propagating their principles by example as well as by precept, in other words, by promoting the establishment of new co-operative fabrics, as well as by teaching and preaching.

(e) In order to prevent co-operative societies from degenerating into ordinary middle-class joint stock companies (*sociétés par actions*), all workmen employed, whether shareholders or not, ought to share alike. As a mere temporary expedient, we are willing to allow shareholders a low rate of interest.

Trades' unions: Their past, present and future

(a) Their past

Capital is concentrated social force, while the workman has only to dispose of his working force. The *contract* between capital and labour can therefore never be struck on equitable terms, equitable even in the sense of a society which places the ownership of the material means of life and labour on one side and the vital productive energies on the opposite side. The only social power of the workmen is their number. The force of numbers, however is broken by disunion. The disunion of the workmen is created and perpetuated by their *unavoidable competition among themselves.*

Trades' Unions originally sprang up from the *spontaneous* attempts of workmen at removing or at least checking that competition, in order to conquer such terms of contract as might raise them at least above the condition of mere slaves. The immediate object of Trades' Unions was therefore confined to everyday necessities, to expediences for the obstruction of the incessant encroachments of capital, in one word, to questions of wages and time of labour. This activity of the Trades' Unions is not only legitimate, it is necessary. It cannot be dispensed with so long as the present system of production lasts. On the contrary, it must be generalised by the formation and the combination of Trades' Unions throughout all countries. On the other hand, unconsciously to themselves, the Trades' Unions were forming *centres of organisation* of the working class, as the mediaeval municipalities and communes did for the middle class. If the Trades' Unions are required for the guerrilla fights between capital and labour, they are still more important as *organised agencies for superseding the very system of wages labour and capital rule.*

(b) Their present

Too exclusively bent upon the local and immediate struggles with capital, the Trades' Unions have not yet fully understood their power of acting against the system of wages slavery itself. They therefore kept too much aloof from general social and political movements. Of late, however, they seem to awaken to some sense of their great historical mission, as appears, for instance, from their participation, in England, in the recent political movement, from the enlarged views taken of their function in the United States, and from the following resolution passed at the recent great conference of Trades' delegates at Sheffield:

"That this Conference, fully appreciating the efforts made by the International Association to unite in one common bond of brotherhood the working men of all countries, most earnestly recommend to the various societies here represented, the advisability of becoming affiliated to that body, believing that it is essential to the progress and prosperity of the entire working community."

(c) Their future

Apart from their original purposes, they must now learn to act deliberately as organising centres of the working class in the broad interest of its *complete emancipation.* They must aid every social and political movement tending in that direction. Considering themselves and acting as the champions and representatives of the whole working class, they cannot fail to enlist the non-society men into their ranks. They must look carefully after the interests of the worst paid trades, such as the agricultural labourers, rendered powerless [French text has: "incapable of organised resistance"] by exceptional circumstances. They must convince the world at large [French and German texts read: "convince the broad masses of workers"] that their efforts, far from being narrow and selfish, aim at the emancipation of the downtrodden millions.

Direct and indirect taxation

(a) No modification of the form of taxation can produce any important change in the relations of labour and capital.

(b) Nevertheless, having to choose between two systems of taxation, we recommend the *total abolition of indirect taxes,* and the *general substitution of direct taxes.* [In Marx's rough manuscript, French and German texts are: "because direct taxes are cheaper to collect and do not interfere with production."]

Because indirect taxes enhance the prices of commodities – the trades-men adding to those prices not only the amount of the indirect taxes, but the interest and profit upon the capital advanced in their payment;

Because indirect taxes conceal from an individual what he is paying to the state, whereas a direct tax is undisguised, unsophisticated, and not to be misunderstood by the meanest capacity. Direct taxation prompts therefore every individual to control the governing powers while indirect taxation destroys all tendency to self-government […]

Armies
[French and German subtitle reads: "Standing armies their relation to production."]

(a) The deleterious influence of large standing armies upon *production,* has been sufficiently exposed at middle-class congresses of all denominations, at peace congresses, economical congresses, statistical congresses, philanthropical congresses, sociological congresses. We think it, therefore, quite superfluous to expatiate upon this point.

(b) We propose the general armament of the people and their general instruction in the use of arms […]

3. Resolutions of the Third Congress of the International Workingmen's Association

Various authors

On October 6, 1868, the GC decided to publish the principal resolutions of the Congresses of Geneva (1866) and Brussels (1868). The *Resolutions of the Third Congress of the International Working Men's Association* were of fundamental importance for the IWMA. They signalled the defeat of the mutualists and, with it, the collectivist turn of the entire organization. This text first appeared in *The Bee-Hive*, between November and December 1868, and, subsequently, still in London, with the Westminster Printing Company, in February of the following year, as a booklet entitled *The International Working Men's Association. Resolutions of the Congress of Geneva, 1866, and the Congress of Brussels, 1868*. For the complete text, see GC, III: 292–298.

Trades unions and strikes

1. That strikes are not a means to the complete emancipation of the working classes, but are frequently a necessity in the actual situation of the struggle between labour and capital.
2. That it is requisite to subject them to certain rules of organization, opportunity, and legitimacy.
3. In trades where no unions and benefit societies exist as yet, it is necessary to create them. The unions of all trades and countries must combine. In each local federation of trade societies a fund destined to support strikes ought to be established. In one word, the work undertaken by International Working Men's Association it to be continued so as to enable working men to enter the association en masse.
4. It is necessary to appoint in each locality a commitee consisting of delegates of the various societies, who shall act as umpires, deciding eventually upon the advisability and legitimacy of a strike. For the rest, the different sections will, of course, in the mode of appointing these committees, follow the particular manners, habit, and laws of their respective places.

The effects of machinery in the hands of the capitalist class

Considering that on the one side machinery has proved a most powerful instrument of despotism and extortion in the hands of the capitalist class, and that on the other side the development of machinery creates the material conditions necessary for the superseding of the wages system by a truly social system of production;

49

Considering that machinery will render no real service to the working men until by a more equitable, social organization, it be put into their own possession, the Congress declares:

1. That it is only by means of co-operative associations and an organisation of mutual credit that the producer can obtain possession of machinery.
2. That even in the existing state of things it is possible for working men organised in trade societies to enforce some guarantees or compensation in cases of sudden displacement by machinery [...]

The question of education

Cognisant that it is impossible at present to organise a rational system of education, the Congress invites the different sections to establish courses of public lectures on scientific and economical subjects, and thus to remedy as much as possible the shortcomings of the education actually received by the working man. It is understood that reduction of the hours of labour is an indispensable preliminary condition of any true system of education.

Property in land, mines, railroads, &c.

1. *In relation to mines, collieries, railways, &c.* – Considering that these great productive forces are fixed in, and occupy a large portion of the soil, the common gift off nature,

that they can only be worked by means of machinery and collective labour power,

that the machinery and the collective labour power, which today exist only for the advantage of the capitalists ought in future to benefit the whole people;

The Congress resolves:

(a) That the quarries, collieries, and other mines, as well as the railways, ought in a normal state of society to belong to the community represented by the state, a state itself subject to the laws of justice.
(b) That the quarries, collierries, and other mines, and Railways, be let [leased] by the state, not to comapnes of capitalists as at present, but to companies of working men bound by contract

to guarantee to society the rational and scientific working of the railyways, etc., at a price nearly as possible approximate to the working expense. The same contract ought to reserve to the state the right to verify the accounts of the companies, so as to present the possibility of any reconsitution of monopolies. A second contract ough to guarantee the mutual right of each member of the companies in respect to his fellow workmen.

2. *In Relation to Agricultural Property* – Considering that the necessities of production and the application of the known laws of agronomy require culture on a large scale, and necessitate the introduction of machinery and the organisation of agricultural labour power, and that generally modern economical development tends to agriculture on a large scale;

Considering that consequently agricultural labour and property in arable soil ought to be put on the same footing as mines;

Considering that the productive properties of the soil are the prime materials of all products, the prime source of all means of production, and of all desirable things that cost no labour;

The Congress thinks that the economical development of modern society will create the social necessity of converting arable land into the common property of society, and of letting the soil on behalf of the state to agricultural companies under conditions analagous to those stated in regard to mines and railways.

3. *In Relation to Canals, Highways and Telegraphs* – Considering that the roads and other means of communication require a common social direction, the Congress thinks they ought to remain the common property of society.

4. *In Relation to Forests* – Considering that the abandonment of forests to private individuals causes the destruction of woods necessary for the conservation of springs, and, as a matter of course, of the good qualities of the soil, as well as the health and lives of the population, the Congress thinks that the forests ought to remain the property of society.

Reduction of the hours of labour

A resolution having been unanimously passed by the Congress of Geneva, 1866, to the effect that the legal limitation of the working day is a preliminary condition to all ulterior social improvement of the working classes, the Congress is of opinion that the time has arrived when practical effect should be given to that resolution, and that it has become the duty of all the branches to agitate that question practically in the different countries where the International Working Men's Association is established.

War and standing armies

Considering that our social institutions as well as the centralization of political power are a permanent cause ot war, which can only be removed by a thorough social reform;

that the people even now can diminish the number of wars by opposing those who declare and make war;

that this concerns above all the working classes, who have almost exclusively to shed their blood;

that to do this there is a practical and legal means which can be immediately acted upon; that as the body politic could not go on for any length of time without labour, it would suffice tor the working men to strike work to render war impossible;

the International Working Men's Congress recommends to all the sections, and to the members of working men's societies in particular and to the working classess in general, to cease war in case a war be declared in their country. The Congress counts upon the spirit of solidarity which animates the working men of all countries, and entertains a hope that means would not be wating in such an emegency to support the people against their government.

4. Emancipation and Independence of Woman

P. Eslens, Eugène Hins, and Paul Robin

[This text is excerpted from the Report of the 5th Commission on Programmatic Questions presented at the Congress of Lausanne (1867). In the debate on the role of man and woman in society, the Belgian branch submitted two reports expressing opposed positions. The first, that of the majority, written by César de Paepe and two other internationalists, expressed conservative views and called for woman to return to the family, arguing that her emancipation could be achieved only through that of the working man. By contrast, the minority report prefigured certain goals that would later be advanced by the feminist movement, such as the socialization of domestic labor. Its three exponents were P. Eslens, of whom nothing is known; Eugène Hins

(1839–1923), first a Proudhonian and later a Bakuninist, director of the newspaper *La Liberté*, member of the Belgian federal committee and a delegate to the Congresses of Brussels (1868) and Basel (1869); and Paul Robin (1837–1912), a French schoolteacher who moved between Belgium, Switzerland and London, a follower of Bakunin since 1869, and member of the IWA's Central Committee in 1870–71. The complete text is in PI, I: 220–221.]

Ancient religions considered work a punishment; today man sees in work his true destiny. Work then becomes a sacred right that cannot be denied to anyone. Woman can therefore claim this right by the same token as man, since only in work will she find independence and dignity.

Many arguments have been made against extending this right to women. We shall examine the most specious of them:

1. Hiring women in industry is said to lower the wages of men. This is simply a result of the current organization of work. One could just as well say that hiring too large a number of men would lower the wages of all of them, and then conclude that it is necessary to limit the number of workers and reestablish the ancient guilds. An easy way to prevent this problem would be to include women in the future system by which work is organized.
2. Workplaces are said to be sites of immoral behavior. This arises from various causes that have nothing to do with the work itself – for example, pressure exercised by licentious bosses and foremen; inadequate wages, which drive women to debauchery; and ignorance, which leaves woman no other pleasures than those of the senses.
3. Woman is said to be weak. But if man is endowed with strength, woman may make up for this with dexterity. The field open to woman is therefore vast, and the machines that more and more diminish the importance of physical strength will increase the number of occupations that she can practice.
4. Motherhood. It is said that woman is destined for marriage and therefore will not have time to work. But one can answer that she may perhaps not marry, or she may be a widow without children, or she may have finished raising her children. Moreover, we should keep in mind that with the division of labor, there are certain work assignments that could be better carried out by married women, such as preparing food, washing and ironing, making clothes, and teaching children in pre-school. Woman will then only be unable to

work during the last months of pregnancy and the first three years of a child's life. During that time, the woman will be supported either by her husband (assuming the continuation of marriage) or by a special fund earmarked for this purpose.

If we reckon an average of four children for each woman, and if we allow roughly four years for each child, this would add up to no more than sixteen years removed from work, and even then, not completely. There will therefore remain in the life of woman a sufficient part to be devoted to work.

A man can be free to support a woman entirely if he wants a full-time housewife, but the woman should not be bound to him as a matter of necessity. If she wants to leave him, she should be able to retrieve, in the exercise of her profession, an independent existence.

Conclusion. The International Workers' Association should promote the development among women of associations that currently exist only for men. The women's associations should federate with the men's associations so as to fight together for the emancipation of labor, which alone will be able to assure independence for everyone.

5. Report of the Commission for Reduction of Work Hours

[This report was prepared by the commission on reduction of the workday of the Brussels Congress (1868). It was read in the session of September 12, 1868, by the Parisian cabinet-maker Eugène Tartaret, who was also a delegate to the Lausanne congress (1869). Part of it was published in B1868. The complete text is in PI, I, 385–387.]

The purpose of reducing the number of hours of work is to assure the material and intellectual development of the workers, to allow them the free exercise of their civil and political rights.

In modern society, work should no longer be punishment, servitude, or a mark of indignity; it should be a duty imposed on all citizens.

If work is to be really the exercise of a common duty, it should be carried out under conditions that guarantee workers their health, the satisfaction of their needs and those of their families, and protection against the pain and misery of old age and disability.

Under present conditions, does work meet the goal set by the *International*? – No.

Work as practiced under the pressure of competition is a struggle to the death among workers, people against people, individual against individual. Everywhere exploitation produces antagonism and servitude of the workers.

Production bears the weight of enormous charges, imposed by excessive taxes, to pay exorbitant salaries to officials whose main occupation is to keep workers subjugated to capital.

Exploitation, fostering and maintaining competition by lowering wages, forces workers to work long hours. In some very painful occupations – construction, digging, etc., etc. – the workers tire quickly and receive no training.

Finally, wherever the workday is not limited, the worker becomes physically and intellectually exhausted. From a citizen destined to learn, carry out responsibilities, and exercise civil and political rights, the worker is turned into a pariah, a slave indifferent to progress and incapable of learning anything. Tired of his pain and his misery, the worker puts up with exploitation and servitude without daring to protest such injustice. And how would he learn, how would he resist? – He doesn't have the time.

This initial goal of reducing work hours is therefore indispensable, because without it, the task of organizing international solidarity, proposed by our Association, would be hopeless [...]

The necessary increase of production and lowering of prices must be achieved [not by forcing workers to work longer hours, but rather] through the use of appropriate raw materials, the professional training of workers, and the wise use of machines.

But the intervention of machines further complicates the unfortunate situation of the workers, because the machines belong exclusively to the owners of capital.

It is sometimes objected that the worker at the machine will play a passive role, as nothing more than the *operator of the machine*. It is also said that in certain occupations the worker will no longer do anything but regular and uniform operations, which will limit his knowledge of the industrial process as a whole. But we are not afraid that this will happen.

Machinery is inert and is a human creation; it cannot function usefully without cooperation and without intelligent direction.

If man's industrial role is diminished through a reduction of working hours, justice is served, because man has not only work to do, but also a family to support, children to educate, civil and political rights to exercise. If machinery when first introduced harms workers through excess production and a forced unemployment that impoverishes them, this is because, as the International has recognized, it is not owned by the workers, who can acquire it only through solidarity.

Machinery, a fruit of human intelligence, must serve man as a means of emancipation and must not be a cause of ruin. If it produces too much, it should run for less time, and its human operator will benefit from the reduction of work hours.

This reduction of work hours should bring man wellbeing, intelligence, and freedom [...]

As the Geneva Congress has resolved unanimously that the limitation of work hours is an indispensable precondition for all subsequent social improvements, the Congress believes that the time has come to give practical effect to this resolution, and that it is the duty of all Sections, in all countries, to agitate this demand wherever the International Workers' Association is established.

6. Strikes, Unions, and the Affiliation of Unions with the International

César De Paepe

[The following text is excerpted from a report by the Brussels branch of the IWA at the September 8, 1868 session of the IWA congress in that city. César De Paepe (1841–1890) was second only to Marx as a theoretician of the IWA. A leader of the Belgian branch, he participated in all IWA congresses except those of Geneva (1866) and The Hague (1872). He belonged to the "autonomist" wing of the IWA and was a delegate at the congresses of Brussels (1874) and Bern (1876). In 1885 he was among the founders of the Belgian Socialist Party. This text was published in B1868 and in PI, I, 271–285.]

We must first declare that, in our view, the strike is not even a partial solution to the great problem of abolishing poverty, but we believe that it is nonetheless an instrument of struggle which will lead decisively in the direction of such a solution. This is why we consider it necessary to react against those who place exclusive emphasis on cooperation, who see, apart from consumer-, producer-, and credit-cooperatives, no serious movement among workers, and who in particular regard strikes as useless and even as fatal to the interests of workers [...]

The strike [...] is just, legitimate, and necessary when agreements are violated by the employer. It can then be undertaken whatever the risk of failure. Is it not always great and beautiful to see the slave protest against barbarous and inhuman measures? And what measure can be more barbarous and inhuman than the practice of incessantly chipping away at the meager ration of those whose lives are already marked by privation?

Given the ridiculously low wages in certain industries (such as manufacturing and coal mining), given the extreme centralization of capital ... given the enormous scale of the capital that the workers would need in order themselves to run vast factories or coal mines, and in the absence of sufficient credit to facilitate the creation of producer cooperatives (*associations de production*) in these industries, we ask what weapon other than the strike – even if unorganized – is left to these proletarians to defend themselves against perpetual wage-reduction? Would it be better for them to die of hunger on the job without emitting a cry of indignation and without making any effort to stand up? Well, even if it were as clear as $2+2=4$ that the strike could bring no improvement, we would at least have to accept it as the supreme protest of the disinherited against the vices of our social order.

We have already said that the strike may be useful and necessary, and therefore that we are in favor of unions (*sociétés de résistance*) to support strikes and to give them wise and energetic leadership. Yes, despite our desire and our certitude that the social order will one day be completely transformed, that is, that the exploitation of man by man will be replaced by equal exchange and reciprocity, we affirm that it is necessary to establish unions as long as there are categories of workers whose complete emancipation is impossible today [...]

The union is necessary because it inspires a certain fear in the exploiter. Unless the exploiter is almost certain of success, he will take care not to violate agreements, knowing that he would lose some of his authority in case of failure [...]

The union (*société de résistance*) will remain indispensable as long as there is exploitation of man by man, as long as the idle extract anything from the labor of others. Moreover, it is only through the union that both the owners and the workers will know who they are dealing with when someone applies for a job. The union (*Association*) gives each of its members a certificate of morality and honesty. Owner and worker alike know that the union accepts only workers of unquestioned integrity.

One cause of the constant decline of wages is that unemployed workers go door to door in search a job, thereby giving the exploiter the impression that there are more unemployed than there really are. Through the union, requests for workers would have to be made directly to committees that would then send workers only to where they are really needed [...]

If strikes must be called and led by unions (*sociétés de résistance*), so in turn unions will only be serious to the extent that they are federated, not only within an occupation and within a country, but also across occupations and across countries. Hence the need for an international federation [...] [Then] the owner will be unable to find anywhere – either in neighboring localities, or anywhere in the country, or abroad – the workers he may need in order to replace those who will have suspended their labor for a legitimate reason [...]

The strike, we admit, has only a provisional utility. The perpetual strike would be the eternalization of wage-labor, and we want wage-labor abolished. The perpetual strike would be the struggle without truce or victory between capital and labor, whereas what we want is not what has come to be called *the association of labor and capital* [...] but rather the absorption of capital by labor. We demand this because since capital is accumulated labor that should have an exchange value equal only to the value of the labor that it has cost, it cannot then be divided up as though it were a product. Produced by labor, capital can only be the [collective] property of the worker.

Then [...] with the universal organization of work and of trade, of production and of circulation, coinciding with a necessary and inevitable transformation in the organization of landed property and an intellectual transformation (made possible by thorough education for everyone), social regeneration will take place at once in the material and the mental domains. Thenceforward based on science and labor – rather than, as at present, on ignorance and capitalist domination – humanity, marching from progress to progress in every branch of the arts, the sciences, and industry, will peacefully fulfill its destiny.

Marx and the Politics of the First International

George C. Comninel

The founding of the First International

In 1859, Karl Marx published *A Contribution to the Critique of Political Economy* in Berlin.[1] This constituted only the first part of the first book of the six books he planned on the subject, and included only a small part of the material already written.[2] In the following year he was distracted by a variety of issues and problems, including lawsuits and polemics following libellous charges made by Karl Vogt (whom he already knew to be, as was subsequently proved, a paid agent of Louis Bonaparte[3]). When he returned to seriously pursue his critique of political economy in mid-1861, he soon transcended the project of completing the second part of the book, as such. Over the next two years he produced an enormous manuscript – 1472 large pages in 23 notebooks – that comprised the first drafts of what would become the three volumes of *Capital* plus the further three volumes of *Theories of Surplus Value*.[4]

Whereas Marx wrote the first (1857–8) manuscript, comprising the *Contribution* and *Grundrisse*, at a time of deepening economic crisis – writing to Frederick Engels that he was "working like mad all night and every night" to get it at least in rough shape before "the *déluge*"[5] – the 1860s were on the whole a relatively prosperous period. The

---

1. Karl Marx, *A Contribution to the Critique of Political Economy*. Karl Marx-Frederick Engels, *Collected Works*. New York: International Publishers [MECW], Vol. 29, 1987: 257–419.
2. Ibid., 540–542, n. 57.
3. Marx's letters of 1860 are preoccupied with Vogt's calumnies, widely reported in Germany, including the astonishing claim that Marx had run a racket during the 1848 Revolution, extorting money from vulnerable communists in Germany (MECW, Vol. 41, 1985), 43. The whole matter is documented in Marx's *Herr Vogt* (MECW, Vol. 17, 1981), 21–329.
4. Karl Marx, *Economic Manuscript of 1861–63* (MECW, Vol. 30, 1888), 455, n. 1.
5. Marx to Engels, 8 Dec. 1861 (MECW, Vol. 40, 1983), 217.

next significant crisis, in fact, did not occur until 1873 (the onset of "the Long Depression," lasting until 1896). Much of the attention of the working class in the 1860s was directed towards issues of international politics, such as the American Civil War, the conflicts attending unification in Italy and Germany, the Polish uprising, and the Irish struggle for independence. Then, with the end of the decade came the Franco-Prussian War – the last major European war before 1914 – and the Paris Commune.

It was, in fact, out of efforts to forge international working-class political solidarity that the International Workingmen's Association (IWA) came into being on September 28, 1864.[6] What is striking is the extent to which it was the International, born entirely from a working-class initiative, that seized and imposed itself on Marx. Not only did he have nothing to do with the idea in the first place, but his correspondence in the years before this historic turning point suggests that if anything he might have been expected to have been sceptical, and to have kept aloof from it.

Only six months earlier, Engels had remarked with respect to the possibility of re-issuing his *The Condition of the Working Class in England* that "this is not a suitable moment in any case, now that the English proletariat's revolutionary energy has all but completely evaporated and the English proletarian has declared himself in full agreement with the dominancy of the bourgeoisie."[7] Writing back the following day, Marx mentioned that he had attended the large meeting called by the London Trades Union Council on March 26 to support the Northern states in their struggle to end slavery, and oppose possible British intervention on the side of the South. "The working men themselves spoke very well indeed," he noted, "without a trace of bourgeois rhetoric or the faintest attempt to conceal their opposition to the capitalists." Yet he continued, "How soon the English workers will throw off what seems to be a bourgeois contagion remains to be seen."[8]

Beyond scepticism as to the readiness of the working class, he was now deeply committed to completing his theoretical critique of political economy and the capitalist system. In the period of his responding to Vogt he had good reason to emphasize that the Communist League

---

6. Marx to Engels, 4 Nov. 1864 (MECW, Vol. 42, 1987) 15–18, nn. 18, 19. For a brief history of the International, and a selection of its most important documents (including those that are cited here) see Marcello Musto, ed., *Workers Unite! The International 150 Years Later*. London: Bloomsbury, 2014.
7. Engels to Marx, 8 April 1863 (MECW, Vol. 41), 465.
8. Marx to Engels, 9 April 1863 (MECW, Vol. 41), 468.

belonged to history, that it was he himself who had moved to dissolve it years before, and even that he had belonged to no organization since. Still, writing to Ferdinand Freiligrath (another Red 48er) in connection with the Vogt affair, Marx went significantly further:

> ... since 1852 I had not been associated with any association and was firmly convinced that my theoretical studies were of greater use to the working class than my meddling with associations which had now had their day on the Continent.... Whereas you are a poet, I am a critic and for me the experiences of 1849–52 were quite enough.[9]

One would hardly anticipate based on this, or anything else he expressed since entering into serious economic study, that from virtually the day of its founding the International would become the constant focus of Marx's efforts and attention for eight years and more. Indeed, he would need to steal time from it to complete *Capital* (occasionally even claiming to be out of town so he could write undisturbed by the press of its business). Yet he did not withdraw from it. The International became the most significant historical development in working-class unity and collective action to his day, and the potential that he perceived in it from its inception made it impossible for him to stand apart.

When the Communist League was formed in 1847 through merger of the League of the Just and the Communist Correspondence Committee of Brussels (of which Marx and Engels were founding members), it was a secret organization committed to a revolution that would end existing class society and usher in a new age of equality and true human freedom. Marx induced the League to set aside the traditional trappings of secret societies as previously established by revolutionary groups and workers in trades. Secrecy was of course still necessary for a group dedicated to revolution. With its reorganization, the League commissioned Marx and Engels to write its statement of purpose, and *The Manifesto of the Communist Party* could hardly have been more explicit in its call for revolution.

What is so striking in contrast is the extent to which the IWA did not take the form of an explicitly revolutionary organization, but instead engaged in what might be called class politics in ordinary times. This is not merely a matter of its rhetoric. To be sure, when Marx wrote to Engels about the founding meeting and its aftermath, which included composing the Association's "Inaugural Address," he noted the real limits as to what could be expected:

---

9. Marx to Ferdinand Freiligrath, 29 Feb. 1860 (MECW, Vol. 41), 81–82.

> It was very difficult to frame the thing so that our view should appear in a form that would make it acceptable to the present outlook of the workers' movement. ... It will take time before the revival of the movement allows the old boldness of language to be used.[10]

If the workers were not ready for bold language, they certainly did not found their Association to undertake revolution. Yet that this clearly was no rebirth of the old revolutionary politics did not prevent Marx from interpreting the fact that the meeting was "chock-full" as a sign that "there is now evidently a revival of the working classes taking place." And, far from holding back from the Association, to the founding of which he was invited as a non-speaking presence on the platform, he accepted membership not only on the provisional organizing committee, but on the sub-committee charged with drafting a statement of rules and principles.

The difference is also not simply a matter of stated objectives. In the *Manifesto*, for example, the stated goals include a "graduated income tax" and "Free education for all children in public schools."[11] The Communist League was nonetheless seriously and immediately committed to revolution. Within the IWA, Marx not only did not hide his ultimately revolutionary goals, but included them from the start in the Inaugural Address and Rules of the Association.

The Address began not with the spectre of revolution haunting Europe, but with the "fact that the misery of the working masses has not diminished from 1848 to 1864."[12] After rehearsing both the facts of that misery and the crushing political defeat after 1848, Marx pointed only to two "compensating features": the Ten Hours Bill and the growth of the cooperative movement. Still, his conclusion was that "To conquer political power has, therefore, become the great duty of the working classes."[13] The Rules – unanimously adopted and published by the Association together with the Address – were even less ambiguous. They stated that "the emancipation of the working classes must be conquered by the working classes themselves," called for "the abolition of all class rule," and asserted that "the economical emancipation of the working classes" was the ultimate

---

10. Marx to Engels, 4 Nov. 1864 (MECW, Vol. 42) spells out his view of the meeting and his intentions in what followed.
11. Marx and Engels, *Manifesto of the Communist Party* (MECW, Vol. 6, 1976), 505.
12. Karl Marx, "Inaugural Address of the International Working Men's Association" (MECW, Vol. 20, 1985), 5.
13. Ibid., 12.

goal.[14] The concluding words of the Address even echoed those of the *Manifesto*: "Proletarians of all countries, Unite!"

Yet, where the *Manifesto* was directly a call for revolution, the founding documents of the International, the policies adopted at its Congresses, and the organizational undertakings over the course of its existence all focussed on precisely the task of building and uniting – in the open – a mass political instrument for the working class. It is not that Marx was ever in any way less committed to revolution, let alone converted to reform. Nor were he and his closest associates alone among IWA members in advocating for revolution. As profoundly different as they were in their politics, Bakunin and his supporters – who eventually outnumbered those who stood with Marx – were no less committed to the idea of revolutionary change rather than reform. The key difference between Marx and Bakunin, indeed, lay precisely in the former's recognition that a revolutionary transformation presupposed a *political* process; that in the first instance a *political* revolution was necessary, and that this required the real and substantial development of working-class political agency. It was to this end, from the beginning, that Marx devoted his energies to the International.

This purpose fit with the whole impetus behind the founding of the IWA. Although the development of capitalist economic relations and of national workers' organizations varied enormously across Europe,[15] there was a great deal shared at the level of progressive political positions, particularly in the international arena, as well as with respect to basic rights and social policies. The founding meeting was called in the wake of a confluence of international issues – Italian unification, American Civil War and Polish Uprising – that had brought British workers together with visiting French workers and resident workers from other countries.[16] In addition to the issues of peace, freedom and an end to slavery, and causes of national self-determination, the leading issues on which workers virtually everywhere agreed involved political rights and electoral democracy, the right to organize with respect to their labour, preventing recourse to foreign strikebreakers, the reduction of working hours, and (*still*) progressive taxation and free public education. Aside from the many issues that

---

14. Karl Marx, "Provisional Rules of the Association" (MECW, Vol. 20), 14.
15. The original Rules of the Association referred specifically to Europe, which only was changed in the revised rules written by Marx and Engels in 1871.
16. David Fernbach, "Introduction," in Karl Marx, *The First International and After.* London: Penguin/NLR, 1974, 10–13.

were directly international, the value of international cooperation could be seen in the fact that, as Marx observed in his Address, continental governments had been obliged to follow the example of English factory legislation after that victory had been won. Even reformist workers embraced the gains to be made on these issues, while for Marx their achievement embodied the real substance of "the political reorganisation of the working men's party" for which he had called in the Address.

Divergences in economic development, working-class organization, and politics

Across Europe, the situation of the working class was different in each country. There existed profound national differences in the form and extent of capitalist production, hugely disparate historical experiences and ideological tendencies, a range of nationally-specific characteristic forms of workers' organization, and enormous divergences with respect to political situations and forms of state.

In the first place, the capitalist mode of production was not old, but very recent; and it had not developed originally throughout Western Europe, but only in England. These claims remain controversial for many, despite a growing body of evidence that supports them.[17] But it is virtually universally recognized that industrial development on the European continent lagged significantly behind that in Britain. Belgium was the first continental nation to undergo significant capitalist development; France grew relatively slowly at least until the 1870s; and Germany came from far behind but then

---

17. I have discussed this in virtually all my previous work, and will cite here only George C. Comninel, *Rethinking the French Revolution*. London: Verso, 1987; and "Critical Thinking and Class Analysis: Historical Materialism and Social Theory," *Socialism and Democracy*, 27 (1) (March 2013): 19–56. The foundation for this historical conception lies in the work of Robert Brenner, most notably two articles collected (with rejoinders) in T.H. Aston, and C.H.E. Philpin, eds. *The Brenner Debate: Agrarian Class Structure and Economic Development in Pre-Industrial Europe*. Cambridge: Cambridge University Press, 1987. Ellen Meiksins Wood has contributed importantly to these ideas in *Democracy Against Capitalism: Rethinking Historical Materialism*. Cambridge: Cambridge University Press, 1995; *The Pristine Culture of Capitalism*. London: Verso, 1991; and *The Origin of Capitalism: A Longer View*. London: Verso, 2002. A recent book by Michael Zmolek, *Rethinking the Industrial Revolution*. Leiden: Brill, 2013, provides a lengthy historical analysis of the long development and late realization of industrial capitalism in England.

rapidly surpassed France.[18] Marx himself weighed in on the unique status of Britain in 1870:

> Although the revolutionary *initiative* will probably start from France, only England can act as a *lever* in any seriously *economic* revolution. It is the only country where there are no longer any peasants, and where land ownership is concentrated in very few hands. It is the only country where almost all production has been taken over by the *capitalist form*, in other words with work combined on a vast scale under capitalist bosses. It is the only country *where the large majority of the population consists of wage-labourers*. It is the only country where the class struggle and the organization of the working class into *trade unions* have actually reached a considerable degree of maturity and universality. Because of its domination of the world market, it is the only country where any revolution in the economic system will have immediate repercussions on the rest of the world.[19]

He concluded, "England cannot be treated simply as a country along with other countries. It must be treated as the metropolis of capital."

The extent to which France truly differed from England has rarely been accorded proper recognition, since it was not simply a matter of degree. An essential condition of the capitalist mode of production is that capital controls the process of production through management, which is referred to as the subordination (or subsumption) of labour to capital. Marx in addition recognized that there was not only the formal subordination of labour to capital, but also its *real* subordination, through which capital not only has the inherent right to control production, but actively intervenes to do so.[20] In France, however, workers – in legal principle and in practice within the workplace – largely retained the right to control production themselves.[21] In labour law there had long existed a fundamental difference between *louage d'ouvrage* (contract for work) and *louage de service* (contract of

---

18. Eric J. Hobsbawm, *The Age of Capital*. London: Sphere, 1977, 56; F. Crouzet, "The Historiography of French Economic Growth in the Nineteenth Century," *Economic History Review*, 56 (2): 223.
19. Karl Marx "The General Council to the Federal Council of Romance Switzerland" (MECW, Vol. 21, 1985), 86.
20. Karl Marx, *Capital* Vol. 1 (MECW, Vol. 35, 1996), 511. There is an enormous literature on this issue, drawing particularly on a chapter in Marx's original manuscript analysing the formal and real "subsumption" of labour to capital, which was not included in *Capital*. I take account of the published text alone here simply because it is entirely sufficient to the point.
21. I am indebted for much of what follows on France to the analysis of Xavier Lafrance in his as yet unpublished doctoral dissertation, *Citizens and Wage-Labourers: Capitalism and the Formation of a Working Class in France*. York University, 2013.

service).[22] This distinction continues to this day: someone working under *louage d'ouvrage* is essentially a "contractor," recognized in law as *not* being a subordinate of the person contracting for service, and retaining rights with respect to the work. The *louage de service*, by contrast, was originally the characteristic contract for a subordinate person, such as in domestic service, and has in the twentieth century become the basis for the standard capitalist contract of employment.[23]

Whereas for much of the nineteenth century British labour law built upon and strengthened the common law relationship of "master and servant," labour law in France from 1789 to the latter part of the ninenteenth century instead built upon the *liberty* of the worker. Legal oversight of labour contracts was transformed from a police matter of public order into a civil issue of mutual contractual obligations, overseen by local labour tribunals.[24] In this regard, "the contrast between France and England between 1789 and 1875 was therefore complete."[25] On the English side, "a logic of industrial subordination" took the employers' good faith for granted; on the French side, "a concern for fairness" instead actively compensated for inequality in economic status, holding employers to account for the consequences of their management.[26] In France there was a formal recognition of the difference between "workers" (*ouvriers*) and "day labourers" (*journaliers*, who were under *louage de service*) with the latter comprising only 10 percent of industrial employees, and enduring real subordination to the commands of the employer – *unlike* the "workers," who continued to enjoy *louage d'ouvrage*. Indeed, there is a "perfect pattern of inverse symmetry" between France and England with respect to collective bargaining versus face to face negotiations by individual workers.[27] In France collective bargaining was banned, but workers benefited from the legal recognition of their rights as individuals relative to their employer; in England workers were personally subject to their employer as "master," but increasingly

22. Alain Cottereau, "Sens du juste et usages du droit du travail: une évolution contrastée entre la France et la Grande-Bretagne au XIXe siècle," *Revue d'histoire du XIXe siècle*, 33 (2) (*Relations sociales et espace public*, 2006), 101–120. (Published in English as "Industrial tribunals and the establishment of a kind of common law of labour in nineteenth-century France," in Willibald Steinmetz, ed., *Private Law and Social Inequality in the Industrial Age*. Oxford: Oxford University Press, 2000.)
23. Ibid., 103, 113–114.
24. Ibid., 105–109.
25. Ibid., 109, my translation.
26. Ibid., 112.
27. Ibid., 116.

the law made room for the "voluntary" choice of collective representation.

As a result of the French Revolution – buttressed locally by workers' demands, and seemingly without concern at higher levels of the state – legal practice insisted on recognizing contractual equality in social terms, not just in formal economic terms. This was grounded upon the liberty of the individual worker, with local labour tribunals acting as conciliators seeking to balance interests and achieve peace and fairness in the workplace. It is clear, therefore, based upon a large and growing body of evidence, that the basic capitalist social relationship of the subordination of labour to capital in industry was very far from fully realizable – if perhaps not actually illegal – down to the last decades of the nineteenth century. Just as the French Revolution had the effect of buttressing the rights and customs of peasants, preventing any development of capitalist production on the land, so also it not merely reinforced but greatly increased the rights of workers in industry. This provided a profoundly different context for labour.

It was not, of course, as if the French state took away all rights of property owners; but it had a predisposition towards benefiting great property holders in relation to the state itself and large-scale trade and industry, while generally neglecting the position of small-scale proprietors in relation to production. This state-centric form of class relations had been characteristic of the old regime, and while important institutional changes certainly followed as a result of the Revolution, the continuity is striking.[28] This entrenchment of pre-capitalist economic patterns goes a long way towards explaining the slow rate of industrialization in France, and sheds light on the historically distinctive development of its labour organizations.

It has long been recognized that, after the Revolution abolished guilds as holdovers from the feudal past, the workers continued to rely upon their *compagnonnages*, journeymen's societies that equally had roots in the middle ages.[29] In addition, workers increasingly developed various forms of mutual-aid society. Together with the legal regime of *louage d'ouvrage*, these forms both expressed and reinforced a corporatist character in workers' organizations. The form of

---

28. See my analysis in *Rethinking the French Revolution*, 200–203.
29. For a classic typology of the forms of working-class organization in France, see Louis Levine, *Syndicalism in France*. New York: Columbia University Press, 1914, 26–33. On the *compagnonnages*, and particularly their political role after the Revolution, see William H. Sewell Jr., *Work and Revolution in France*. Cambridge: Cambridge University Press, 1980.

workers' associations stood in integral, yet ironic, connection with the recognition of the rights of workers relative to employers: workers in a given trade developed a *collective* identity with respect to social needs and political participation, in part on the basis of their relative security and strongly held identity as *individual* members of that trade. This relative strength of French workers as individuals contrasted greatly with the characteristic form of capitalist social relations of wage labour, above all as realized in England, and provided a powerful historical foundation for the development of syndicalism in France.

Of course, workers' interests were not always met through the conciliation of the labour tribunals, and strikes did occur. In keeping with the strong legal recognition of their rights as individuals, as well as the role of the state in preserving "public order," strikes were entirely illegal until 1864, and strikers were frequently prosecuted.[30] In the absence of collective bargaining, with most terms of employment recognized with respect to the trade as a whole in each locality, there were no trade unions as such. When, therefore, workers did resort to strikes, they organized ad hoc, secret, *sociétés de resistance* solely for that purpose – yet another development that underpinned French syndicalism. All of these tendencies were profoundly reinforced by the small scale and artisanal production typical of French industry – as late as 1896, 36 percent of industrial workers were employed in workshops of five or fewer, and 64 percent in workplaces of less than 50.[31]

These syndicalist tendencies were expressed not only in the strength of various anarchist movements, but also in the difficulty of forging a socialist political organization. In 1880, Jules Guesde met with Marx to draft the program for the French Workers' Party. Marx dictated its preamble, and collaborated on the sections of minimum political and economic demands.[32] Ironically, however, it was after Guesde (with Marx's own son-in-law Paul Lafargue and other leaders of the party) demonstrated that the minimum demands were

---

30. There were 14,000 prosecutions between 1825 and 1864, and 9,000 strikers were imprisoned (Robert J. Goldstein, *Political Repression in 19th Century Europe*. New York: Routledge, 2010, 58.

31. Roger Magraw, "Socialism, Syndicalism and French Labour Before 1914," in Dick Geary, ed., *Labour and Socialist Movements in Europe Before 1914*. Oxford: Berg, 1989, 49. Magraw offers an excellent overview of the role of syndicalism in French politics.

32. Karl Marx, "Preamble to the Programme of the French Workers' Party" (MECW, Vol. 24, 1989), 340; Karl Marx and Jules Guesde, "The Programme of the Parti Ouvrier," https://www.marxists.org/archive/marx/works/1880/05/parti-ouvrier.htm. See also Engels' letter to Eduard Bernstein, 25 Oct. 1881 (MECW, Vol. 46, 1992), 144–151.

to be little more than a lure to attract workers – as opposed to means both to develop class organization and ameliorate social conditions – that Marx made the famous assertion that if this was Marxism then "If anything is certain, it is that I myself am not a Marxist."[33] Far from being a potent political force, this party was challenged by several other socialist parties, to say nothing of the anarchists. With the heavy repression of the left after the Paris Commune, and unions only given real status in 1884, the strong syndicalist currents and relatively weak formal economic organization of the working class continued long after the end of the nineteenth century.

While, unlike Britain, France remained a largely rural society in the period of the International – indeed, even in 1914 60 percent of the population was rural[34] – there was nonetheless a good deal of industrial production, albeit mostly on a small scale and with limited subordination of workers to capital. Germany, by contrast, had seen much less development of industry in any form prior to the mid-nineteenth century, but rapid growth from that point led its manufacturing to surpass even that of Britain before the First World War.[35] Yet, at the time of the founding of the International, Germany was the only country in which a real socialist party existed, the General German Workers' Association established by Ferdinand Lassalle in 1863. Not only did Lassalle support German unification even under the reactionary Prussian monarchy, but he met with and sought to work with its chief minister, Bismarck.[36] This seemingly strange political cooperation, however, made sense on both sides. On the one hand, unification of Germany was long a goal of the left (though Marx, as well as like-minded socialists and radical democrats, rejected the idea of doing so through the Prussian monarchy). On the other, Bismarck was not afraid to work with working-class leaders who would contribute to his nationalist project (witness his appointment of Lothar Bucher, a radical democrat of 1848 and intimate of Lassalle, as an aide[37]).

Bismarck's willingness to coopt even socialist revolutionaries, and to introduce extensive measures of state welfare – while also wielding the power of the state in the Anti-Socialist Laws – combined with the state-centric legacy of Lassalle's politics, gave a peculiar stamp to the development of the labour movement in Germany. What is most

---

33.   A remark to Paul Lafargue that Engels reported to Bernstein (MECW, Vol. 46), 356.
34.   Magraw, "Socialism, Syndicalism and French Labour before 1914," 49.
35.   Dick Geary, "Socialism and the German Labour Movement Before 1914," in Geary, *Labour and Socialist Movements in Europe Before 1914*, 102–103.
36.   Jonathan Steinberg, *Bismarck: A Life*. Oxford: Oxford University Press, 2011, 199ff.
37.   Ibid., 206–207.

striking is the extent of working-class political development relative to that of trade unions. Not only did Germany have the first working-class socialist political organization, but it had the second as well: the "Eisenach" Social Democratic Workers' Party of Germany, founded in 1869. Under the leadership of Wilhelm Liebknecht and August Bebel, the Eisenachers declared themselves from their founding to be a branch of the International, and lent important support to Marx in its last years. After these parties merged into the Social Democratic Party in 1875 (adopting a statement of principles that was, however, importantly criticized by Marx[38]), it rapidly developed into a powerful political force and the largest socialist party in the world.[39] While it is famously recognized that the labour unions associated with the Social Democratic Party became strongly reformist, notwithstanding the party's formal commitment to Marx's ideas and the cause of socialist revolution, it is the prior development of significant socialist political organizations that is truly distinctive in Germany, and it shaped the working class movement there as a whole.

The working-class movement in England differed from those of both France and Germany in profoundly important ways. As noted above, Marx recognized it to be capitalist to a unique degree even in the 1870s. It was England that held priority in developing the form of industrial production that characterized capitalist social relations, proper. The long battle through which capitalists established their subordination of workers in production was fought here first, and in response the working-class trade union movement developed early.[40] Despite heavy legal suppression in the first quarter of the nineteenth century, there was a long history of workers' economic organization, and effective mobilization to achieve gains such as the Ten Hours Bill, prior to the formal legalization of unions in 1871. Although important political organization existed in the era of Chartism, no political party ensued from this, and English workers through their unions mostly collaborated with the Liberal party through the end of the nineteenth century. It had been British trade unionists who were instrumental in founding the IWA, and despite the founding of such parties as the Social Democratic Federation in 1881 and (more

---

38. Karl Marx, "Critique of the Gotha Programme" (MECW, Vol. 24, 1989), 75–99.
39. Geary, "Socialism and the German Labour Movement Before 1914," 101.
40. Zmolek, *Rethinking the Industrial Revolution* provides an excellent history of this struggle over control of production. The are many histories of English unions and working-class organization, but one would be hard pressed to recommend any work ahead of E.P. Thompson's *The Making of the English Working Class*. Harmondsworth: Penguin, 1968.

significantly) the Independent Labour Party a decade later, the workers' movement remained dominated by the unions until they themselves finally established the Labour Party in 1900.[41]

At the founding of the International, therefore, it is clear that even considering only the three major countries of European industrial capitalism[42] there was enormous variation in the development of the capitalist mode of production, and correspondingly great differences in the forms of workers' organization, both economic and political. This is evident even apart from the profound differences in the forms of state across Europe. Britain had its liberal parliamentary regime, yet even after the Second Reform Act less than 60 percent of urban male workers – and far fewer in the countryside – had the vote.[43] Although France had adult male suffrage, and Prussia the three-class franchise,[44] elections had little meaning in either, and Prussia had yet to unify Germany. These variations in the form of state were enormously significant. While Marx's reasons for dedicating himself to building a working-class political movement internationally may be readily understood, the challenges of doing so under such varied conditions can hardly be overstated.

Political currents within the International

One of the greatest challenges lay in the profusion of cross-cutting political movements. As is clear from the forgoing, there were many different political tendencies among the European working classes. All the major currents, moreover, co-existed within the IWA. Among them were several with which Marx had to deal.

British workers were above all committed to their trade unionism, though there were numbers of individuals – especially former Chartists and emigrés from the aftermath of 1848 – who adhered to developed political perspectives. The London Trades Council was particularly active politically, having organized meetings such as those supporting the struggle against slavery and the Polish Uprising, to say nothing of the founding of the International itself. Outside the circle of those immediately involved in the IWA, however, support

---

41. See Gordon Phillips, "The British Labour Movement Before 1914," in Geary, *Labour and Socialist Movements in Europe Before 1914.*
42. Though Belgium was far more developed in industry on a per capita basis than either France or Germany, and its workers played a crucial role in the International, its small size undercut the impact it might otherwise have had.
43. Phillips, "The British Labour Movement Before 1914," 39.
44. Geary, "Socialism and the German Labour Movement Before 1914," 125.

for progressive causes did not much translate into active politics. While it may well be a mistake to attribute inherent "trade union consciousness" to those primarily committed to the economic organization of the working class, it is certainly the case that the British membership of the International was overwhelmingly reformist in orientation.

The French workers who had joined in the founding meeting of the International were very largely influenced by Pierre-Joseph Proudhon. His emphasis on the right of the individual to the proceeds of labour; his opposition to political organization, but also to strikes; the great role that "mutualism"[45] played in his thought: all these resonated powerfully with the largely artisanal French workers.[46] A case can be made that Proudhonism was the primary current against which Marx had to struggle down to 1867, when the beginning of a wave of strikes – in which active support by the IWA played an important role – signalled an important shift away from Proudhon.[47]

Mikhail Bakunin was a very different anarchist thinker (though that term was no more common at that time than was "Marxist"). The relationship between Marx and Bakunin changed tremendously over time. At the time of the International's founding, Marx wrote to Engels that he had seen him for the first time since 1848, and liked him very much, "more so than previously," adding: "On the whole, he is one of the few people whom after 16 years I find to have moved forwards and not backwards."[48] Yet the history of the second half of the brief life of the International revolved around the growing opposition between Marx and his supporters, and Bakunin and his own.[49]

Another French current was represented by Louis Auguste Blanqui, revolutionist par excellence, who had taken part in numerous conspiracies and every uprising and revolution, from joining the Carbonari in the 1820s, to being elected president of the Paris Commune in 1871 (though already under arrest by the Versailles government).

---

45. Proudhon anticipated the transformation of society largely through the formation of producer cooperatives, and it was largely to the end of realizing this that he strongly advocated the idea of "the People's Bank."

46. Albert S Lindemann, *A History of European Socialism*. New Haven, CT: Yale University Press, 1983, 106.

47. Fernbach does see the history of the IWA in these terms, "Introduction" (note 16), 16–19.

48. Marx to Engels, 4 Nov. 1864 (MECW, Vol. 42, 1987), 18–19.

49. In 1874–75, Marx commented importantly on the text of Bakunin's *Statehood and Anarchy*, throughout which Bakunin criticized Marx explicitly (MECW, Vol. 24), 485–526. Bakunin died in 1876. The literature on Marx and Bakunin is enormous.

While he was undoubtedly a socialist in at least the broad sense of the term, his primary commitment was to making political revolution, from which change would be introduced. As Engels characterized the man and his movement:

> Blanqui is essentially a political revolutionary, a socialist only in sentiment, because of his sympathy for the sufferings of the people, but he has neither socialist theory nor definite practical proposals for social reforms. In his political activities he was essentially a "man of action," believing that, if a small well-organised minority should attempt to effect a revolutionary uprising at the right moment, it might, after scoring a few initial successes, carry the mass of the people and thus accomplish a victorious revolution.[50]

If perhaps many socialists would not meet the stringent criteria of Engels, it is still true that for Blanqui the revolution itself came first. Blanquism, however, was not a significant force in the International before 1870. But after the bloody suppression of the Commune, many surviving Blanquists fled to London, where they immediately made an impact and were a force in the IWA's last year.[51] They opposed moving the General Council of the International to New York, and officially split to create a specifically Blanquist organization in opposition.[52]

The last significant political current of the period reflected the ideas of Lassalle. To a great extent, Lassalle's nationalism and founding of a specifically German socialist party – to say nothing of his death immediately before the founding of the International – limited the influence of his ideas within the IWA. Marx and Engels had been in regular communication with him, and despite growing differences they mourned his passing. Although in many ways the primary influence of Lassalleanism was as an absence from, and even barrier to, the IWA, the doctrine of "the Iron Law of Wages" that Lassalle espoused did figure among the ideas to which members of the International adhered. That there was a limited "wages fund" in the economy, as a result of which efforts by trade unions to increase wages must be frustrated, was an idea that predated Lassalle; but the name he gave to the doctrine lent unwarranted "scientific" credibility to it and

---

50. Frederick Engels, "Programme of the Blanquist Commune Refugees" (MECW, Vol. 24), 13.
51. For more on Blanquism as a political force, see Patrick H. Hutton, *The Cult of the Revolutionary Tradition: The Blanquists in French Politics*. Berkeley, CA: University of California Press, 1981.
52. Engels, "Programme of the Blanquist Commune Refugees," 13.

helped make it a force to be reckoned with. Many of the Germans who did belong to the International were influenced by Lassalle.

Marx's politics and interventions in the International

Marx's contributions to the International can be seen to correspond broadly to the course of its history. This was not, however, because he dominated it, however great his influence. The members of the International were never afraid to express their opinion or stand their ground, and eventually the tide turned against Marx and towards Bakunin. His success, particularly in the early years, followed in the first place from his deep and energetic commitment and constant attention to maintaining the vision he had for it. Again and again, Marx undertook obligations for day-to-day matters as well as grand statements of purpose and policy (which, of course, always had to be voted upon). At the same time, he revealed real talent in political organization, strategy and manoeuvring, which became particularly important in the later years.[53]

Marx's role was especially important in relation to international issues. Soon after the Inaugural Address and Rules were adopted, the Central Council sent a message of congratulations written by Marx to Abraham Lincoln – "the single-minded son of the working class" – on his re-election:

> The working men of Europe feel sure that, as the American War of Independence initiated a new era of ascendancy for the middle class, so the American Anti-Slavery War will do for the working classes.[54]

He wrote in a similar vein on behalf of the International to President Johnson after Lincoln's assassination, and subsequently (citing the letter to Lincoln) to the National Labor Union of the United States urging them to work for peace, to allow the working class to advance, at a time when "their would-be masters shout war."[55]

---

53. This was, however, evident as early as his first letter to Engels on the founding of the IWA, in which he related finessing a dreadful statement of principles through his unanticipated preparation of the Inaugural Address, which was then met with unanimous approval in its stead.

54. Karl Marx, "To Abraham Lincoln, President of the United States of America" (MECW, Vol. 20), 20.

55. Karl Marx, "Address to the National Labour Union of the United States" (MECW, Vol. 21, 1985), 53–55. The threat of war loomed in 1869 as the US pressed claims against Britain for damages resulting from the *Alabama,* a ship built in Britain and delivered to the Confederacy, and other violations of neutrality. The chair of the

Among his other interventions in relation to international issues were the well-known addresses on the Franco-Prussian War.

Marx also drafted a number of resolutions that were among those adopted at the Congresses of the International in 1866 and 1868.[56] These covered such issues as: limitation of the working day to 8 hours; abolition of child labour (other than in connection with education); elimination of indirect taxes; replacement of standing armies with armed citizens; and general strikes as a means to prevent war.[57] In 1869 he advocated a policy of free and compulsory public education, using the example of US states but arguing for nationally regulated systems to ensure equal quality regardless of local conditions.[58] At the London Conference of 1871, Marx himself moved that "The Conference recommends the formation of female branches among the working class."[59] At the same conference he also moved that reports be prepared on "the means of securing the adhesion of the agricultural producers to the movement of the industrial proletariat." By 1871, however, the struggle with the Bakuninists had already begun in earnest.

Although much of what he wrote reflected the progressive stances with which the International was founded, pressing for stronger but widely accepted policies of social justice, it was in putting forward positions dealing directly with the economic and political struggles of the working class that Marx was increasingly compelled to contend with opposing views within the IWA. In June 1865, he addressed two consecutive meetings of the General Council in London in order to refute the idea of a fixed wages fund in the economy (the "Iron Law of Wages").[60] This followed a series of speeches by the former

---

Senate Foreign Relations Committee sought the enormous sum of $2 billion, with the possible alternative of annexation of British Columbia, the Red River Colony, and Nova Scotia. The claims ultimately were resolved through arbitration.

56. Marx did not himself attend any of the Congresses until the last, at The Hague, in 1872, but he submitted resolutions through the General Council. There were, of course, other resolutions as well.

57. Office of General Council, International Working Men's Association, *Resolutions of the Congress of Geneva, 1866, and the Congress of Brussels, 1868*. London: IWMA, 1868.

58. Karl Marx, Synopses of Speeches on Education (August 10 and 17, 1869), in General Council, International Workingmen's Association, *The General Council of the First International, Minutes, 1868–1870*. Moscow: Progress Publishers, 1964, 140–141, 146–147.

59. Karl Marx and Frederick Engels, "Resolutions of the Conference of Delegates of the International Working Men's Association" (MECW, Vol. 22, 1986), 424.

60. Karl Marx, *Value, Price and Profit* [sometimes published as *Wages, Price and Profit*] (MECW, Vol. 20), 102–159.

Owenite and Chartist John Weston that maintained this view and argued that trade union efforts to raise wages would therefore necessarily have negative consequences. Marx's intervention – virtually a short course in what he would publish as *Capital* – opened into weeks of debate on the subject, involving other members as well, until his view generally carried the day.

Subsequently, Marx defended trade unions in a resolution for the Geneva Congress of 1866: in the first instance, as necessary to workers' struggle around "questions of wages and time of labour"; but, further, as "unconsciously ... forming *centres of organization* of the working class" and having a crucial role "as *organized agencies for superseding the very system of wages labour and capital rule*." Then, as a result of the growing wave of successful strikes organized with support from the International, his resolution to the 1868 Brussels Congress went further to assert that while "strikes are not a means to the complete emancipation of the working classes" they "are frequently a necessity in the actual situation of the struggle between labour and capital," as well as to call for the organization of unions in trades where they did not exist, and for their joining together both locally and internationally. Through tireless efforts of this kind, Marx won growing support for his views, and increasingly displaced the influence of Lassalle and Proudhon on economic and labour issues.

The politics of Blanquism did not present such a great problem. It was neither nationalist, as Lassalle had been, nor anti-political, like Proudhon. Although, given their insurrectionary orientation, the Blanquists were not inclined to see the International in the same terms as Marx, their strong support for political organization and action meant they were not infrequently on the same side as Marx. The real issues were more deeply strategic: the difference between: (a) building a workers' movement that in the end would not only represent the whole of the class, but even be able to mobilize them *as* a class; and (b) organizing revolutionary insurrection in essentially the classic form of taking to the barricades.

Few Blanquists had been drawn to the International initially, because of the dominant role of Proudhonists among its French membership. But as the International's success and recognition grew, and with the decline of Proudhonism after 1868, some Blanquists joined even before the Commune. Although Marx worked with the Blanquists, particularly against Bakunin, the basis for his politics was never similar, as became evident with the move of the General Council to New York. Marx's interpretation of the Commune underscores the extent to which he saw revolutionary struggle in terms that differed greatly from theirs.

Already in early August 1870, a month before the stunning French defeat at Sedan, Marx wrote to Engels that:

> If a revolution breaks out in Paris, it is questionable whether they will have the means and the leaders capable of offering serious resistance to the Prussians. One cannot remain blind to the fact that the 20-year-long Bonapartist farce has brought tremendous demoralisation in its wake. One would hardly be justified to rely on revolutionary heroism.[61]

This was not so much a question of whether a "Commune" might be formed, given the history of both 1789 and 1848. The question was whether a revolutionary insurrection in the 1870s – with France defeated, the Prussian army on the doorstep of Paris, and a National Assembly of all the old parties sitting at Versailles – could succeed.

There was, of course, no doubt once the Commune was established that Marx would support it. As he wrote to Ludwig Kugelmann,

> If you look at the last chapter of my Eighteenth Brumaire you will find that I say that the next attempt of the French revolution will be no longer, as before, to transfer the bureaucratic military machine from one hand to another, but to break it, and that is essential for every real people's revolution on the Continent. And this is what our heroic Party comrades in Paris are attempting.[62]

Notwithstanding his frustration at their wasting time with trivia, failing to seize opportunities, and neglecting even to prepare adequately for the onslaught that was coming, it is clear not only in his published writing but also his letters that his admiration for the Communards in "storming the heavens" knew no bounds.[63]

Yet despite Marx's several suggestions that success might have been possible, it is not only their many mistakes but the objective situation that seem to argue otherwise. Revolutionary heroism, as he had predicted, was not enough. At least ten thousand were left dead in the street, tens of thousands more transported, and the militant working class of Paris was depleted for a generation. As Marx well knew, a revolution requires more than heroic insurrection.

The greatest conflict Marx faced in the International was of course that with Bakunin, culminating in removal of the General Council to

---

61. Marx to Engels, 8 Aug 1870 (MECW, Vol. 44, 1989) p. 39.
62. Marx to Kugelmann, 12 April 1871 (MECW, Vol. 44), 131.
63. Aside from *The Civil War in France* (MECW, Vol. 22), 307–359, see Marx's letters of 12, 17 and 26 April, 13 May and 12 June, 1871 (MECW, Vol. 44).

New York. Skirmishes were fought on several issues of policy, though the major battles were mainly organizational. Bakunin and his associates joined the IWA in 1868. The following year the subject of inheritance – abolition of which was a central tenet for Bakunin, and one of the few goals that might precede revolutionary abolition of the state – figured importantly as a policy issue. Marx produced a report, adopted by the General Council, that stressed that inheritance was only a problem because of the social power inherent in capital, and that in the struggle against capital "To proclaim the abolition of the right of inheritance as the starting point of the social revolution would only tend to lead the working class away from the true point of attack against present society."[64] After Bakunin spoke against the position, however, this report became the first from the General Council that failed to be adopted at an IWA Congress.

The most pointed policy struggle directly focussed upon the issue of political organization and action, against which the Bakunists were solidly arrayed. In this regard, Marx had the great advantage of having included the centrality of political struggle in both the Inaugural Address and Rules of the Association, though this was challenged (in part on the basis of bad translation). There were, therefore, several motions confirming the importance of workers' political liberties and active political engagement in the last years of the International, and it is testimony to Marx's own political skill that they passed. In offsetting the influence of Bakuninists, he drew support particularly from German delegates (whose increased involvement broadly corresponded to his own growing stature in Germany following the publication of *Capital*) and from the Blanquists.

At the London Conference of 1871, it was the leading Blanquist (and Communard) Édouard Vaillant who moved:

> In the presence of an unbridled and momentarily victorious reaction, which stifles any claims of socialist democracy and intends to maintain by force the distinction between classes, the Conference reminds members of the Association that the political and social questions are indissolubly linked, that they are two sides of the same question meant to be resolved by the International: the abolition of class.
>
> Workers must recognize no less than the economic solidarity that unites them and join their forces, on the political terrain as much as on the economic terrain, for the triumph of their cause.[65]

---

64. Karl Marx, "Report of the General Council on the Right of Inheritance," in *General Council of the First International, Minutes, 1868–1870,* 322–324.
65. Jacques Freymond, *et al.* eds., *La Première Internationale,* Vol. II (Geneva: E. Droz, 1962), 191–193.

In response, the London Conference commissioned a resolution – subsequently drafted by Marx and Engels – for submission to the next Congress to supplement the revised Rules already adopted at the Conference in order to clarify the importance of political organization. This new Section 7a of the Rules, adopted by the 1872 Congress at The Hague, began

> In its struggle against the collective power of the propertied classes, the working class cannot act as a class except by constituting itself into a political party, distinct from, and opposed to all old parties formed by the propertied classes.[66]

This was of course a major political achievement for Marx.

With, however, German socialists focussing primarily on their two national parties and on the newly established Reich, the Blanquists committed to a fundamentally different conception of what the International should be, and the Bakuninists growing in strength, Marx recognized that the Association had reached a limit to what it might at the time achieve in terms of the politics to which he was committed. Indeed, there was a real possibility of its becoming either a Bakuninist association opposed to political organization, or a Blanquist association that largely ignored economic organization and struggle in favour of fomenting insurrection. In either case, the potential of the IWA to build a working-class political force and its capacity to advance progressive social policies in meaningful ways would be profoundly compromised. He therefore adroitly undertook to frustrate both political tendencies at the Hague Congress: on the one hand through a report that led to Bakunin being expelled (though the Congress balked at expelling all members of Bakunin's secret organization within the IWA), and on the other, largely responding to the looming presence of Blanquist emigrés in London, by relocating the General Council to New York. In consequence, these fractious internal forces took their separate paths, leaving few behind with Marx and Engels. It really was this fact of fundamental political fragmentation and opposition, rather than the move to New York as such, that spelled the end of the International. The idea of a broad international movement, working together despite national differences and comprising a wide range of political ideas, with the common objective of building the capacity of the working class for revolutionary transformation of society while ameliorating their condition in the present, was – not for the last time – undone.

---

66. International Workingmen's Association, 5th Congress, *The Hague Congress of the First International: September 2–7, 1872, Vol. 1, Minutes and Documents.* Moscow: Progress Publishers, 1976, 282.

Marx was not a Leninist

Of course Marx was not a Leninist. When Marx died, Lenin had not yet turned 13. Yet issues of Marx's politics have been approached from Lenin's perspective for more than one hundred years now, often even by non-Leninists. This is not the place to take up a serious critique of Lenin,[67] and one must be careful not to trivialize or reduce his ideas to simplistic caricatures. It is instructive, however, to locate Marx's politics concretely in relation to those proposed by Lenin, and to contrast the two.

If the emancipation of the working class – and with it the whole of humanity – was to be the task of the workers themselves, then the first requirement was development of the capacity of that class to act in their own interests. It is precisely in this regard that Marx's conception of class politics comes to the fore, and can be seen to be inherently different from the politics of reformists, insurrectionists, anarchists and Leninists alike. Marx was prepared to make great sacrifices to help the working class advance in its struggle. It always remained, however, the self-organization of the workers that was central. Workers had to make themselves collectively into agents who would end the state's role as instrument of class-rule, and remake their lifetime of labour from a means of enriching the few into a collective realization and enjoyment of human potential. No single institution, leader, or ideological conception was either sufficient or irreplaceable for that to be achieved. It is this commitment to development of the working class, *as such*, into a social and political force that is most clearly revealed by Marx's participation in the International.

Marx never became a reformist – contrary to the views of Eduard Bernstein, most notably[68] – despite his efforts to ameliorate conditions of workers, engage in politics within existing states, and resist irresponsible calls to provocative action. By the same token, despite his abiding commitment to revolution and genuine support for the Commune, he was never an insurrectionist, and he certainly could conceive revolutionary change being achieved without taking to barricades. Marx also was never an anarchist, as such, though as early as

---

67. Which in any case would also have to take account of Lenin as a Marxist – an entirely different matter – as well as the unique historical context created by the Bolshevik Revolution.

68. Bernstein did not deny that Marx was a revolutionary, especially originally, but saw a second, reformist current in his ideas, which he sought particularly to develop. Eduard Bernstein, *Evolutionary Socialism: A Criticism and Affirmation*. New York: B.W. Huebsch, 1912.

1843 he became the first political theorist ever to view the state – *in itself, and regardless of how democratic it might be* – as inherently a form of human alienation that needed to be transcended in achieving human emancipation.[69] In this regard, he was so profoundly anti-statist to the end of his life that it might be said that his disagreement with anarchism[70] was not with its end, but over the feasibility of its means. Finally, beyond all this, he was never a Leninist, and if anything more clearly not in his maturity than in his youth.

Fifty-four years passed between the *Communist Manifesto* and Lenin's *What is to Be Done?*, with the transfer of the International to New York not quite half-way between the two. As noted above, the International was very different from the Communist League, and had a different purpose. Moreover, the IWA clearly never had any of the characteristics that Lenin called for, either in a party as such, or subsequently in the Third International, which was founded directly on the Bolshevik party model.[71] Most importantly, Marx never made any effort to introduce such characteristics.

To begin with, when Marx stressed that "the emancipation of the working classes must be conquered by the working classes themselves" (as the first rule of the Association had it), he meant exactly that. In Marx's resolutions submitted to and adopted at the Geneva Congress, the call for workers themselves to undertake "a statistical inquiry into the situation of the working classes of all countries" was posited not only to be able to know what needed to be done, but to demonstrate "their ability to take their own fate into their own hands." His resolution on cooperative labour went on to hold that:

> It is the business of the International Working Men's Association to combine and generalize the *spontaneous movements* of the working classes, but not to dictate or impose any doctrinary system whatever.[72]

The extent to which the democratic practice of the IWA was real – and anything but a form of "democratic centralism" – can be seen in the

---

69. George C. Comninel, "Emancipation in Marx's Early Work," *Socialism and Democracy*, 24 (3) (November 2010), 72.
70. That is, socialist or communist – not "libertarian" – anarchism.
71. On Lenin's conception of the party, see V.I. Lenin, *What Is to Be Done?* in *Collected Works*, Vol. 5. Moscow: Progress, 1961, 347–530. On the organization of the Third International see Helmut Gruber (ed.), *International Communism in the Era of Lenin: A Documentary History*. Ithaca, NY: Cornell University Press, 1967; and Fernando Claudin, *The Communist movement: from Comintern to Cominform*. Harmondsworth: Penguin, 1975.
72. General Council, *Resolutions of the Congress of Geneva* (note 57), emphasis in original.

difficulty Marx continuously had in dealing with the various other political currents. Yet, despite the growing battle with Bakunin, he made no effort to limit membership, a basic principle of the Bolshevik model. Indeed, the revised Rules of 1871 made the openness of membership even more explicit than the original Rules, stating that "Everybody who acknowledges and defends the principles of the International Working Men's Association is eligible to become a member."[73] When Marx's participation in the International is viewed in full, and without the filter of one or another expression of Leninism, the vivacity, openness and democracy of the politics that can be discerned is not merely a revelation, but an inspiration.

It is an inspiration that is desperately needed today. The situation of the working class internationally has (in relative terms) worsened even more in recent decades than it had when Marx wrote the Inaugural Address. The gains that workers achieved following the decisive global defeat of fascism more than two generations ago – a defeat won by working-class men and women determined to end not only rapacious and horrific oppression, but also economic vulnerability and immiseration – have been rolled back dramatically. Yet, as Marx noted then, there are compensating factors.

On the one hand, globalization and the extension of genuinely capitalist social relations of production have brought about a far greater economic commonality than existed in the era of the First International. National historical and cultural differences are of course still very real even within the confines of Europe, let alone globally. Yet, with Chinese capitalists now opening sweatshops in Italy, and with urbanization and digital communications bridging – if far from eliminating – many cultural divides, the capacity for international cooperation among labour movements is greater than ever. At the same time, on the other hand, despite the enormous oppressive power of states, and intimidating anti-labour practices of multinational giants and small-scale employers alike, significant advances have been achieved with respect to the rights of workers. These rights certainly are abused on a daily basis, but they exist in ways that they did not 150 years ago. If, therefore, the situation then called for workers to come together – and to find means to overcome not only profound social differences, but political differences as well – how much greater is both the need and the potential today. An important first step would be to recognize the value Marx himself saw in a movement like the International.

---

73. Karl Marx, "General Rules of the International Working Men's Association" (MECW, Vol. 23, 1988), 7.

Capitalist Crisis, Cooperative Labor, and the Conquest of Political Power: Marx's 'Inaugural Address' (1864) and its Relevance in the Current Moment

Michael Joseph Roberto

In the fall of 1864, Karl Marx was hard at work in London completing the first volume of *Capital* when he chose to exit the study and put theory at the service of practice. Marx had done something similar in Brussels almost 20 years earlier. He and Frederick Engels had "settled accounts" with former associates, an assortment of Left Hegelians and proponents of "true socialism," in a lengthy manuscript that was never to be published in their lifetimes. For Marx, it appeared that the decision to terminate work on *The German Ideology* would free him to resume his studies in political economy. But not for long! He and Engels had already recognized that an unprecedented economic crisis had struck much of Europe and that it was time to act. So in early 1846 they established the Communist Correspondence Committee, the first proletarian International. From Brussels, Marx had hoped to build in key cities a network of similar committees whose main objective would be the continuous exchange of information on socialist movements in England, France, Germany, and elsewhere in Europe. Although the plan never materialized, Marx's efforts were seminal to the formation of the Communist League and to the spirit of proletarian internationalism that spread through much of Europe in 1848 – until the democratic revolutions launched by workers against the "old order" were betrayed by their temporary partners, the bourgeois republicans of various stripes. With defeat came the counterrevolution and a decade of stifling reaction, from which emerged a new type of politics characterized by Marx in *The Eighteenth Brumaire of Louis Bonaparte* (1851) as the first form of modern-capitalist dictatorship, and which Engels ably summed up a few years later when he called Bonapartism "the true religion of the bourgeoisie."[1]

All this was central to Marx's thinking on the evening of September 28, 1864 as he entered St. Martin's Hall to attend a meeting called by British trade unionists and a contingent of Parisian workers to support the nationalist movement in Poland and Italy. For Marx, whose decision to attend marked a break with his longstanding rule of refusing such invitations, more was at stake than the national questions in Poland and Italy. The unprecedented economic boom of the 1850s turned to bust, as rampant speculation brought a new crisis and, with it, a resurgent workers' movement in Britain and parts of the Continent. This raised new historic possibilities for the European working classes. "This much is certain," he had written Engels more than a year earlier: "the era of revolution has now fairly opened up in Europe once more. And the general state of affairs is good." Yet for all his excitement, Marx cautioned that the next wave of action required revolutionaries to learn from the "comfortable delusions and almost childish enthusiasm" of the politics they had pursued in the years leading up to 1848.[2]

Indeed the long retreat after 1848 had helped Marx to deal with his own delusions. For one thing, he had learned that social revolution was only possible as an outcome of capitalist crisis, and the next one would require revolutionaries to push aside all romantic notions of the past and organize the majority rather than clinging to the politics of a self-purifying, delusional minority. Marx thought that this moment had come in 1857 when a series of bank failures brought a sharp and dramatic financial crisis. But the crisis quickly passed, driving him deeper into his studies to figure out why. As it turned out, his decision to reengage politically on the night of September 28, 1864 would further delay completion of the first volume of *Capital* – and prevent subsequent planned volumes from appearing during his lifetime. But everything he had learned since Brussels told him to do just that. Something quite momentous was underway and, given what he had jotted in one of his Brussels notebooks in 1845 (later known to the world as his *Theses on Feuerbach*), Marx knew well that theory was of little use if not validated by practice. So he could hardly refuse to be present that night, especially considering who

---

1. Engels to Marx, April 13, 1866, *Karl Marx-Frederick Engels Collected Works* (hereafter cited as *MECW*), vol. 42 (New York: International Publishers, 1987), 266.
2. Marx to Engels, February 13, 1863, *MECW*, vol. 41 (Moscow: Progress Publishers, 1985), 453.

had called the meeting. As he later told Engels, "I knew that on this occasion 'people who really count' were appearing, both from London and from Paris," and the meeting "which was chock full" plainly showed that "a revival of the working classes [was] taking place." Quite simply, Marx had put himself squarely in the midst of an historic occasion since those present "resolved to found a 'Workingmen's International Association', whose General Council would be located in London and whose purpose was to "'intermediate' between the workers' societies in Germany, Italy, France, and England."[3]

As we commemorate the 150th anniversary of the founding of the International Workingmen's Association – the First International – we also reaffirm Marx's key role in shaping its structure and politics. Engels made this clear enough in 1877, when he wrote that Marx's activity in the International was synonymous with its history, that he was the "soul" of the organization who drafted nearly every document issued by the General Council from 1864 to 1871.[4] Indeed, the large corpus of historiography and political commentary we now have has proven Engels right. But it also makes one wonder, is there anything more to say? To this I respond: Is it not Marx who seems always to remind us that the past must always be revisited from the standpoint of the present? And is it not this very principle that makes Marx's method central to the historian's craft, or at least to those who grasp and then embrace it? And if the answer to both is 'yes' is it not this kind of history that allows us to arrive at Marx's understanding of theory, which cannot remain as theory unless put into practice?

From these questions, I call attention to four cardinal points in Marx's Inaugural Address to the First International in 1864: (1) his grasp of the character of the crisis of the 1860s and the role it played in fueling a resurgent working-class movement of historic proportions; (2) why he considered the principle of cooperative labor to be a transformative process and transitional step toward socialism; (3) why cooperative labor as a primary passage to social emancipation could not be achieved without the conquest of state power by the working class; and (4) how his approach to political organizing in the 1860s demonstrated a keen understanding of what had to be

---

3. Marx to Engels, November 4, 1864, *MECW*, vol. 42, 16.
4. Frederick Engels, "Karl Marx," *MECW*, vol. 24 (New York: International, 1989), 190. Engels wrote the article in 1877 for the *Volks-Kalendar*, a publication of the Social-Democratic Workers Party.

done at that moment in order to advance toward the ultimate objective, communism. I then close with a brief discussion of why all four cardinal points made by Marx in 1864 resonate in the current moment.

Capitalist crisis: increasing misery in a sea of plenty

Keenly and adeptly, Marx opens the Address by describing the link between crisis conditions typical of a new phase of capitalist development and the resurgence of the working-class movement. In so doing, he focuses on a cardinal feature of the crisis – increasing misery in a rising sea of plenty – which resulted from the contradictions of industrial production. Marx had detected the origins of this phase and its peculiar conditions in the lead-up to the commercial and trade crisis of 1845–47. Rapid industrialization in the 1820s and 1830s had put a new twist on the meaning of demand which, as Marx had determined in 1846, dictated the further development of machinery as "the necessary consequence of market requirements" and, consequently, the coming of the "first world crisis of capitalism."[5] As British employers displaced workers with machines, their counterparts on the Continent and in North America were compelled to do the same, setting into motion "crisis tendencies in capitalist accumulation" as capitalists increasingly looked to transform the forces of production as a means of appropriating surplus value from workers.[6] By the late 1830s and early 1840s, these tendencies were evident in other parts of Europe as crisis conditions fully materialized in 1847.

To our knowledge, Marx and Engels were the first to analyze the crisis, in a review they wrote in 1850, describing the boom–bust intervals in the decade leading up to the 1848 revolutions.[7] The "uninterrupted depression" of industry in the years 1837–42 was followed by two years of commercial and industrial prosperity (1843–45), which fueled massive speculation. Sub-crises, i.e., the Europe-wide famine in 1846 and rising speculation in cotton and railroads, converged to create the conditions for a general commercial and trade crisis in 1847. The crisis seemingly began in 1845 with the potato blight, devastating Ireland and spreading to the Continent though with far less

---

5. Marx to Pavel Vasilyvich Annenkov, December 28, 1846, *MECW*, vol. 38 (Moscow: Progress, 1982), 99.
6. Simon Clarke, *Marx's Theory of Crisis* (New York: St. Martin's Press, 1994), 86.
7. Marx and Engels, "Review," *MECW*, vol. 10 (Moscow: Progress, 1978), 490–95. This was the third review by Marx and Engels for the *Neue Rheinische Zeitung: Politcisch-ökonimische Revue*.

catastrophic results. A year later, the grain harvest failed in much of Europe, "the worst in a generation."[8] The consequent doubling of food prices was disastrous for two-thirds of the European population still living below or barely above subsistence levels. Relief rolls expanded in many European cities, as food riots and other public disorders were frequent and widespread.[9] In England, railroad speculation had driven up share prices, resulting in a speculative "whirlpool" that turned unproductive investments into a "superstructure of fraud."[10] A wave of bankruptcies followed and soon spread to the Continent, causing shareholders to sell at reduced prices. The rising number of bankers and brokers in European cities who went bankrupt served to depress other areas of trade and commerce. Deposits made on railroad loans to the Bank of England, already earmarked for railroad expansion in other countries, found their way instead to overseas markets in sugar, coffee and other colonial products, thus pushing up prices and providing the impetus for even greater speculation. These developments accompanied the downturn in the cotton industry caused by overproduction of English cloth, which then, fueled by speculation in East Indian and Chinese markets, led to an industry-wide recession and huge production and employment cuts in English factories.[11] Meanwhile, the steady outflow of gold and silver from the Bank created panic over dwindling bullion in the money market. By May 1847, the first stage of the general crisis hit, and all credit transactions in Great Britain came to a halt. By September, speculation in the corn trade following the repeal of the Corn Laws a year earlier led to still more bankruptcies, which dovetailed with the collapse of East Asian trade caused by the routing of surplus capital into industrial production and the subsequent glut of commodities in those markets – all contributing to the collapse of the entire credit system. For Marx and Engels, the bankruptcies of 1847–48 were "unprecedented in the history of commerce."[12]

Such were the makings of a *general crisis*, the first of its kind in the European capitalist core of the expanding world market system, seemingly caused by speculation in certain commodities but essentially a contradiction arising from over-accumulation that triggered

---

8. Jonathan Sperber, *Revolutionary Europe, 1780–1850* (London & New York: Longman, 2000), 392.
9. Robert Justin Goldstein, *Political Repression in 19th-Century Europe* (London & Canberra: Croom Helm, 1983), 180.
10. Marx and Engels, "Review," 491.
11. Ibid., 493–94.
12. Ibid., 495.

overproduction. The superabundant investment of English capital in railroads at home and abroad led to the creation of many new enterprises and their rampant speculation, making it appear the cause of the crisis. Yet Marx and Engels saw through the appearances and concluded that at root it was a crisis of overproduction.[13] But it turned out to be much more: the first *general crisis* of the capitalist core, or more properly, a crisis rooted in the passage of one hegemonic form of capital to another.[14] Industrialization in Europe had coincided with the lateral extension of capital into the non-capitalist world on the basis of the older, hegemonic form of commerce. In both cases, speculation played a major role, but fundamentally this crisis marked an historic watershed in the history of capitalism, the birth of one phase and demise of another. "For the historian," as Eric Hobsbawm has written, "the great boom of the 1850s marks the foundation of a global industrial economy and a single world history."[15] The trade crisis of 1847, therefore, was the last of its kind. The ensuing wave of industrialization made Europe the undisputed core of the world capitalist market, constituting a pivotal moment in the history of world capitalism.

The key point here is that the general crisis of 1845–47 made possible the paradox of capitalist progress on a qualitatively new scale, increasing poverty and misery is a rising sea of plenty. Marx had experienced this in Brussels; in the winter of 1847–48, as he was writing *The Communist Manifesto*, almost one-quarter of the entire population received assistance of some kind despite the tremendous growth in textiles.[16] He had also addressed the causes of the paradox in *The Poverty of Philosophy*, his 1847 polemic against Pierre Joseph Proudhon. Proudhon, who also saw the paradox but could not grasp its main cause, had sought to reconcile the irreconcilable, attempting to bridge the contradictions of capitalist production and exchange through acts of free will and bonds of mutual assistance. In his mammoth *System of Economical Contradictions, or the Philosophy of*

13. Ernest Mandel, *The Formation of the Economic Thought of Karl Marx* (New York & London: Monthly Review Press, 1971), 71–72.

14. Michael Joseph Roberto, "Crisis, Revolution, and the Meaning of Progress: *The Poverty of Philosophy* and Its Contemporary Relevance," *Cultural Logic: Marxist Theory and Practice*, 2009, http://clogic.eserver.org/2009/Roberto.pdf

15. Eric Hobsbawm, *The Age of Capital, 1848–1875* (New York: Vintage Books, 1975), 69.

16. Edward De Maesschalck, *Marx in Brussel, 1845–1848* (Leuven: Davidfonds, 2005), 31. I am grateful to Liesebeth Deporter for translating key passages from the Dutch edition of De Maesschalck's very informative account of Marx's experience in Brussels.

Poverty, Proudhon had set all this down in proposing a new political economy that Marx called a "phantasmagoria." Against Proudhon, Marx argued that the paradox of rising poverty in a sea of plenty required its transcendence, a revolutionary overhaul of existing economic conditions through the conscious activity of working-class theoreticians guided by the knowledge of "profane history" and scientific political economy.[17] As Marx wrote in *The Poverty of Philosophy*, or the *Anti-Proudhon* as it was commonly known, the transcendent moment or moments would materialize when proletarian theoreticians no longer needed to find science "in their minds" but only to recognize what was occurring before them and "become its mouthpiece. So long as they look for science and merely make systems ... they see in poverty nothing but poverty, without seeing its revolutionary, subversive side, which will overthrow the old society. From this moment, science, which is a product of the historical movement, has associated itself consciously with it, has ceased to be doctrinaire and has become revolutionary"[18]

This was Marx's mindset when he drafted the Inaugural Address almost 20 years later. Through his ongoing studies and journalism, he had come to understand the paradoxical contradiction of capitalist progress as a primary feature of industrial development, specifically, the tendency of rising poverty as a necessary consequence of capital accumulation. His explanation of this tendency appears in volume 1, chapter 25 of *Capital*, "The General Law of Capitalist Accumulation." Marx's explanation, which is based on conditions in England between 1846 and 1866, is also a core argument in the Address. For Marx, all that is plausible for the working-class movement depends on the character of the crisis.

"It is a great fact," he begins, "that the misery of the working masses has not diminished from 1848 to 1864, and yet this period is unrivalled for the development of its industry and the growth of its commerce."[19] It also brought "astonishing" wealth to the capitalists. He cites William Gladstone, the Chancellor of Exchequer, who informed Parliament in April 1864 that the total import and export trade of England had tripled since 1843. A year earlier, Gladstone had boasted to Parliament in a speech entitled "Progress of the Nation" that taxable income had

---

17. Marx to Annenkov, 97.
18. Marx, *The Poverty of Philosophy: Answer to the Philosophy of Poverty by M. Proudhon*, MECW, vol. 6 (Moscow: Progress Publishers, 1976), 177–78.
19. Marx, "Inaugural Address of the Working Men's International Association," MECW, vol. 20 (Moscow: Progress Publishers, 1985), 5.

risen 6 percent from 1842 to 1852, then another 20 percent since 1853, a fact "so astonishing [as] to be almost incredible." From his research on *Capital*, Marx could have thrown in much more data, with respect not only to the augmentation of income but also to the increasing concentration and centralization of capital.[20] Progress, for sure, but for whom? Gladstone freely admitted that "this intoxicating augmentation of wealth and power [was] entirely confined to classes of property." But that wasn't enough. Gladstone also deemed it necessary to trumpet capitalist prosperity for the richest of the capitalists as evidence that the war on poverty could be won since, as he claimed, nine out of ten workers whose wages remained unchanged and whose lives were all about the "struggle for existence" still "lived on the border of that region."[21] In other words, the exploited masses needed to hold on because prosperity might still come their way.

Skillfully, Marx exposed Gladstone's view of progress in England with evidence – also found in *Capital* – from property and income tax returns and public health reports. Gladstone had declared that the average condition of the British laborer had improved to an "extraordinary degree" and was unrivalled "in the history of any country or any age." Marx countered with statistics from income and property tax returns in 1864 showing that about 3,000 of the wealthiest in the nation reaped more income than "the whole mass of agricultural laborers in England and Wales." From parliamentary reports, Marx also cited examples of deprivation and misery among various categories of workers, their children, and even prisoners. He then concluded that workers in England and on the Continent all had one thing in common. We cite Marx's passage in full because it is a pivotal point of the Address:

> Everywhere, the great mass of the working classes were sinking down to a lower depth, at the same rate, at least, that those above them were rising in the social scale. In all countries of Europe it has now become a truth demonstrable to every unprejudiced mind, and only denied by those whose purpose it is to hedge people in a fool's paradise, that no improvement of machinery, no appliance of science to production, no contrivances of communication, no new colonies, no emigration, no opening of markets, no free trade, nor all these things put together, will do away with the miseries of the industrious masses; but that on the present false base, every fresh development of the productive powers of labour must tend to deepen social contrast and point to social antagonisms. Death of starvation rose almost to the rank of an

---

20. Marx, *Capital: A Critique of Political Economy, Vol. I,* trans. Ben Fowkes (London: Penguin, 1990), 802–18.
21. Marx, "Inaugural Address," 7.

institution, during this intoxicating epoch of economical progress, in the metropolis of the British Empire. That epoch is marked in the annals of the world by the quickened return, the widening compass, and the deadlier effects of the social pest called a commercial and industrial crisis.[22]

To write this passage, Marx had drawn from his journalistic writings and his research for *Capital*. Two years before the International was formed, he had clearly recognized that capitalists always had the upper hand, whether in boom or bust times. As he wrote in *Capital*, the aim of every capitalist:

> ... is the valorization of his capital, the production of commodities which contain more labour than he paid for, and therefore contain a portion of value which costs him nothing and is nevertheless realized [*realisiert*] through the sale of those commodities. The production of surplus-value, or the making of profits, is the absolute law of this mode of production. Labour-power can be sold only to the extent that it preserves and maintains the means of production as capital, reproduces its own value as capital, and provides a source of additional capital in the shape of unpaid labour.[23]

These same processes sharpened during a crisis of overproduction, which brought greater poverty and misery to an ever-growing labor force. Marx had made this point in an article in *Die Presse* in February 1862, when he wrote about the impact of the cotton crisis on Lancashire, the largest industrial district of Great Britain and the center of cotton manufacturing. Marx reported that the main cause of the crisis was not the impact of the American Civil War on the cotton trade but the problem of overproduction in English mills. He quoted one of the biggest cotton barons, who admitted that "since 1858 an unprecedented glutting of the Asian markets had taken place and that in consequence of steadily continuing overproduction on a mass scale the present crisis was bound to occur," even without the war, tariffs and the North's blockade of the South.[24] And what impact did this crisis of overproduction have on workers? It led to the Lancashire Cotton Famine of 1861–65. In December 1862, at the height of the famine, 49 percent of all mill operatives in the cotton districts in Lancashire were unemployed; another 35 percent were on short-time, leaving only 16 percent employed full time. But just as Gladstone and others saw possibilities for workers on the threshold of newfound

---

22. *Ibid.*, 9–10.
23. Marx, *Capital*, I, 769.
24. Marx, "On the Cotton Crisis," *MECW*, vol. 19 (Moscow, Progress Publishers, 1984), 161.

wealth, "some disingenuous observers" like the social reformer Edwin Chadwick saw in all the poverty and suffering the possibility of improvements in public health. It was not a case of starvation when a man was deprived of beer, gin, or even tea ... but the case of men having bread, simple food with better air, as against a high or ordinary diet with impure air."[25]

In the end, the underlying theoretical principles for Marx's explanation of capitalist progress in the Inaugural Address also appear in volume 1 of *Capital*. Together, they demonstrate that Marx continued, as earlier in Brussels, to put theory at the service of practice. The difference now was his deeper understanding of the complex processes of capitalist production and exchange. From sections of Chapter 25 one cannot doubt how thoroughly Marx had come to understand the dialectics of capital accumulation and poverty. "The greater the social wealth, the functioning capital, the extent and energy of its growth," Marx wrote, "and therefore also the greater the absolute mass of the proletariat and the productivity of its labour, the greater is the industrial reserve army." Marx then added:

> The same causes which develop the expansive power of capital, also develop the labour-power at its disposal. The relative mass of the industrial army thus increases with the potential energy of wealth. But the greater this reserve army in proportion to the active labour-army, the greater is the mass of a consolidated surplus population, whose misery is in reverse ratio to the amount of torture it has to undergo in the form of labour. The more extensive, finally, the pauperized sections of the working class and the industrial reserve army, the greater is official pauperism. *This is the absolute general law of capitalist accumulation.*[26]

For Marx, the law governing capitalist accumulation was the same law that governed the extraction of unpaid labor, surplus-value from the worker:

> Within the capitalist system all methods for raising the social productivity of labour are put into effect at the cost of the individual worker; that all means for the development of production undergo a dialectical inversion so that they become means of domination and exploitation of the producers; they distort the worker into a fragment of a man, they degrade him to the level of an appendage of a machine. ... They transform his life-time into working-time, and drag his wife and child beneath the wheels of the juggernaut of capital. But all methods for the production of surplus-value are at the same time methods of accumulation, and every extension of accumulation becomes, conversely, a means for the development of those methods. It

---

25. John Belcham, *Industrialization and the Working Class: The English Experience, 1750–1900* (Portland, OR: Areopagitica Press, 1990), 157–58.

26. Marx, *Capital*, I, 798.

follows therefore that in proportion as capital accumulates, the situation of the worker, be his payment high or low, must grow worse.... Accumulation of wealth at one pole is, therefore, at the same time accumulation of misery, the torment of labour, slavery, ignorance, brutalization and moral degradation at the opposite pole, i.e. on the side of the class that produces its own product in the form of capital.[27]

Such was the theory that Marx began turning into a material force when the International agreed to accept his draft of the Inaugural Address. By theorizing the paradox of capitalist progress, Marx had himself become what he had described in the *Anti-Proudhon* years earlier, a theoretician who had found science not in his mind but before his very eyes and had then become its mouthpiece. Against those like Proudhon, who saw in poverty nothing but poverty, Marx's intent in the Inaugural Address was an extension of what he wrote in 1847, to see in poverty "the revolutionary, subversive side, which will overthrow the old society." No wonder that later in life, Marx would refer to the *Anti-Proudhon* as the embryo of *Capital*. In the Inaugural Address we see some of this offspring.

Cooperative labor as a lever of socialist transition

From his discussion of the crisis, Marx briefly described the set-backs European workers had experienced in the post-1848 political climate. "The short-lived dreams of emancipation," he wrote, "vanished before an epoch of industrial fever, moral marasme and political reaction." Working-class party organizations and journals on the Continent were "crushed by the iron hand of force" and many of its political leaders had fled to England. British workers, too, had lost much ground. Some gave it up willingly to join the "immense exodus" to California and Australia in search of gold, while those who remained found themselves in the tightening grip of capital. Class-conscious workers once in the forefront of political radicalism were bribed by more work and higher wages; in the eyes of fellow workers, they had become "political blacks." Meanwhile, all efforts to revitalize the Chartist movement came to naught, and the many once-vital working-class publications went down from mass apathy. Marx summed it all up cleverly: "No solidarity of action between the British and the continental working classes" had become "a solidarity of defeat."[28]

---

27. Ibid., 799.
28. Marx, "Inaugural Address," 10.

Still, he found two great victories achieved by the conscious political activity of workers during the previous two decades. First was the
passage of the Ten Hours Bill, which had limited the working day for
women and children in British factories – whenever the law was
enforced. Moreover, the bill's passage had signaled a widening
divide between the landed aristocracy and industrial bourgeoisie;
Tories in support of landed, aristocratic interests voted for the bill
against the commercial bourgeoisie, which had infuriated the aristocracy by repealing the Corn Laws nearly two years earlier. Then, too,
the legislation discredited middle-class reformers who, in defense of
capitalism, had argued that legal restrictions on the length of the
working day would be ruinous to British industry and, therefore, cala-
mitous for workers. It was the defeat of the reformers, Marx said, that
showed how British workers had triumphed "over the blind rule of
supply and demand which forms the political economy of the
middle class." Even more significant than the bill's practical success,
"the victory of a principle" meant that for "the first time in broad daylight the political economy of the middle class succumbed to the political economy of the working class."[29]

But Marx saw an even greater triumph of the political economy
of labor in the cooperative movement, especially the cooperative factories established, organized and run solely by workers. Here, "the
unassisted efforts of a few bold 'hands'" demonstrated what
workers could accomplish on their own "by deed instead of by
argument"; in other words, workers reaping success from their practical efforts without direction or meddling from bourgeois intellectuals. Cooperatives were the "great social experiments" of the day
whose importance to the working class movement could not be overstated because they demonstrated to the world how large-scale
production:

> ... in accord with the behests of modern science, may be carried out without
> the existence of a class of masters employing a class of hands; that to bear
> fruit, the means of labour need not be monopolized as a means of dominion
> over, and of extortion against, the laboring man himself; and that like slave
> labour, like serf labour, hired labour is but a transitory and inferior form, des-
> tined to disappear before associated labor, plying its toil with a willing hand, a
> ready mind, and a joyous heart.[30]

Marx leaves no doubt that workers engaged in cooperative
production were true pathfinders in the struggle against

---

29. Ibid., 11.
30. Ibid. See also *MECW*, 42, 54–55, note on Rochdale Pioneers.

capitalism.[31] Compare his strong support for this segment of the working class to his glaring omission of the many accomplishments of British trade unions since the 1840s. Since "the real worker-kings of London" had invited him to the meeting, the omission is jarring.[32] But it demonstrates that Marx was already wary of the reformist tendency of British trade unionism and was likely pondering the harder line he would take against it a year later when he criticized trade unions that fail the working class by "limiting themselves to a guerrilla war against the effects of the existing system, instead of simultaneously trying to change it, instead of using their organized forces as a lever for the final emancipation of the working class, that is to say, the ultimate abolition of the wages system."[33] On the other hand, Marx's championing of the cooperative movement is the only section of the Address where he explicitly points to socialist transition.[34] Insisting that all forms of labor, including the hired labor of cooperatives, are "transitory and inferior," he demonstrated his historical-materialist grasp of the long trajectory that made the coming of a superior form, the labor of associated producers, plausible.

At the same time, the historical realities since 1848 also revealed equally concrete forces that stood in the way of this trajectory, all to prove that "however excellent in principle, and however useful in practice, cooperative labour, if kept within the narrow circle of the casual efforts of private workmen, will never be able to arrest the growth in geometrical progression of monopoly, to free the masses, nor even to perceptibly lighten the burden of their miseries." On this point Marx could not be clearer about the solution:

---

31. Marx credits Robert Owen with sowing "the seeds of the cooperative movement" in England. He was also aware of the Rochdale Society of Equitable Pioneers, one of the earliest and most successful of England's cooperatives, formed in 1844 in Manchester by weavers from a cotton thread factory. As we shall see, Marx eventually pushed the International to recognize the superiority of producer over consumer cooperatives. But the inclusiveness of the Rochdale cooperative, whose members were communists, chartists, trade union leaders, and others, demonstrated what Marx meant by workers joining together to avoid "the class of masters" over them. For more details on the particulars of the Rochdale Pioneers, see the old but still valuable study by Sydney R. Elliot, *The English Cooperatives* (New Haven, CT: Yale University Press, 1937), and the brief but recent discussion of the cooperative by Jesús Cruz Reyes and Camilia Piñeiro Harnecker, "An Introduction to Cooperatives," in *Cooperatives and Socialism: A View from Cuba* (New York: Palgrave Macmillan, 2013), 31–33.
32. Marx to Joseph Weydemeyer, November 29, 1864, *MECW*, 42, 44.
33. Marx, "Value, Price and Profit," *MECW*, 20, 149.
34. Henry Collins and Chimen Abramsky, *Karl Marx and the British Labour Movement: Years of the First International* (London: Macmillan, 1965), 50.

> To save the industrious masses, cooperative labour ought to be developed to
> national dimensions, and consequently, to be fostered by national means.
> Yet the lords of land and the lords of capital will always use their political pri-
> vileges for the defence and perpetuation of their economical monopolies. So far
> from promoting, they will continue to lay every possible impediment in the
> way of the emancipation of labour.[35]

Undoubtedly, the development of cooperative labor on a national scale
and by "national means" required political struggle at all levels of
society that ultimately aimed at the taking of state power. But on this
point the issue of cooperative labor became a source of deep and
lasting conflict in the International. The Marx "party" – not an organization but "a party in the broadest historical sense" as Marx described
it – stressed the absolute necessity of political struggle in the long
march to a revolutionary society based on free, associated labor.[36] In
opposition, the Proudhonists insisted that the social emancipation of
labor could – and should – be achieved without it. Consequently,
the growing divide between the Marxists and the Proudhonists
during the first four years of the International only represented the
deepening of the political chasm created by its two principals, Marx
and Proudhon, during the crisis years of the mid-1840s.

Proudhon had proposed a new political economy based on the
principle of reciprocity; i.e., equal exchange of goods based on values
"constituting" equal amounts of labor put into their making, and all
done by voluntary agreement. For Proudhon, value so constituted
was easily achievable if made integral to the practices of cooperatives
and mutual aid societies that had been operating in France and elsewhere on the Continent since the 1830s. Why abolish the existing
system, Proudhon asked, when all that was "good" in commodity
exchange could be preserved simply by eliminating all the "bad"?
The struggle to attain this, Proudhon insisted, was purely economic
and in no way political. Accordingly, he rejected any call for workers
to engage in political activity aimed at the restructuring of society –
in short, a revolution.[37]

As is well known, Marx had sought Proudhon as a key ally in
building the European workers' movement – until Proudhon's book

---

35. Marx, "Inaugural Address," 11–12.
36. Marx to Ferdinand Freiligrath, February 29, 1860, *MECW*, 41, 87.
37. Charles Sabel and Jonathan Zeitlin, "Historical Alternatives to Mass Production:
    Politics and Technology in Nineteenth-Century Industrialization," *Past and
    Present*, 108 (August, 1985), 143; Steven K. Vincent, *Pierre-Joseph Proudhon and the
    Rise of French Republican Socialism* (New York: Oxford University Press, 1984),
    160–61.

appeared. In 1846, Marx called on Proudhon to take the lead in establishing a correspondence committee in Paris just like the one he and his associates had set up in Brussels. His invitation to Proudhon stressed the importance of breaking down national barriers to prepare for concerted European working-class action, a prescient internationalism that Marx sought to develop fully later on in the International. But Proudhon said no, wanting no part in the creation of any new authority, opposing participation in unions, strikes, and any revolutionary "jolt ... as the means of social reform."[38] Revolution was nowhere on Proudhon's table. For Marx, the final break came with the appearance of Proudhon's book. Proudhon's "phantasmagoria" of political economy would do great harm to the working-class movement if not ruthlessly criticized. And so Marx quickly wrote the *Anti-Proudhon*.[39]

All of this was replayed two decades later but at a much deeper level and with considerably more at stake. In the International, Proudhonists pushed for societal transformation strictly on their terms, which meant promoting cooperative enterprise in the main and solely on the basis of self-help, mutual assistance and gratuitous credit. The Marx party saw matters differently: the cooperative movement was one of many key parts in the broad struggle to build a new society. Marx made this clear in Section 5 ("Co-operative labour") of the "Instructions" he wrote for the delegates to the first congress of the International in Geneva in September 1866. The "business of the International," Marx wrote, was "to combine and generalize the spontaneous movements of the working classes, but not to dictate or impose any doctrinary system whatever." Instead, support was limited to "a few general principles" that nonetheless made cooperatives central to the International's broader and long-term political objectives. The great value of the cooperative movement as a transformative force was to demonstrate how the working class could build "a republican and beneficent system of *the association of free and equal producers*." The Instructions also affirmed Marx's position in the Inaugural Address that cooperatives alone could never achieve this end. They were but one of many "*changes of the general conditions of society*" only to be realized by "the transfer of the organized forces of society, viz. the state power, from capitalists and landlords to the producers themselves." Moreover, the Instructions also signaled Marx's view that the real transformative power of

---

38. Robert L. Hoffman, *Revolutionary Justice: The Social and Political Theory of P.-J. Proudhon* (Urbana, Chicago, IL and London: University of Illinois Press, 1972), 343–44.
39. Marx to Annenkov, 97.

cooperative enterprise lay in the production of goods rather than in their distribution (via cooperative stores).[40]

The Proudhonists battled this position at Geneva and lost, but the struggles over the character of cooperative labor were far from over. Indeed, the arguments grew more intense at the next two congresses. When discussion about collective ownership first emerged at the second congress at Lausanne in 1867, the Proudhonists called for the transfer of all large-scale industry to small-scale cooperative societies. The Marxists countered that the tasks involved would prove to be unmanageable for small-scale, local cooperatives and argued for the necessity of state control and management. Horrified at the prospects of even greater augmentation of state power, the Proudhonists quickly retreated to a vacuous position by merely calling for their transfer to "social ownership" and without stipulating its forms. The Marxists had no objection to such emptiness and were willing to let it pass. Though the whole matter was tabled for the next congress, the discussions sharpened the Marx-Proudhon divide on collective ownership and the role of the state. The last gasp of the Proudhonists came at the third congress in Brussels in 1868, when they sought a resolution calling for people's banks to provide gratuitous credit in order to free labor from the dominion of capital and thereby restore capital to "its natural and legitimate function, that of being the agent of labour." For the Marx party, the resolution smacked of Proudhon's phantasmagoria of an historic reversion to preindustrial, petty-capitalist society. Despite the fact that the resolution was tabled, the Proudhonists thought they had achieved a great victory. But it proved to be their last. By the time of the fourth congress at Basel, Proudhonism had been swept away by the pace of capitalist development, as the sharpening of class antagonisms had made its doctrines ridiculously anachronistic, a vestige of earlier times. The Marxist position on cooperatives and the principle of cooperative labor in the context of the broader struggle against capital had prevailed – only to face a new threat from Bakunin and his followers.[41]

---

40. Marx, "Instructions for the Delegates of the Provisional General Council. The Different Questions," *MECW*, vol. 20, 190; see also *The General Council of the First International 1864–1866: The London Conference, Minutes* (Moscow: Foreign Languages Publishing House), 346–47. Since Marx was ever mindful of the necessity for cooperative production to expand on a national level, the Instructions also recommended that the income generated by each cooperative be put into a fund for the propagation of new enterprises. See the entire document in the documents section of this issue.

41. Julius Braunthal, *History of the International, Volume 1: 1864–1914*, trans. Henry Collins and Kenneth Mitchell (New York & Washington: Frederick A. Praeger,

The necessity of political power in the march to associated labor

Marx closes the Address with a call to action: "To conquer political power has therefore become the great duty of the working classes." No matter what the gains of workers through strikes and protests or the spread of cooperative enterprise, none were alone sufficient for a revolutionary transformation of society and the end to capitalism. Victory depended mainly on the workers being "united by combination and led by knowledge."[42] For Marx, only a scientific and collective grasp of material conditions made possible the concerted, conscious political action required for the proletariat's *line of march* to communism. Here again, we find the embryo of Marx's thinking on these matters in the practical and theoretical work he forged in Brussels nearly 20 years earlier. In the *Anti-Proudhon* he had argued that working-class theoreticians who had found science before their very eyes could then articulate that knowledge to build the working-class movement. "Of all the instruments of production," Marx wrote, "the greatest productive power is the revolutionary class itself."[43] A year later, he and Engels had themselves become its leading advocates. Relying on their theoretical grasp of the general crisis of the 1840s in the *Manifesto of the Communist Party*, they called on the working class to take "the first step in the revolution" to win "the battle of democracy" and then "use its political supremacy to wrest, by degrees, all capital from the bourgeoisie, to centralize all production in the hands of the State, i.e. of the proletariat organized as the ruling class, and to increase the total of productive forces as rapidly as possible."[44] Two decades later all this came to bear on Marx as he sat down to write the Inaugural Address, which he crafted as a review of the working class since the 1840s. A new crisis was underway and the moment had arrived to renew revolutionary struggle. The delusions of the past must give way to new thinking and practice but with the same goal – the conquest of state power by the working class as an independent political force.

As political struggle within and beyond the International intensified in the late 1860s and early 1870s, Marx remained steadfast in his conviction that social emancipation could only proceed from that political struggle. Whatever the particular forms of political struggle dictated by national and or regional conditions, this objective remained

---

1967), 128–31; G.M. Stekloff, *History of the First International* (New York: International Publishers, 1928), 99–132.

42. Marx, "Inaugural Address," 12.
43. Marx, *The Poverty of Philosophy*, 211.
44. Marx and Engels, *Manifesto of the Communist Party, MECW*, vol. 6, 504.

its central task and prime duty. The economic struggles, whether to achieve cooperative enterprise or to build trade unions, would not of themselves lead to a new society based on associated labor. The ultimate challenge lay in building movements in various capitalist nations whose objective would be to conquer state power in order to democratize the political system and then to engage in the processes aimed at the emancipation of labor. The task of creating a revolutionary society built on the principles and practices of associated labor could only proceed once state power was achieved. The political revolution once made had to vanquish all vestiges of the counterrevolution in order to advance the social revolution. And it could only be successful if done *internationally*.

This much was certain even in the fifth and final congress held in The Hague in 1872, the only one Marx attended. Within less than a year after the International was established, the Marx party had waged constant internal struggles against two main camps, a politically indifferent and often truculent Proudhonism, and the reformism of the British trade unions. By then history had swept away the abstract fantasies of Proudhonism, while the British labor movement sought greater accommodation and acquiescence to capital. As delegates convened in The Hague, the European working classes faced the growing power of monopoly capital and political reaction. The Paris Commune had been crushed the previous year, and European capitalism would soon generate a new and unprecedented round of imperial expansion that would bring the carving up of Africa, the race for new markets in the East, and, eventually, a global conflagration. Meanwhile, the likelihood of a Bakuninist majority at the next congress and the increasing factionalism in the various European sections suggested that the International had done its part in facilitating the growth of proletarian consciousness, though it now seemed clear that new vehicles were necessary for further development. For these reasons, the Marx party boldly engineered a vote to move the General Council to New York, thereby signaling its view that further development of the working-class movement in Europe required a new vehicle or vehicles.

Nevertheless, Marx was relentless in reminding the International that the primary duty of the working class was still, in the end, the conquest of political power. The Commune's crushing defeat had dramatized that imperative. For this reason, the Marx party proposed a resolution at the congress that was adopted by a wide margin and inserted into the Rules under Article 7a. It read:

In its struggle against the collective power of the propertied classes, the working class cannot act as a class except by constituting itself into a political party, distinct from, and opposed to, all old parties formed by the propertied classes.

This constitution of the working class into a political party is indispensable in order to ensure the triumph of the social revolution, and of its ultimate end, the abolition of classes.

The combination of forces which the working class has already effected by its economic struggles ought, at the same time, to serve as the lever for its struggles against the political power of the landlords and capitalists.

The lords of land and capital will always use their political privileges for the defence and perpetuation of their economic monopolies, and for the enslavement of labour. The conquest of political power has therefore become the great duty of the working class.[45]

Ironically, perhaps, this call to the working class which Marx made central to the cause of the International would ultimately transform his and Engels' meaning of the party, if not the role of communists in it. Almost from the beginning of their collaboration, both had viewed "their" party as likeminded individuals with consensus on the character of revolutionary struggle at any moment and on the seminal analysis which defined that struggle. As August Nimitz reminds us, the "Marx–Engels team" logged more time in the International than any other political group. But outside of the General Council, where they anticipated what Nimtz calls "Leninist organizational norms" for discipline within a centralized but democratic body, the team rejected any idea of an organizational model that might risk putting the International at the service of an existing bourgeois political party.

Nevertheless, Marx came to see the International as a transformative phase of party building. In 1873, a year after the decision at the Hague congress to transfer the General Council to New York, Marx advised its secretary, Friedrich Sorge, to allow the "formal organization" of the International to "recede into the background for the time being," since the struggle to win political power had now passed "to the most capable in the various countries." Party-building would now occur within the "various countries."[46] At the same time, Marx and Engels retained their longstanding position that communists "do not form their own political party opposed to other working class parties ... have no interests separate and apart from the proletariat as a

---

45. Marx and Engels, "Resolutions of the General Congress Held at The Hague," *MECW*, vol. 23 (New York: International Publishers, 1988), 243.
46. August Nimtz, Jr., *Marx and Engels: Their Contribution to the Democratic Breakthrough* (Albany, NY: State University of New York Press, 2000), 234–35.

whole ... [and] do not set up sectarian principles of their own, by which to shape and mould the proletarian movement."[47]

"Strong in deed, mild in manner"

Marx's astute use of content and analysis in his crafting of the Inaugural Address often overshadows the political sensitivity he brought to its delivery. To his understanding of theory and practice we must also add his grasp of the moment and the method and style it required. As a member of the committee charged with drafting a declaration of principles and provisional rules, Marx was asked to complete the task after all efforts by committee had failed. Quickly discarding a confusing jumble of ideas and sentiments offered by other committee members, Marx drafted what he described to Engels as "a sort of review of the working class since 1845," along with a list of 10 provisional rules. For Marx, the main purpose of the address was to unite politicized workers of varying viewpoints – "the people who really counted" – on the basis of content that all would find more or less acceptable. This, he told Engels, was difficult to do since the reawakening of the workers was still in its early stages and direct, plain-speaking calls for revolution that characterized the old boldness, were premature. So, he wrote Engels, "we must be strong in deed, mild in manner."[48]

Marx showed tremendous skill in employing language to unite distinct factions of workers, though there could be no mistaking the bold communist principles beneath the moderate phrasing that called for a revolution aimed at the transition to socialism. Long ago, one of the first historians of the International to write from a communist viewpoint observed that Marx's scientific training and his political experiences empowered him to explain the historical course of the proletarian struggle to those around him. From the various currents of workers' movements since the 1840s, Marx saw the essence and historical trajectory of the class itself by grasping its fundamental causes and hence its laws of development. On this basis, Marx then directed all his knowledge toward helping workers think of themselves as a *class for itself*. To that end, Marx the great thinker became also a respected and likeable person. When we read about Marx's work in the International, we begin to feel the vibe that Marx had generated to secure genuine acceptance among those he believed "really counted" but were not like him. Marx's sensitivity to language in the Inaugural

---

47. Marx and Engels, *Manifesto of the Communist Party*, 497.
48. Marx to Engels, *MECE*, vol. 42, 18.

Address reflected his sensitivity to the cause and the enormous responsibilities it required to be human. While he recognized how important it was theoretically to be one step ahead of the masses, he realized politically that it could be "no more than one step."[49]

The Inaugural Address from our vantage point

From our studies and practical work, many of us understand that the current crisis points to a global capitalist system beyond repair. Indeed, the human toll in the core and periphery, as well as on nature itself, is unprecedented. Nor has so-called progress under capitalism ever been more paradoxical. Consider that a million people living on the streets in Mumbai routinely go to work every day in the informal sector, while India's richest man – some media accounts say the world's fourth richest – enjoys unfathomable pleasures with his wife and three children in their 27-story house, replete with a ballroom, lounges, and ceilings on the top floors high enough to accommodate a small forest of trees. As capitalism draws to an historic close, so do its extremes. But how difficult it is to grasp them in today's spectacle of capitalist prosperity! Gladstone's promises of "intoxicating" wealth to the workers of nineteenth century England pale in comparison to the corporate propaganda mills of today, which call on us to consume ever more, though each act of consumption often means submission to more debt and the moral degradation now inseparable from the coming ecological catastrophe – all resulting from the incessant drive for capital accumulation.

Yet for all its dysfunctional features and dystopian elements, this crisis points to the plausibility of another world beyond capitalism. Transitional and transformative forces are at work that connect our moment of transition to the one that Marx and the founders of the First International considered theirs.

First, there is the long tradition of working-class internationalism itself. At the end of the Inaugural Address, Marx calls attention to the unbounded potential of "fraternal concurrence" that arose from the historic struggles against capital and the old order. None were more central than the "heroic resistance" of English workers who kept their leaders from "plunging headlong into an infamous crusade for the perpetuation and propagation of slavery on the other side of the Atlantic." Here, for Marx, was the archetype of "criminal designs" by European rulers whose lust for profit required the survival

49. Stekloff, *History of the First International*, 77.

of pre-capitalist barbarisms. And just as that same, most advanced of all European nations sought to keep alive the Confederacy and its barbarous and anachronistic mode of production, so too did it give credence to czarist Russia, that most backward and reactionary giant and Poland's assassin. In the name of the International, Marx called on the working classes of Europe and North America to forge their respective paths to political power, and to simultaneously "vindicate the simple laws of morals and justice" through a growing spirit of internationalism.[50]

I will not venture here on the necessary scope of a New International and the monumental efforts it will take to create one. But in the past quarter-century, we have seen moments of "fraternal concurrence" that have given rise to optimism and a coherent vision of the future. The anti-globalization protests of the late 1990s and early 2000s galvanized popular support against corporate power and its massive malfeasance toward hundreds of millions of people in the peripheries of the world capitalist system. The protests in Seattle and elsewhere sparked the formation of counter-hegemonic forces against neoliberalism and imperialism, manifest in the meetings of the World Social Forum. Then came the Occupy movement, which exploded in New York in September of 2011, and quickly spread across the United States and beyond, its participants propelled by a desire "to vindicate the simple laws of morals and justice" against the power of the 1 percent whose prosperity has meant growing deprivation among the remaining 99. More recently, the courageous stand by Walmart employees and fast-food workers has given the rest of us some insight into the desperate lives of the working poor. Though far from socialist, all these efforts are byproducts of a nascent global movement that owes much to the legacy of the First International.

I have sought to explain why Marx's grasp of *his* historical moment should resonate in *ours*. The cardinal points in the Address – crisis, cooperative labor, and the conquest of political power by the workers themselves – are all relevant to the current moment, albeit in more complex forms and in infinitely more dangerous times.

The global capitalist crisis of the 1860s marked the beginning of the end of capitalism. This explains on the one hand why the International emerged and, on the other, why it failed. As István Mészáros has recently suggested,[51] the worldwide rise of imperialism against the

---

50. Marx, "Inaugural Address," 13.
51. István Mészáros, "Reflections on the New International," *Monthly Review*, vol. 65, no. 9 (February, 2014), 47.

forces of international labor brought the latter's defeat, of which the demise of the International was symptomatic. During this last stage of capitalism – in which the reproduction of capital itself increasingly depends on financialization and ecological degradation – the gap between wealth and poverty advances dialectically with a titanic effort to conceal it; hence the paradox of appearance and essence on an unprecedented scale. For Gladstone, national progress flowed from the profits of the propertied classes, which held the claim that the vast majority of workers "on the borders" would one day reap its benefits as they actually fell into greater poverty. We find the same realities and baseless claims in the United States today. Recovery from the 2008 financial collapse, which concealed the deeper and longstanding crisis in the so-called productive economy, has been steady and increasingly profitable – but mainly for the owners and high-level managers of capital. But that's the extent of it. For workers, official unemployment is dropping, but that masks the more significant statistics of underemployment and depressed wages. Even in the manufacturing sectors where some job growth has occurred, corporate profits are soaring while wages are sometimes no more than half of what they were in past times. One could say that more Americans are back at work though they are squeezed of surplus value in absolute terms. Meanwhile, the message they get from corporate media gurus about better times ahead echoes Gladstone's.

Secondly, the magnitude of the current crisis is fueling the US cooperative movement, sometimes with the aid of Occupy groups. The best known case is in Chicago where occupiers supported workers at Republic Windows and Doors who took over the plant in January 2012 after owners illegally shut it down for the second time in four years. Occupiers raised a groundswell of community support that gave Republic's workers time to develop a proposal for cooperative ownership. Their plan called for the creation of the New Era Windows Cooperative as the first large industrial cooperative in the US. The value of their efforts, typical of many others, is that they are involving individuals whose ideological dispositions vary quite significantly but who in working together create "the potentiality of class consciousness based on learned experiences in the process of production" as well as playing a role in the wider anti-capitalist struggle.[52]

---

52. Peter Ranis, "Worker Cooperatives: Creating Participatory Socialism in Capitalism and State Socialism," *Democracy at Work*, October 1, 2012, http://www. democracyatwork.info/articles/2012/10/worker-cooperatives-creating-participato ry-socialism-in-capitalism-and-state-socialism/

Why not? The cooperative movement has deep roots in the US and also an historic connection with the First International. For example, the International took its position on the legal limit of an eight hour working day from a declaration of the National Labor Union (NLU) at its 1866 convention in Baltimore, a hallmark in the history of trade unionism.[53] Nevertheless, the NLU put cooperation on an even higher plane, and the subsequent development of the cooperative movement in the parts of the United States during the late 1860s and 1870s was substantial, though decidedly Proudhonist and anarchist rather than socialist.[54] Cooperatives also developed along regional lines. In the South, African Americans forged local consumer cooperatives that demonstrated community control and democratic decision-making within the wider framework of self-help. Their leading theoretician, W.E.B. Du Bois, called for "a cooperative Negro industrial system in America" as part of a broader vision and belief that what lay in the future was "the ultimate triumph of some form of Socialism the world over; that is, common ownership and control of the means of production and equality of income."[55]

Nevertheless, as Marx reminds us, we cannot afford to restrict these efforts to narrow circles of workers developing cooperatives in their respective cities. Nor should we regard cooperatives operating within existing capitalist relations of production and exchange as anything more than transitional forms and measures. If this is indeed a structural crisis of world capitalism, then our moment of transition compels us to build a national force that is at once a movement and a political party. More than ever, our duty is the conquest of political power to facilitate the democratic-socialist revolution – or face our common ruin.

---

53. Marx, "Instructions for the Delegates of the Provisional General Council," 187.
54. Samuel Bernstein, *The First International in America* (New York: Augustus M. Kelley, 1965), 24, 93–98.
55. W.E.B. Du Bois, *Dusk of Dawn: An Essay Toward an Autobiography of a Race Concept*, in *Du Bois: Writings*, ed. Nathan Huggins (New York: Library of America, 1986), 788–89.

A Common Banner: Marxists and Anarchists in the First International

Michael Löwy

I

Marxists and Anarchists (these terms were not usual at that time) were part of the International Workingmen's Association (IWA) – the First International – since its origin in 1864. The disagreements between partisans of Marx and of Bakunin led to a bitter split in 1872. Soon afterwards, the "Marxist" IWA de facto dissolved itself, while the Bakuninists created, in a conference at Saint-Imier, Switzerland (1872), their own IWA, which, in precarious ways, still exists today. For Marx, the reasons for the split are Bakunin's Pan-Slavist tendencies and his anti-democratic, conspiratorial fractionalism. According to Bakunin, the division resulted from Marx's Pan-German orientation, as well as his authoritarian and intolerant behavior. In spite of the obvious exaggerations, both accusations contain some truth, and the wrongs can hardly be placed only on one side. Marxist and Anarchist historians reproduced these arguments, each one blaming the other for the crisis of the IWA. Academic scholars, even if they don't take sides, also emphasize the conflict of ideas and practices between the two.[1]

What is lost in this approach, which largely predominates in the literature on the First International, is the simple and important fact that this was an open and pluralistic Association, where, in spite of disagreements and conflicts, partisans of Proudhon, Marx, Bakunin, Blanqui, and others, were able to work together for several years, eventually adopting common resolutions, and fighting side by side in the greatest revolutionary event of the nineteenth century, the Paris Commune. Let us briefly sketch some of the main moments of this

---

1. A recent example is Robert Graham, "Marxism and Anarchism on Communism: The Debate between the Two Bastions of the Left," in Shannon Brincat (ed.) *Communism in the 21st Century*. Vol 2 *Whither Communism?* Oxford, Praeger, 2014.

forgotten history of the "coming together" of Marxists and Anarchists in the IWA.

II

Soon after the founding of the First International, its Central Council assigned Karl Marx to write the Provisional Rules of the Association. The document begins with the famous call – "The emancipation of the working classes must be conquered by the working classes themselves" – which has remained a common ground for Marxists and Anarchists.

From the beginning, Anarchists and *Libertaires* – I use the French term, which refers to a broad anti-authoritarian *revolutionary socialist* tendency, because its English equivalent, *libertarians*, has been hijacked by an ultra-liberal *capitalist* reactionary ideology – were present, next to other socialists, in the First International. This applies first of all to the followers of Proudhon (1809–1865), whose relations with the Marxian socialists were not necessarily conflictive. Between Marx's friends and the representatives of the Left Proudhonian current, such as the Belgian César de Paepe and the French Eugène Varlin, there was considerable agreement. Both opposed the right-wing (petty-bourgeois) Proudhonians, partisans of so-called "mutualism," an economic project based on "equal exchange" among small proprietors. One of the main proponents of mutualism and private property was the French delegate Henri Tolain, who would later be expelled from the First International for treason because of his support for the bourgeois Versailles government against the Paris Commune.

At the Brussels Congress of the IWA in 1868, the alliance between the two leftist tendencies resulted in the adoption, against the "mutualists," of a *collectivist* program, presented by the Belgian *libertaire* socialist César de Paepe. This resolution proposed collective ownership of the means of production – land, mines, forests, machines, means of transportation.[2] The resolution on the forests appears, in retrospect, one of the most interesting, in view of its *socialist and ecological* implications:

> Considering that abandoning the forests to private owners leads to their destruction;
> That this destruction in certain parts of the territory will harm the conservation of water sources, and therefore, the good quality of the land, as well as public health and the life of the citizens;

---

2. See Gaetano Manfredonia, *L'anarchisme en Europe*, Paris, PUF, Que sais-je? 2001, 36.

The Congress decides that the forests should become the property of the social collectivity.[3]

Both tendencies also supported a resolution stating that workers should react to war by a general strike. Karl Marx (who wasn't present in Brussels) didn't like this resolution, which he appears to have considered unrealistic, although it was proposed by one of his followers – soon to become his son-in-law by marrying Jenny Marx – Charles Longuet.

It was at that moment, in 1868, that Bakunin joined the First International. He considered himself, on several issues, sympathetic to Marx's ideas. He met Marx during a visit to London in 1864, and in 1867 Marx sent him a copy of *Das Kapital*. Bakunin's reaction was enthusiastic; he celebrated "M. Karl Marx, the illustrious leader of German Communism," and "his magnificent work *Das Kapital*." He believed the book should be translated into French:

> ... because, as far as I know, no other book contains such a profound, luminous, scientific analysis, such a decisive one, and, if I may say so, is so pitiless in unmasking the formation of bourgeois capital and the systematic and cruel exploitation that it continues to impose on proletarian labor. The only shortcoming of the book ... is that it is written, in part only, in a too metaphysical and abstract style ... which makes its reading difficult and almost impossible for most workers. However, it is the workers that should read it. The bourgeois will never do it, or, if they read it, wouldn't understand it, and if they understand it, will never mention it; this book being nothing else but their death sentence, scientifically motivated and irrevocably uttered, not as individuals but as a class.[4]

It is not by chance that as late as 1879, several years after the split, a close follower of Bakunin, the Italian anarchist Carlo Cafiero, produced a popular version of *Capital*, which was considered very useful by Marx.

Of course, there were from the beginning strong disagreements between Marx and Bakunin. In an October 28, 1869 letter to Herzen, Bakunin mentioned his principled opposition to what he called Marx's "state-communism." But in the same letter he added, about Marx: "we should not underestimate, and I certainly don't, the immense services that he rendered to the cause of socialism, which he has served with intelligence, energy and sincerity for the last 25 years, in which endeavor he has undoubtedly surpassed us all."[5]

---

3. Amaro del Rosal, *Los congresos obreros internacionales en el siglo XIX*, Mexico, Grijalbo, 1958, 159.
4. Quoted in G.P. Maximoff (ed.), *The Political Philosophy of Bakunin*, London, The Free Press of Glencoe, 1953, 187. Also Bakounine, *Œuvres*, Paris, Champ libre, VIII, 357.
5. Quoted in «Association Internationale des Travailleurs», *Wikipedia*.

In 1869, at the Basel Conference of the IWA, the two collectivist tendencies approved a common resolution proposing the socialization of land. However, the Anarchists obtained a symbolic victory by winning significant support – but not the required majority – for their resolution in favor of the abolition of inheritance: 32 votes among 68 delegates (23 were against, 13 abstained). Marx and his friends on the General Council argued that inheritance was only a consequence of the economic system, based on private property of the means of production, and was not the cause of exploitation. Their proposal – to tax, rather than suppress inheritance – got only 19 votes (37 against, six abstentions). Bakunin viewed the latter vote as a "complete victory" for his ideas.

III

With the Paris Commune of 1871, Anarchists and Marxists cooperated in the first great attempt at proletarian power in modern history. Already in 1870, Leo Frankel, a Hungarian worker activist living in France, a close friend of Marx, and Eugene Varlin, the dissident Proudhonian, worked together for the reorganization of the French section of the IWA. After March 18, 1871, the two cooperated closely in the leadership of the Paris Commune: Frankel as Delegate on Labor, Varlin as Delegate on War. Both took part, in May 1871, in the fight against the Versailles army. Varlin was shot after the defeat of the Commune, while Frankel was able to emigrate to London.

In spite of its short-lived character – only a few months – the Commune was the first historical example of workers' revolutionary power, democratically organized – delegates elected by universal suffrage – and suppressing the bureaucratic apparatus of the bourgeois State. It was also a truly *pluralist* experience, associating in the same struggle "Marxists" (a word which didn't yet exist), left Proudhonians, Jacobins, Blanquists and Social Republicans.

Of course, Marx's and Bakunin's respective analyses of this revolutionary event were entirely opposed. One could summarize Marx's interpretation by the following quote:

> The situation of the small number of convinced socialists in the Commune was excessively difficult. They had to oppose a revolutionary government and army to the Versailles government and army.

Against this understanding of the civil war in France as being between two governments and their respective armies, Bakunin developed a strong anti-statist viewpoint:

> The Paris commune was a revolution against *the State* itself, this supernatural monster produced by society.

Well informed readers have already corrected this presentation: the first statement was in fact written by Bakunin, in his essay "The Paris Commune and the notion of the State."[6] And the second one was written by Marx, in his first draft of *The Civil War in France 1871*.[7] We inverted the statements on purpose, to show that the – undeniable – divergences between Marx and Bakunin, Marxists and Anarchists, are not as simple and obvious as one usually believes.

Interestingly, Marx rejoiced in the fact that during the events of the Commune the Proudhonians forgot their mentor's hostility to revolutionary political action, while certain Anarchists were pleased that Marx's writings on the Commune forgot centralism and adopted federalism. It is true that *The Civil War in France 1871*, which Marx wrote on behalf of the First International (along with the several drafts and materials preparing this document), bears witness to Marx's ferocious anti-statism. Defining the Commune as the political form, finally found, for the social emancipation of the workers, he insisted on the break with the State, this artificial body, this *boa constrictor* as he called it, this suffocating nightmare, this parasitical overgrowth.[8]

In fact, this was not the first time that Marx voiced strongly anti-statist views. He did so in his manuscript *Critique of Hegel's Philosophy of Right* (1843), where he opposes "true democracy" to the state, and in several political writings, for instance in the *18th Brumaire of Louis Bonaparte* (1852), where he writes that "the state enmeshes, controls, regulates, superintends, and tutors civil society from its most comprehensive manifestations of life down to its most insignificant stirrings, from its most general modes of being to the private existence of individuals." In modern bourgeois society "this parasitic body acquires a ubiquity, an omniscience, a capacity for accelerated mobility, and an elasticity which finds a counterpart only in the helpless dependence, the loose shapelessness of the actual social body

---

6. M. Bakounine, *De la Guerre à la Commune*, textes ed. Fernand Rudé, Paris, Anthropos, 1972, 412.

7. Marx, Engels, Lénine, *Sur la Commune de Paris*, Moscow, Ed. du Progrès, 1971, 45.

8. Karl Marx and Friedrich Engels, *Inventer l'inconnu. Textes et correspondances autour de la Commune*, introduced by Daniel Bensaïd, in "Politiques de Marx" series, Paris, Editions de La Fabrique, 2008.

(*Gesellschaftskörper*)."[9] The essay on the Commune is the sharpest expression of this revolutionary rejection of the state.

However, after the Commune, the conflict between the two revolutionary tendencies of international socialism intensified, leading, at the Hague Congress of the IWA (1872), to the exclusion of Bakunin and Guillaume (his Swiss follower), and the transfer of the IWA headquarters to New York – in fact, its dissolution. Following the split, the Anarchists, as mentioned above, founded their own International Workers Association.

In spite of the split, Marx and Engels did not ignore Bakunin's writings, and in some cases, had to agree with his anti-Statist arguments. One striking example is the *Critique of the Gotha Program* (1875). In his book *Statism and Anarchy* (1873), Bakunin sharply criticized the concept of "People's State," used by German Social-Democrats, which he attributed (rightly) to Ferdinand Lassalle and (wrongly) to Marx. When the followers of Marx and Lassalle united in 1875 in the city of Gotha to found the German Social-Democratic Party (SPD), their common Program raised the proposition of a People's State (*Volksstaat*) for Germany. In his *Critique of the Gotha Program* – written as an internal document, and only published after his death – Marx openly rejects the concept of People's State. Moreover, in the letter to his friend Wilhelm Bracke – one of the leaders of the Party – which he sent together with the *Critique*, he explained that one of his reasons for writing this document is that "Bakunin ... makes me responsible not only for all the programs of the Party, but even for all the steps taken by [Wilhelm] Liebknecht since the days of his cooperation with the People's Party (*Volkspartei*)."[10] Engels, in a March 1875 letter to August Bebel, is even more explicit : "The Anarchists threw the *Volksstaat* in our faces to the point of saturation, even though Marx's piece against Proudhon as well as the *Communist Manifesto* had already openly stated that with

---

9. On the Manuscript of 1843 see Miguel Abensour, *La Démocratie contre l'Etat. Marx et le moment machiavélien,* Paris, Le Felin, 2004, 137–42, and K. Marx, *The Eighteenth Brumaire of Louis Bonaparte,* Moscow, Progress Publishers, 1937, 30 (corrected after the German original, in Marx and Engels, *Ausgewählte Schriften,* Zürich, Ringverlag, 1934, 369).

10. Document annexed in Marx and Engels, *Critique des Programme de Gotha et d'Erfurt,* Paris, Editions Sociales, 1950, 46. The Party mentioned is the Workers' Social-Democratic Party (SDAP) founded by Liebknecht and Bebel in 1869 in the city of Eisenach (the precursor to the SPD). The *Volkspartei* was a liberal bourgeois Party, in which Liebknecht participated before the foundation of the SDAP.

the establishment of socialist society the State dissolves itself and disappears."[11]

One can therefore conclude that the argument against Lassallean statism in the *Critique of the Gotha Program* was, to a certain extent, motivated by Bakunin's polemics against the German Social-Democrats. In the same letter to Bebel, Engels goes even further in the direction of Anarchism: "One should drop all this idle talk on the State, particularly after the Paris Commune, which was no longer a State in the proper meaning of the word. ... I propose therefore to replace everywhere [in the Program] *State* by *Gemeinwesen*, a good old German word, which may well correspond to the French 'Commune.'"[12]

IV

Instead of trying to book-keep the mistakes and blunders of each side in the conflict – there is no lack of mutual accusations – I have tried to emphasize the positive aspect of the First International: a diverse, multiple, democratic internationalist movement, where participants with distinct political approaches were able not only to coexist, but to cooperate in thought and action over a period of several years, playing a vanguard role in the first great modern proletarian revolution. It was an International in which Marxists and *Libertaires*, either as individuals or as political organizations (such as the Marxist German Social-Democratic Workers' Party) could – in spite of the conflicts – work together and engage in common actions.

The later Internationals – the Second, the Third and the Fourth – did not have much space for the Anarchists. However, at several important moments in the history of the twentieth century, Anarchists and Socialists or Communists were able to join forces: (1) In the first years of the October Revolution (1917–21), many Anarchists, such as Emma Goldman and Alexander Berkman, gave (critical) support to the Bolshevik leaders; (2) During the Spanish Revolution, the Anarchists of the CNT-FAI (Confederación Nacional del Trabajo – Federación Anarquista Ibérica) and the Trotsky-sympathizers of the POUM (Partido Obrero de Unificación Marxista) fought side by side against fascism, and opposed the non-revolutionary orientation of Stalinists and right-wing Social-Democrats; and (3) In May '68, one of the first revolutionary initiatives was the foundation of the

---

11. Ibid., 99.
12. Ibid.

March 22 Movement, under the leadership of the Anarchist Daniel Cohn-Bendit and the Trotskyist Daniel Bensaïd. There were also several significant intellectual attempts to bring together the two revolutionary traditions, among writers such as William Morris or Victor Serge, poets such as André Breton (the founder of the Surrealist movement), philosophers such as Walter Benjamin, and historians such as Daniel Guérin.

The experience of the First International cannot repeat itself, of course, but it is highly relevant to us, at the beginning of the twenty-first century, when again Marxists and Anarchists – or Autonomists, *Libertaires*, etc. – join forces and act together, as individuals, as networks, or as political organizations (whose existence is not an obstacle to cooperation), in support of the Zapatistas of Chiapas, in the Global Justice movement, in radical ecological struggles, in the mass mobilizations of the *Indignados* (Spain, Greece), or in Occupy Wall Street.

Race, Internationalism and Labor: Reflections upon the 150th Anniversary of the First International

Race, Internationalism and Labor:
Reflections upon the 150th Anniversary
of the First International

Bill Fletcher Jr.

> If the emancipation of the working classes requires their fraternal concurrence, how are they to fulfill that great mission with a foreign policy in pursuit of criminal designs, playing upon national prejudices, and squandering in piratical wars the people's blood and treasure? ... [The working class has the duty] ... to master themselves the mysteries of international politics; to watch the diplomatic acts of their respective governments; to counteract them, if necessary, by all means in their power; when unable to prevent, to combine in simultaneous denunciations, and to vindicate the simple laws or morals and justice, which ought to govern the relations of private individuals, as the rules paramount to the intercourse of nations.
>
> The fight for such a foreign policy forms part of the general struggle for the emancipation of the working classes.
>
> Proletarians of all countries, unite![1]

As strong and as relevant as are Marx's words from 1864, there has been a tendency in much of the Left to assume that Marx and Engels, and perhaps the First International more generally, were *the* architects of working class internationalism. Though neither Marx nor Engels laid such a claim, if one's starting point for examining class struggle and internationalism is nineteenth century Europe, one can easily get that impression. This essay attempts to look at the question of internationalism through a somewhat different lens, specifically one that centers on matters of "race" and the "national question."[2]

---

1. Karl Marx, "Inaugural Address of the International Working Men's Association," www.marxists.org/archive/marx/works/1864/10/27.htm, p. 7.
2. "Race," as we will explain, is a social-political construct. The "national question" refers to the matter of oppressed nations and nationalities. In some cases this has overlapped with matters of "race."

I

... when the proletariat was rebellious and self-active, it was described [by propagandists of the elite classes during the construction of Atlantic capitalism – BF] as a monster, a many-headed hydra. Its heads included food rioters (according to Shakespeare); heretics (Thomas Edwards); army agitators (Thomas Fairfax); antinomians and independent women (Cotton Mather); maroons (Governor Mauricius); motley urban mobs (Peter Oliver); general strikers (J. Cunningham); rural barbarians of the commons (Thomas Malthus); aquatic laborers (Patrick Colquhoun); free thinkers (William Reid); and striking textile workers (Andrew Ure). Nameless commentators added peasant rebels, Levellers, pirates, and slave insurrectionists to the long list. Fearful of the energy, mobility, and growth of social forces beyond their control, the writers, heresy hunters, generals, ministers, officials, population theorists, policemen, merchants, manufacturers, and planters offered up their curses, which called down Herculean destruction upon the hydra's heads: the debellation of the Irish, the extermination of the pirates, the annihilation of the outcasts of the nations of the Earth.[3]

Though it has become something of a cliché within the Left to note that capitalism, from its inception, has been global, the point itself remains quite profound. Contrary to mainstream economic history and also, unfortunately, to certain currents within the Left, capitalism *began* as a global enterprise. Though rising at a faster rate in England – along with the building of the nation-state – capitalism emerged in numerous settings, including city-states. From its origins the capitalist enterprise did not restrict itself to any single location. Although it fought to secure domestic markets, it never accepted territorial limits.

The trade in African slaves, politely known as a component of the "Triangular Trade," was, along with the pillage of the lands of the Native Americans/First Nations in the Western Hemisphere, critical to the growth and expansion of capitalism. As Marx and Engels famously noted:

The discovery of America, the rounding of the Cape, opened up fresh ground for the rising bourgeoisie. The East-Indian and Chinese markets, the colonisation of America, trade with the colonies, the increase in the means of exchange and in commodities generally, gave to commerce, to navigation, to industry, an impulse never before known, and thereby, to the revolutionary element in the tottering feudal society, a rapid development.[4]

---

3. Peter Linebaugh and Marcus Rediker, *The Many-Headed Hydra: Sailors, Slaves, Commoners, and the Hidden History of the Revolutionary Atlantic* (Boston, MA: Beacon Press, 2000), 329.
4. Karl Marx and Friedrich Engels, "Manifesto of the Communist Party," in Robert C. Tucker, ed., *The Marx-Engels Reader* (New York: W.W. Norton, 1972), 336.

Yet the period of the construction of Atlantic capitalism (to borrow from Linebaugh and Rediker) is regularly disconnected from discussions of proletarian resistance and the notion of internationalism. While slave insurrections, revolts of indentured servants, and movements such as the Levellers and Luddites are mentioned in mainstream history, such phenomena are regularly viewed in isolation. Worse yet, they are too often viewed not as resistance by the oppressed to their oppression, but instead as resistance to forward progress by decaying classes and, in some cases, allegedly decaying civilizations.

Nevertheless, in order to grasp the notion of proletarian internationalism, it is important to begin at the beginning and appreciate the extent and depth of the resistance to barbaric capitalism as it came out of the starting blocks, so to speak. And it is here that much of the First International missed the mark, leaving something of a legacy that has affected both the Left and the broader labor movement. For in the thinking of the First International, the notion of working-class internationalism was largely envisioned as a European and North American affair rather than a truly global enterprise. And while there were those, such as Marx and Engels, who recognized the debt that Europe owed the rest of the world for the pillage that "developed" both Europe and North America, this also did not translate into the sort of internationalism that was necessary in the nineteenth century, and certainly on through today.

II

Haunting working-class internationalism in the global North – and especially in the USA – have been the twin specters of race and empire, the two integrally linked. In proceeding forward one must understand that "internationalism" does not refer exclusively to cross-border interactions, but refers as well to a practice that transcends the national identity of a given working class.[5] In that sense, internationalism can refer to an approach that may be advanced *within* a multi-ethnic or multinational state. Thus, in examining the question of working-class internationalism in the USA, we are confronting not only the matter of foreign policy – as referenced in Marx's quote at the beginning of this essay – but also the practice of working-class politics *within* the USA given its multi-national/multi-ethnic character and, indeed, its character as an empire.

---

5. "National" does not necessarily refer to "nation-state"; it can refer to an ethnological identification, particularly in the context of multinational or multi-ethnic states.

Let us consider in this context an issue that plagued the European working-class movement of the nineteenth century: the Irish Question. There are many things noteworthy about the Irish Question, but one in particular is that it was not only a matter of "foreign policy," narrowly defined. In a peculiar manner it was about race *and* the national question, at least with regard to the British working class. Though Marx did not use those precise terms, this perspective is implicit in the arguments that he raised. Marx recognized in the Irish Question a key to understanding the inability of the British working class to attain genuine class consciousness. Not only did he see the upper echelons of the British working class as blinded by national chauvinism; he viewed the entire British working class as affected by a national *privilege* that directly corresponded to the racial and national oppression of the Irish people.

Yet what is striking, in reviewing the history, is that while Marx raised both the Irish Question and the matter of chattel slavery as central issues around which the working class needed to struggle, this did not translate into a more general approach by the First International and its affiliates to the broader matters of race and national oppression. One could argue that the First International displayed a "blind spot" (to borrow from Theodore Allen) when it came to national questions outside of Europe itself.

In order to better understand the implications of this challenge for today, we must briefly digress to a discussion of both race and national oppression. In a most peculiar way, it starts in Ireland.

The significance of the Irish Question was not only its impact on the British working class but also the extent to which, as Allen shows, the British subjugation of Ireland served as a model or prototype for the construction of "race" in North America and much of the rest of the world.[6] In a manner recalling the Spanish *Reconquista*,[7] the defeat of the Irish people and their colonization by the English resulted not in the absorption of the Irish ruling class by the English ruling class, but instead the all-round suppression of the Irish people, including language, culture, politics and land control. Although this suppression came to be seen through the prism of religion, the conflict was not driven by religion but instead by the colonial

---

6. Theodore Allen, *The Invention of the White Race, Vol. 1: Racial Oppression and Social Control* (New York: Verso, 2012).
7. The *Reconquista* was the process of "cleansing" the Iberian peninsula of Moors and Jews. It culminated in the defeat of the Moors in Granada in 1492 and the transformation of Iberia generally, and Spain in particular, into a "white" Catholic kingdom.

ambitions of the British. The subjugation involved the introduction of a settler population from outside of Ireland and the "creation" by the English of a "race" of allegedly inferior, indigenous people. The English were very conscious in doing this and saw it as their destiny. This translated, over time, into a differential in treatment and existence between the British working class and anything Irish. Marx understood that insofar as the British working class was *complicit* in the oppression of the Irish, they would never achieve their own class emancipation.

Thus, race was not about prejudice or bad ideas in an abstract sense. Rather, as Allen continuously pointed out, it was and is about social control and oppression. It was/is a system cleverly devised in order to create the most fundamental of forms of class collaboration whereby, in the case of Ireland, the settler population along with the British working class swore allegiance, literally and figuratively, to a system that was oppressing the Irish people. In so doing, they ensured, to borrow an old African American aphorism, that they, too, would not be able to leave the sewer.

"Race" exists on the foundation of oppression and privilege, i.e., the oppression of the subjugated group and a differential in treatment between the oppressed and the oppressor population – racial and/or national privilege, including but not limited to the working class of that oppressor state. As such, race collides directly with the possibility of working-class internationalism, a fact that the power bloc of capitalists understood from the very beginning.[8]

Race, further, overlaps with matters relative to imperial consciousness. This became obvious when many working-class organizations – parties and unions – in Europe and North America refused to speak out against empire and colonialism. The examples are innumerable. In the popular mind it is a matter of "patriotism" within the global North that excuses away silence in the face of colonialism or, now, neo-colonialism. Trade unions in the global North, for much too long, accepted the prerogative of empire. They took the reality of empire as an unchanging context for their activities. While some unions based in the "metropoles" might assist workers in the colonies in their immediate economic struggles, this was not seen by these unions as necessarily inconsistent with the existence of empire.

In the US context there are countless examples of this problem, beginning, of course, with the attitude of most of white organized labor towards the African American during the period of slavery and

---

8. As explained in excellent fashion by Linebaugh and Rediker in *The Many-Headed Hydra.*

immediately after; the attitude toward westward expansion and the aggression against Native Americans and Mexicans; and various foreign ventures, beginning in the late nineteenth century.[9] The challenge at each point revolved around patriotism (defined in racial and/or nation-state terms) and narrow self-interest.

The contradiction between race and internationalism, if not resolved in favor of working-class internationalism, can only result in various forms of class collaboration, either with a set of capitalists, or with the imperial state. The subordination of internationalism to so-called national interests and (racial or nation-state) patriotism has resulted in the trade union movement forfeiting its right and ability to become a *labor movement* in the broad sense in which that notion should be interpreted. The outcome has been not solidarity, but rather practices ranging from charity to active cooperation with the imperial state in undermining progressive social movements abroad (e.g., the role of the AFL-CIO in the Chilean coup in 1973).

There are important exceptions in the USA that are worthy of mention. While there is a long history to Left-initiated solidarity projects within the trade union movement, in the late 1980s there was an open break by leaders of several key unions with the policy of the AFL-CIO toward Central America and South Africa. In both cases the AFL-CIO leadership cooperated with the US government in subverting efforts at sovereignty and national liberation. The United Auto Workers, among others, broke with this and, in 1987, came out against the AFL-CIO's approach and against the policies of the Reagan Administration.

Yet these were exceptions, and the official leadership of most of the trade union movement has for the most part been reluctant to offer significant challenges to US foreign policy. Needless to say, this reflects a deeply racial conception as to whose interests are key, whose experiences are relevant, and how one defines interests in the first place.

III

A striking feature of early resistance to Atlantic capitalism was the lack of coordination among the various acts of solidarity. While there

---

9. It is worth noting that Samuel Gompers, founding president of the American Federation of Labor, initially opposed the Spanish-American War. Once war was declared, however, Gompers, along with many other union leaders, supported the aggression. In subsequent years Gompers proved himself to be an apologist for both racism and imperial expansion.

were organizations, conspiracies, insurrections, etc., there was no systematic contact between them.

The other feature of that early resistance was that it sought to define the nature and character of "the people." In many respects this is the task of internationalism in any era, and most especially today. How does one define who is on which side of the line between the oppressed and the oppressor? The Occupy Movement, for example, spoke domestically about what it termed the 99 percent, suggesting that the overwhelming majority of the people were being stepped on by a small, elite rich segment. While the percentage is probably more like 80–90 percent, the issue is not so much one of sociological precision as it is one of enabling the oppressed to self-identify in positive terms.

A story from the 1741 New York slave conspiracy has come to be a critical image in my mind. The conspirators included Africans and Irish. When they were caught and interrogated, they were asked the objective of the uprising. The Africans were alleged to have said " … to kill the white people." That was not a particular surprise. But when the Irish were asked the same question, they also reportedly said " … to kill the white people."

What is remarkable is not just that the Irish failed to consider themselves "white" (and were not considered "white" by the larger society); it is that "white" was understood as the characteristic or character of the oppressor group. The rebels saw themselves as *not white*; the "people," in other words, were *not white*. And, further, "white" was less a color than a description of the way in which the oppressor self-conceptualized.

The nature of the early resistance to Atlantic capitalism, along with the self-conceptualization of the developing proletariat, raises questions regarding another aspect of internationalism. Indeed, it raises a potential critique of the internationalism of the First International. Specifically, how should one define proletarian internationalism or working-class internationalism? Furthermore, does working-class internationalism mean the internationalism of workers in relation to one another, or does it mean something far broader? It is critical that we approach this question not as sociologists nor even as trade unionists, but as "insurgents," as radicals of the Left.

The First International described itself as the International Workingmen's Association. Leaving aside the important matter of the gendered description, the First and Second Internationals saw their responsibilities as being largely toward workers, most especially workers in manufacturing and transportation. In the First International there were unions, leagues, parties and other groupings. In the case of the Second International, it was a situation of political parties that self-identified as "social democratic" and, at least at the time, claimed *some* level of allegiance to the teachings of Marx and Engels.

Neither the First nor the Second Internationals seemed to appreciate the need for a practice of internationalism that exceeded the solidarity of explicitly working-class struggles (and for that matter, certain sectors of the working class). While there were certain exceptions, e.g., the support for Ireland, this did not extend into the colonial and semi-colonial world.

It is on this matter that the contributions of Lenin became very important in the early twentieth century. Lenin recognized that internationalism had to be more than the unity of trade unions or social democratic parties across geographic boundaries. It had to be working-class parties (and other organizations) taking on a special role as *tribunes of the people* – a term that he made famous. Though Lenin designed an international organization – the Third (Communist) International – that was ideologically more exclusive than its two predecessors, he contended that internationalism should have a different direction and a different point of emphasis: *workers and oppressed peoples of the world, unite!*

The slogan "workers and oppressed peoples of the world, unite!" (WOPWU) is actually more in keeping with the nature of the struggles that accompanied the emergence of Atlantic capitalism than was the internationalism of the First and certainly the Second Internationals. It is also dramatically different from the various forms of "trade union internationalism" that arose in the early twentieth century and that have continued through to this day. While quite revolutionary, it is nevertheless a slogan that should express even the scope of the reform work undertaken by today's working class.

The notion of "WOPWU" if viewed narrowly, is simply about alliances of forces in struggle. Yet it has deeper implications for the mission of working-class organizations and parties. Rather than conceptualizing internationalism in terms of relationships among existing organizations, WOPWU suggests that internationalism is principally about addressing capitalist/imperialist oppression, irrespective of whether it is suffered by workers, trade unions, etc., or by unrelated organizations and movements among other subaltern strata. It is also arguing that the "oppressed peoples" (in Lenin's time, most especially the colonized and semi-colonized peoples) have a special role in the struggle against capitalism and imperialism. To recognize both of

these conclusions means going face to face with race and imperial consciousness in the attitudes and practices of workers in the global North
– particularly workers in the USA.

In the late twentieth century, the US trade union movement began
to consider more seriously the question of global solidarity. In so
doing, it was up against several challenges: (1) breaking with Cold
War trade unionism (and collaboration with imperial adventures); (2)
various forms of isolationism or agnosticism with regard to the rest
of the world, which exist within much of the membership and leadership of organized labor; and (3) pragmatic solidarity.[10] The suppression of the Left within the US union movement has meant that
internationalism, as a current, has largely been absent, though there
have been examples of specific internationalist actions or approaches.
Pragmatic solidarity has emerged in such a way that it seems to
pass for internationalism in many quarters. Yet it misses what is contained in the notion of WOPWU, that is, a search for a broader array
of allies and the need for working-class organizations – including
but not limited to political parties – to address broader levels of
oppression.

A final point about pragmatic solidarity. As Gapasin and I
explored in *Solidarity Divided*, the relatively new interest in global
trade union solidarity within the US movement can be not only very
transactional, but also very self-centered. In the early 2000s when
UNITE, the union that emerged from the textile and garment sectors,
worked to form a global coalition of textile and garment unions, their
objective, it turned out, was less about building genuine multilateral
solidarity than about building a reserve of international support for
its own domestic agenda. Such approaches, needless to say, cause
other labor movements to look at overtures from the US trade union
movement with a jaundiced eye.

IV

If proletarian or working-class internationalism is to move beyond
the stage of what is sarcastically referenced as "resolutionary

---

10. Fernando Gapasin and I discuss the notion of "pragmatic solidarity." in *Solidarity
     Divided* (Berkeley, CA: University of California Press, 2008). The idea is that while
     there has been renewed interest in the global stage, one current of opinion advocates
     what could almost be described as transactional relationships with other union
     movements. Solidarity is then limited to working with unions in the same industrial
     sector or with those that share a common employer. While such solidarity is impor-
     tant, it should not be considered the be all and end all.

socialism,"[11] then it must be reconceptualized. Internationalism must be more than a ritual or slogan (or set of slogans); it must be an actual theory and practice. It must also have vehicles through which to manifest itself; otherwise it becomes nothing more than rhetoric and sentiment.

For much of the Left, both inside and outside the labor movement, internationalism is primarily a "spirit." It is something to raise at conferences and conventions, and periodically something around which a degree of organizing is to take place. At certain moments, as in the 1980s, leftists in the labor movement (and in some other social movements) did an exceptionally good job initiating solidarity efforts around South Africa and Central America, even helping shift the leaderships of some of the US unions. But this was not the rule. We need to think about a consistent internationalism.

Internationalism, within labor, must be manifested through the combination of a narrative and a strategic practice. The narrative needs to flow from three points highlighted in this essay: (1) capitalism, as a global system, has from its inception been the target of resistance from a global proletariat; (2) race has created the most effective means to ensure capitalist/working class collaboration in what we now term the global North, through the complicity of workers with the imperial projects; (3) internationalism today implies including the broad oppressed strata in struggles for social, political, economic and environmental justice, and not viewing such alliances through a transactional set of lenses.

In the absence of such a framework, internationalism will continue to oscillate between episodic actions and efforts at moralistic persuasion. An internationalist framework needs to work its way into left-initiated educational projects, materials, etc. It must be part of the larger account of class struggle and efforts at justice in the USA. It must, in other words, be an essential part of the *counter-narrative* that the Left offers in response to right-wing populism, to explain the crisis of capitalism and the misery that has been befalling the working classes in the global North over the last 30+ years.

The practice of internationalism – linked with the narrative – can be manifested through a variety of concrete struggles.[12] None of these

---

11. A reference to the way many leftists think of change as being about the resolutions passed by mass organizations rather than about the results that emerge through struggle.

12. The emphasis on the linkage reflects the view that experience alone is not the best teacher. Individuals draw various conclusions from actual experiences. Experience in the absence of a progressive, if not radical, theoretical framework can frequently lead to dead-ends. Every Left activist has lived the situation where a grassroots fighter who grasps the essence of a particular struggle may, upon the conclusion

struggles should come as any surprise. Yet they can each be embraced as coherent parts of an internationalist project.

Anti-racism is a good starting place. If anti-racism is understood as qualitatively different from so-called diversity programs, it can be integral to internationalist practice. Anti-racism has both a domestic and a global content. Anti-racism, in the US context, means winning white workers to an internationalism that appreciates the significance of racial and national privilege and the devastating impact of racist and national oppression. Anti-racism serves as a foundation for internationalism in the USA because it challenges the ideological conception of the preeminence of one culture over another, of one national-cultural experience (and history) over another. Anti-racism, in fact, represents an effort on the part of the populations of oppressor nations to regain their humanity.

A case in point can be found in how we understand holocausts. The holocaust carried out by the Nazis against Jews is held up in the global North as being, in effect, the only holocaust worth mentioning. It is held up as exceptional. In point of fact it was far from exceptional on virtually every scale. The difference, as Aimé Césaire pointed out, was that the holocaust against the Jews was carried out by one European population against another. Much of what the Nazis embarked upon had been practiced over centuries in the global South by the European colonial powers. Yet the holocausts witnessed in the global South are rarely given the same or similar attention as those carried out against the Jews.[13]

An additional case in point, of direct relevance to the USA, is that of the Philippines. The US occupation of the Philippines in the early twentieth century was conducted via what can only be described as a genocidal race war. Somewhere in the range of 1,000,000 to 2,000,000 Filipinos lost their lives as the US took control over the islands, defeated the legitimate government, and carried out massacres. Yet these facts have largely been expunged from official US history. This trauma lives with the people of the archipelago to this day. The US has never apologized for this aggression.

---

of that struggle, retreat into inaction or, worse, may develop very backward views on a whole set of questions. Individuals have their own sets of frameworks through which they analyze reality. Such frameworks may not be consistent, but they can frequently serve as a comforting lens.

13. This in no way downplays the holocaust against the Jews. Rather, in exceptionalizing that holocaust, we leave people open to attributing it to a genetic insanity within the German population, rather than understanding it as emerging out of a drive inherent in capitalism since the beginning.

This is not just a matter of history. Though the US granted independence to the Philippines in 1946, it carried out a neocolonial tutelage over the nation-state from that point onward. The US has remained deeply embedded in Philippine politics and continues to support massive repression and government intransigence in the face of a multi-decades long civil war with the Communist-led National Democratic Front. Despite the integral relationship of the USA to the Philippines, there is little discussion in the mainstream media; the US trade union movement knows almost nothing about the situation there (or if and where it does, it tends to cooperate with neocolonial trade unionists in the Philippines); and, while human rights abuses by the government and its paramilitary allies take place at an astounding rate, they are not on the "radar screen" for the US public and for much of the US progressive and Left social forces.[14] Anti-racism, in this context, means not only expressing solidarity with the popular democratic forces in the Philippines; it also involves breaking the silence surrounding events in that country and discussing with the US public the role that the US plays there. In a nutshell, it means that the atrocities faced by the people of the Philippines must become relevant to the US public.

Immigration is another front-line in the construction of a new internationalism in the USA. Addressing immigration from the standpoint of internationalism begins with distinguishing the waves of immigration to the US. Until 1965, immigration was very much weighted against migrants of color. But migration of people from the global South was not new. In the aftermath of the Spanish–American War, migrants arrived in the mainland USA from Puerto Rico, the English and Dutch Caribbean, and the Philippines, in addition to the relatively continuous Mexican migration that dates from the end of US War against Mexico (1848). These migrants were never provided the opportunities that migrants from Europe were granted.

Addressing immigration/migration today means addressing the relationship of the global North to the global South, making this a cutting-edge front in advancing internationalism. This involves addressing the social, political, economic and environmental causes of migration, which in turn means confronting the question of empire. It is here that many advocates for immigrant rights stumble. Rather than tackle the question of US foreign policy and empire, they

---

14. See, for example, the report from the Filipino human rights group Karapatan [Alliance for the Advancement of Human Rights], 2012 *Karapatan Year End Report on the Human Rights Situation in the Philippines.*

tend to rely on moralistic pleas to government or comparisons with the Black Freedom Movement (and the demand for civil and human rights). Though there are clear analogies with other freedom movements in the US and there is a need for fight for complete civil and human rights, the battle around migration raises global issues and is driven by very different factors.

The fight for the migrant, therefore, is a fight around US foreign policy specifically, and about the relationship of global capitalism to the countries and peoples of the global South generally.

The fight to support *national self-determination* has always been a defining battle in identifying internationalism. This was a point that Marx and Engels recognized, but the scope of the fight has greatly expanded.

Many European labor and left-wing movements stumbled on the question of national self-determination when the colonial world was struggling for independence. This has been just as true in the USA. Organized labor in the mainland USA, for example, while periodically devoting resources to organizing workers in Puerto Rico, has shied away from addressing, or even acknowledging, the Puerto Rican struggle for national sovereignty. Organized labor in the USA was not at the forefront in supporting independence for the Philippines. In almost every case, taking an anti-colonial stand has been viewed as opening up labor and the Left to charges of being unpatriotic. And fear of being called unpatriotic has been something that most union leaders have been unwilling to challenge.

National self-determination, *ipso facto*, stands against imperial prerogative. And introducing it into mass struggles represents a concrete internationalist practice, particularly if one shies away from lecturing and one-dimensional rhetoric. Take, for instance, free trade. Much of organized labor in the USA, and many progressives, have tended to oppose free trade agreements on the basis of the destruction that they have brought to US workers. The famous imagery created in H. Ross Perot's description of the North American Free Trade Agreement (NAFTA) as the "giant sucking sound" epitomizes the problem. While there was certainly truth to Perot's reference to the destruction resulting from NAFTA, what was completely ignored was the impact of NAFTA on Canada and, more decisively, on Mexico. The havoc in the agricultural sector and public sector, and the implications for migration into the cities of Mexico and later to the USA, has largely been discounted, except among some sectors of the Left. Yet it is possible to oppose NAFTA from a national self-determination perspective without ignoring the plight of US workers.

Opposition to *wars of aggression*, of course, is central to genuine internationalist practice and needs little elaboration. Support for demands for *reparations*, however, is an aspect that receives far too little attention. Mainstream political and social movements largely reject reparations demands by victims of US imperialism. Here the race factor more often than not raises its ugly head. Take, for instance, Vietnam.

In the aftermath of the US war of aggression against Vietnam, reparations were supposed to be paid to the Vietnamese. The US reneged. In particular, it has failed to take responsibility for the genocidal impact of the dispersal of Agent Orange over Indochina as a whole and Vietnam in particular. There are few groups that address this matter.[15] This is a concrete situation where the demand for reparations is clear and should be unequivocal.

The demand for reparations *within* the context of the USA – as an imperial state – remains a central feature of genuine internationalism, but is all but abandoned by most domestic social movements (except those that have a direct interest in the fight against racist and national oppression). The difficulty in seeking support for reparations – whether to internal or to foreign victims – is that it requires popular discussions of history. The prevailing approach to history in the USA is to avoid it. In addition, the mainstream US approach denies the need for and permissibility of apologies. Without apologies for atrocities and other crimes, it is inconceivable that discussions of reparations can take place. This is why the Left must make history very much present.

V

So, what conclusions can we derive?

First, for much of the Left, internationalism is more about rhetoric and positioning than about trying to unite masses around an alternative practice. In order to build an alternative practice, one must begin with an alternative framework rather than moralistic principles. Uniting education with actual struggles is, as with any other change in consciousness, essential in order to introduce a new "common sense."

---

15. There are groups that have taken up this issue. The "Vietnam Agent Orange Relief & Responsibility Campaign," with which I have the honor of being affiliated, has worked to keep this issue before the people of the USA. See: http://www.vn-agentorange.org/.

Second, internationalism, in the context of the global North, is integrally connected with race. Though Marx and Engels recognized this relationship to a great degree, much of the Left, and certainly the mainstream labor movement, fails to see it. Internationalism within the mainstream labor movement is seen in terms of solidarity between unions rather than solidarity against racial and national privilege, and against racist and national oppression.

Third, internationalism is not a transactional relationship but should be best understood within the context of the slogan "workers and oppressed peoples of the world, unite!" Genuine internationalism, including and especially at the popular level, must be a matter of addressing all forms of oppression. To put it another way, it represents an understanding of *interconnections*.

None of this can coalesce into an alternative movement in the absence of organization. Building internationalism is more than an episode. In that regard it is worth returning to the 1860s. To the credit of many members of the First International, British workers were organized to oppose British government support for the Confederate States of America. From 1862–63, the British government gave serious consideration to intervening in the US Civil War on the side of the Confederacy. Along with France they both wanted to weaken the USA and to join hands instead with a partner in free trade and Atlantic economic liberalism. But British workers adamantly opposed such support for the Confederacy, and took steps to boycott shipping to the CSA. These actions represented the peak of classical working-class internationalism and helped restrain the British from formally intervening.[16]

Yet, at the same time, British workers took a very different stand toward the Irish Question. Paradoxically, while opposing the British government's pro-Confederate leanings, British workers situated themselves differently vis-à-vis that government's colonial relationship to Ireland and the racial/national oppression of the Irish.[17] At

---

16. The British government was also restrained by the possible response of Russia. Having been defeated by the British, French and Ottomans in the Crimean War, the Russians were in a vengeful mood and suggested a possible intervention on the side of North if the British and French chose to intervene in favor of the Confederacy.

17. The oppression of the Irish, as noted earlier, was both racial and national. The "racial" oppression, as Theodore Allen demonstrated, was obviously not about skin color, but rather manifested itself in the total suppression of the Irish. When Irish workers migrated to Britain in search of work, they found themselves in a second-class status and subject to demonization and systematic discrimination.

best, British workers were silent, but silence was not the only character-istic. Active support for the British colonial relationship vis-à-vis Ireland and the Irish was the main feature of the British working class's approach.

Internationalism in one arena – the US Civil War – did not carry over into another area – Ireland and the Irish. In the USA we have had a similar experience. The internationalism that began to emerge in the context of opposition to US aggression in Indochina, did not necessarily translate into challenges to the US empire in other realms. There are myriad examples of this, such as the relative silence in the USA in the face of the CIA-backed coup in Chile (1973); a very slow response to US aggression in Central America during the 1980s (El Salvador, Nicaragua, Honduras and Guatemala, in particular); and the invisibility of US/apartheid South African aggression against Angola.

Internationalism must be constantly reinforced and, absent organ-ization, this is simply not going to happen. Organization, whether within or outside the mainstream labor movement, is necessary in order to wage battles for global justice. Organization makes the differ-ence in terms of building and reinforcing the need for a new "common sense" with regard to US foreign policy and taking on the empire. It is on this point that further exploration is necessary.

Quite ironically, after the mid-nineteenth century, when Irish were utilized as set-tlers within the British Empire, they found themselves frequently playing a role as supporters of the empire.

130

The International Working Class in 1864 and Today

Ricardo Antunes

Introduction

The International Workingmen's Association (IWA) was born in London on September 28, 1864. Its founders, together with Marx, were a distinguished group of communist, socialist and anarchist intellectuals and activists, who dedicated to the project an important part of their lives.

The history of the IWA, which lasted only until 1876, was short but seminal. During the era of formation of the world market, it was necessary to bring together the various working-class organizations from different parts of the world, so that they could share their experiences of struggle and weave ties of solidarity. As capital acquired global contours, so also should the working-class movement. The working class would need to become organically international, capable of exerting power at an international level while at the same time respecting the distinctive features of each of its national components. This was the leitmotif underlying the IWA.

Already in its inaugural manifesto, the First International noted the increasing impoverishment of the working class: "It is a great fact that the misery of the working masses has not diminished from 1848 to 1864, and yet this period is unrivaled for the development of its industry and the growth of its commerce."[1] Given this hard reality, the nascent international movement recognized the urgent necessity of developing a political economy of labor in opposition to the political economy of capital. As stated by Marx in the inaugural manifesto:

> ... to bear fruit, the means of labor need not be monopolized as a means of dominion over, and of extortion against, the laboring man himself; ... like slave labor, like serf labor, hired labor is but a transitory and inferior form,

---

1. Karl Marx, "Inaugural Address of the International Working Men's Association, The First International," *Marx-Engels Collected Works* (*MECW*), vol. 20, 5.

131

destined to disappear before associated labor plying its toil with a willing hand, a ready mind, and a joyous heart.[2]

The First International thus pronounced in its Statutes the essential principle, "the emancipation of the working classes must be conquered by the working classes themselves." Further, "the economical emancipation of the working classes is therefore the great end to which every political movement ought to be subordinate. ... All societies and individuals adhering to it will acknowledge truth, justice, and morality as the basis of their conduct toward each other and toward all men, without regard to color, creed, or nationality"[3] The General Council of the IWA would act as an international organ linking "the different co-operating associations, so that the working men in one country be consistently informed of the movements of their class in every other country." And, "when immediate practical steps should be needed, as, for instance, in case of international quarrels, the action of the associated societies [would] be simultaneous and uniform." Nonetheless, "While united in a perpetual bond of fraternal co-operation, the working men's societies joining the International Association, will preserve their existent organizations intact."[4]

If these were the goals of the IWA 150 years ago, what does it mean to think of an international organization of the working class today? Would its most general principles become dated? Or would they, on the contrary, become even more relevant? If today's working class needs an international organization, how can we imagine what it would look like? Is it even possible, in fact, to defeat the social metabolic system of capital with forms of struggle that are carried out only at the national level? Or, on the contrary, given the globalized shape of capitalism, has it not become even more urgent to create a new project of international working-class organization?

In order to explore these crucial questions, we must try to understand the new morphology of labor and some of its principal tendencies.

The new morphology of labor: informality, casualization, infoproletariat, and value

Particularly since the widespread restructuring of capital, unleashed on a global scale in the early 1970s, the contemporary

---

2. Ibid.
3. Marx, "Provisional rules of the association," *MECW*, vol. 20, 14–15.
4. Ibid., 15–16.

world of production has shown increased levels of casualization of workers.[5] Work has become more and more destructive. As new mechanisms for extracting surplus labor are generated, jobs become more precarious, and masses of workers become disposable and unemployed. This has a downward effect on the wages of workers who are employed. The latest global crisis has amplified this effect. We now witness a huge 'waste' of human labor power, as the secure industrial jobs that were typical during much of the twentieth century have become increasingly scarce.

ICT (information and communications technology) has invaded the world of commodities, providing greater *intellectual* capability (here understood in its narrow meaning given by the market). In this universe characterized by the subsumption of labor to the machine, stable work – associated with Taylorism/Fordism – is being replaced by *atypical work*, outsourced work, 'cooperativism,' 'entrepreneurship,' 'volunteer labor,' etc. At the same time, this new morphology of labor has been expanding the range of *invisible labor*, using new and old mechanisms of labor-intensification. It is as if all possible activities – whether manual or intellectual – were converted into generators of surplus-value. The most important example is that of the service sector: whereas in the early period of industrial capitalism its activities were mostly unproductive, with the financialization of capital and with neoliberal privatization, the activities of the privatized service sector became productive for capital, even though they had the *appearance* of being unproductive. They also became generators of surplus-value.

Already in Marx's time certain service activities added value. This role is even more prevalent nowadays. Enterprises that provide services such as information and communications technology, telemarketing, fast food, hypermarkets, transport, etc., can no longer be considered as simply unproductive, but must be carefully analyzed in relation to global production networks and the production of value.

In *Capital* vol. 2, Marx recognized that certain transport and warehousing activities could produce surplus value. In his words:

> ... what the transportation industry sells is change of location. The useful effect is inseparably connected with the process of transportation, i.e., the productive process of the transport industry. Men and goods travel together with the means of transportation, and this travelling, this locomotion, constitutes the process of production effected by these means. The useful effect can be consumed only during this process of production. It does not exist as a utility

5. See Ricardo Antunes, "La nueva morfologia del trabajo y sus principales tendencias," *Sociologia del Trabajo* 74 (2012), Madrid: Siglo XXI, 47–65.

different from this process, a use thing which does not function as an article of commerce, does not circulate as a commodity, until after it has been produced. But the exchange value of this useful effect is determined, like that of any other commodity, by the value of the elements of production (labour power and means of production) consumed in it plus the surplus value created by the surplus labour of the labourers employed in transportation.[6]

Thus, the theory of value does not lose its relevance. Instead, we witness new and more complex methods of extracting surplus-value, including in activities considered non-material in Marx's terms.[7]

Our hypothesis is that various service activities are taking on an increasing role in constituting value, insofar as, in their interaction with *dead labor*, they participate in the process of valorization of capital. In the early stages of capitalism, productive activities (generators of value) were mainly linked to industry and agriculture, mostly excluding services.[8] With the new forms of interaction between material and non-material labor, as well as the prevalence of collective labor in global production networks, the production of surplus-value grew significantly beyond what was possible in the traditional factory.

Today, the new contingent of workers in ICT [information and communications technology] has been called *cybertariat* (by Ursula Huws)[9] or *infoproletariat* (by Ruy Braga and myself).[10] Huws's study remains central for understanding the interactions between material and non-material labor, as well as their connections with value's new modalities. As we know, telecommunications privatization led to an intensified process of outsourcing and introduced multiple forms of labor casualization and intensification of the labor process.

Contrary to what was argued in theories of "post-industrial society" and creative "informational activity," work in the telemarketing industry has been marked by a contradictory process, since:

1. It combines twenty-first century technologies (ICT) with twentieth-century working conditions.

6. Marx, *Capital*, vol. II, *MECW*, vol. 36, New York: International Publishers, 1997, 62.
7. Marx, *Capital*, vol. I, *MECW*, vol. 35, New York: International Publishers, 1998, chapter XVI, "Absolute and Relative Surplus Value," 509–510.
8. Ricardo Antunes, *The Meanings of Work: Essay on the Affirmation and Negation of Work*, Historical Materialism Book Series, vol. 43, Leiden/Boston: Brill, 2013, chapter 7.
9. See Ursula Huws, *The Making of a Cybertariat: Virtual Work in a Real World*, New York/London: Monthly Review Press/Merlin Press, 2003.
10. See Ricardo Antunes and Ruy Braga, *Infoproletários: Degradação Real do Trabalho Virtual*, São Paulo: Boitempo, 2009.

2. It combines strategies of toyotized flexibility[11] with Taylorist rigidity.
3. It combines group work with the individualization of labor relations, encouraging both cooperation and competition between workers.

A preliminary phenomenology of labor informality demonstrates a sharp increase in the number of workers subjected to a succession of short-term contracts: they have neither stability nor formal status; they work in temporary activities, under the direct threat of unemployment. Workforce casualization has been a central mechanism used by capital to intensify the rhythms and motions of labor, and thereby to extract more value from it.

Otherwise, why, in the middle of São Paulo, the most important industrial area of Brazil, would there exist today a 17-hour shift in the clothing industry, to be performed by Bolivian or Peruvian or other Latin American immigrant workers, who are informally hired and controlled by usually Korean or Chinese employers? We can also cite the case of African workers who pack textile and clothing products in Bom Retiro and Brás, small businesses in the city of São Paulo, whose products for the African market are produced by arduous manual labor.

Other examples can be taken from the sugar agribusiness sector. Even though there is some formal labor in this sector, the rights of *boias-frias* (rural laborers) continue to be circumvented. Rural laborers cut 10 tons of sugarcane per day in the State of São Paulo and as

---

11. Toyotism, the Japanese model for the expansion and consolidation of monopolistic industrial capitalism, is a form of labor organization that emerged in Toyota after 1945, and that rapidly expanded amongst other large Japanese companies. It differs from Fordism in the following ways: it is a form of production closely tied to demand that seeks to respond to the most individualized needs of the consumer-market; it is based on team-work, with cross-functional teams; the production process is flexible, allowing a worker to simultaneously operate various machines (at Toyota, on average five machines); it is based on the just-in-time principle, the best possible use of production time; it works according to the kanban system, command-tags or -boards for the replacement of parts and stock (under Toyotism, stocks are minimal when compared with Fordism); firms have a horizontal structure, as opposed to the vertical Fordist one; this horizontalization extends to subcontracted firms, leading to the expansion of these methods and procedures across the whole network of suppliers. Thus, flexibilization, subcontracting, total-quality control, kanban, just-in-time production, Kaizen, teamwork, the elimination of waste, 'participatory management' and enterprise-unionism, among many other features, become part of the wider arena of the productive process; and quality-control circles (QCCs) are instituted – groups of workers who are encouraged by management to discuss their work and performance with a view to improving productivity. See Antunes, *The Meanings of Work*, chapter 4, 38–39.

much as 18 tons per day in the north eastern region. Their workdays are exhausting, and their production is often undercounted by management. This scenario of work-intensification causes many fatalities among workers. Between 2003 and 2008, some 21 cane-cutters died from overwork in the State of São Paulo.[12]

In Japan, there is the recent case of *cyber-refugees* – young workers from the outskirts of Tokyo who do not have money to rent rooms. They stay in cybercafés at night to rest, use the Internet, and search for new contingent jobs. The best known example is that of young workers in various parts of the world (known as *dekasegis* in Japan) who migrate to cities in search of jobs. Without fixed residences, they sleep and rest in small rooms (glass capsules). I call them *encapsulated workers*.

In China, since the beginning of the century, there have been high rates of unemployment as transnational capital stretches to the limit the *superexploitation* of the working class. The case of Foxconn is illuminating. Foxconn, a computing and information technology enterprise, is an example of Electronic Contract Manufacturing (ECM), a firm that assembles electronic products by subcontracting from Apple, Nokia and other transnationals. At its Longhua plant where the iPhone is assembled, there have been several suicides among the workforce since 2010, most caused by the intense exploitation and isolation of the work. According Pun Ngai and Jenny Chan

> The Foxconn tragedy has been dubbed the "suicide express" by Chinese and international media. In the first eight months of 2010, a startling 17 young workers attempted or committed suicide at the Foxconn production facilities in China, bringing worldwide attention to all Foxconn's customers. Thirteen died, while four survived their injuries. All were between 17- and 25-years-old ... and their loss called upon concerned academics to closely study the changing pattern of global capital accumulation and its impacts on workers. Foxconn is a microcosm of the conditions that dominate the lives of Chinese migrant workers. When *Time* magazine nominated workers in China as runners-up to the 2009 Person of the Year, the editor commented that Chinese workers have brightened the future of humanity by "leading the world to economic recovery." The new generation of Chinese migrant workers, however, seem to perceive themselves as losing their futures. More than 900,000 young workers, who have been placed in the "best" Foxconn factory-cum-dormitory environment, seemed only to show more anxieties, and see fewer alternatives, than their peers.[13]

---

12. See Ricardo Antunes, *Riqueza e Miséria do Trabalho no Brasil II,* Boitempo, São Paulo, 2013, ch. 17.
13. See Ngai and Chan, "The Advent of Capital Expansion in China: A Case Study of Foxconn Production and the Impacts on its Workers," p. 2, http://rdln.files. wordpress.com/2012/01/pun-ngai_chan-jenny_on-foxconn.pdf

This pattern is repeated in many other plants across China. According to SACOM (Students and Scholars against Corporate Misbehavior), at the beginning of 2010, Foxconn workers work an average of 12 hours per day with a basic monthly wage of 900 yuan (just under US$150) which can reach 2,000 yuan for extra hours or for more strenuous work.

Immigrants are perhaps the most conspicuous victims of the structural trend toward casualization. Given the enormous growth of the new informal proletariat, including the manufacturing and services sub-proletariat, new jobs are being filled by *Gastarbeiter* in Germany, *lavoratori in nero* in Italy, Mexican immigrants in the United States, East European immigrants (from Poland, Hungary, Romania, and Albania) in western Europe, *dekasegis* in Japan, Bolivians and Africans in Brazil, and so on.

The cleavages that exist today between stable and precarious workers, men and women, young and elderly, white, black and Indian, and between skilled and unskilled workers are expressions of the new morphology of labor. Pietro Basso, who has studied this phenomenon in Europe, summarizes the reality as follows:

> Once a continent of emigrants and settlers, as it had been for centuries, Western Europe has become a land of an increased flow of immigration from the entire globe. Today, 30 million immigrants live on its territory. And if we add to the immigrants without citizenship those who have obtained citizenship in one of the European countries, the total reaches 50 million, about 15 percent of the entire population of "15-Europe" [referring to when the EU consisted of 15 countries].[14]

Among the immigrants, 22 percent come from Africa, 16 percent from Asia – half of these from the Far East (mainly China), and the other half from the Indian subcontinent. Fifteen percent are from Central and South America, and the remaining 45–47 percent come from other European countries, including those outside the EU (e.g., Turkey, the Balkans, Ukraine, Russia).[15]

Immigrant workers are paid the lowest wages and work during the least desired times, at night and on weekends. Yet Basso states that it is not about:

> ... 'just' overexploitation. In Europe, the whole existence of immigrants and their children is marked by *discrimination*. There is discrimination at the

14. Pietro Basso, "L'immigrazione in Europa: caratteristiche e prospettive," Università Ca' Foscari Venezia (working paper), 1.
15. Ibid.

workplace, or when looking for a job, for unemployment insurance, and for retirement. Immigrants are discriminated against when they apply for housing benefits, when they must pay the highest rents to inhabit dilapidated dwellings in the most degraded areas. In fact, they suffer discrimination even in schools (in Germany there are very few children of immigrants who go to university; in Italy 42.5 percent of students who are children of immigrants are behind in their studies). They are discriminated against in their chances to reunite with their families, and, especially if they are Islamic, they suffer religious discrimination as well (being regarded as potential 'terrorists').[16]

Immigrants are thus at once the *most unprotected* and the *most global'* category of worker. Hence, they constitute a sector of the working class which is, "objectively and more than any other, the carrier of equalitarian and antiracist aspirations, even amid a plethora of contradictions, opportunism and individualism." They thus become "a collective subject which carries a need for social emancipation," as they refuse to "passively accept the condition of legal, material, social, cultural inferiority" associated with their immigrant status.[17] Citing the Italian case, Basso stresses that there have been some successful experiences of unionized immigrants. If, in the beginning, immigrants resorted to unions for aid, with the passage of time and with the consolidation of their presence in the workplace, they increasingly participate in union activities, as they come to represent the general interests of workers.[18]

The recent demonstrations in Europe by immigrant workers and unemployed youth are emblematic. Precarious workers in Portugal organized a movement called *Precári@s Inflexíveis* [literally, Inflexible Precarious Workers].[19] Their *Manifesto* affirms the following:

> We are precarious in work and in life. We work without contract or on short-term contracts. [We have] temporary, uncertain jobs, without guarantees. We are call-center workers, interns, unemployed people, independent workers, immigrant workers, casual workers, student-workers. . . .
> We are not represented in statistics. . . . We live off filler jobs. We can hardly provide a home. We can't take leave; we can't have children or become sick. Not to mention the right to strike. "Flexicurity"? The 'flexi' is for us, while the 'security' is for our bosses. This 'modernization' is tricky and it has been planned and implemented by businessmen and Government, hand in hand. We are in the shadows but we are not silent.

---

16. Ibid.
17. Ibid., 6.
18. Ibid., 8. See also Pietro Basso and Fabio Perocco, *Razzismo di stato: Stati Uniti, Europa, Italia*, Milan: Angeli, 2010.
19. [*Translator's note*: The @ symbol is used in Portuguese (and Spanish) to combine the masculine "o" with the feminine "a."]

We won't stop fighting for fundamental rights alongside the workers in Portugal or abroad. This struggle is not about trade-union or government statistics. ... We don't fit in those figures.
We won't let our conditions be forgotten. And using the same force with which we are attacked by our bosses, we will respond and reinvent our struggle. In the end, there are many more of us than of them. Yes, we are precarious, but we are inflexible.[20]

They are *discriminated against but not submissive;* as members of the working class, they seek to improve their living conditions *through work.* Immigrant workers in Western Europe are perhaps the tip of the iceberg, in terms of their working conditions and the precariousness of their jobs.

The new era of *structural casualization of labor,* in sum, has these features:

1. Erosion of contracted and regulated work, and its replacement by various forms of atypical, precarious and 'volunteer' employment;
2. Creation of bogus cooperative societies, aimed at further squeezing wages by eroding workers' rights and intensifying exploitation;
3. Configuring 'entrepreneurship' as a hidden form of wage-labor, by proliferating various forms of wages, schedules, and functional or organizational flexibility;
4. An ever more intense degradation of immigrant labor on a global scale.

In the last few decades, we have been experiencing new forms of casualization, a phase of "toyotised" flexibility, which displays both continuity and discontinuity in relation to the Taylorist-Fordist modality. On the one hand, there are more highly skilled jobs for a reduced contingent (as exemplified by the workers of software industries and ICT companies); on the other hand, work is increasingly unstable for a growing number of workers at the other end of the spectrum. Meanwhile, in the *middle* of the pyramid, we find hybridity, i.e., skilled labor that may disappear or be eroded by the temporal and spatial changes that have affected production and services worldwide.

Casualization of labor seems to have become a constitutive feature of capital accumulation. The various manifestations of informality/ casualization entail a break with contractual obligations and regulations of the labor force such as prevailed under the Taylorist/ Fordist regime of the twentieth century. Informalization/causalization is an important instrument used by capital to increase the rate of

---

20. www.precariosinflexiveis.org/p/manifesto-do-pi.html.

exploitation of labor and to make jobs globally more precarious. Although casualization is not synonymous with precariousness, they are interrelated, insofar as informality and casualization deprive workers of rights.

In this sense, lean production, team work, layoffs, productivity increases, and subcontracting constitute a model of the flexible enterprise governed by *organizational lyophilization*.[21] Whereas during the apogee Taylorism/Fordism – the era of the mass working class – the strength of an enterprise was proportional to the number of its employees, one can say that in the era of lean production and flexible accumulation, the enterprises that stand out are those that combine the smallest number of workers with high rates productivity.

Understanding this process gives us better insight into why the world of labor tends increasingly toward informality: The shift from Taylorism/Fordism to flexible accumulation means that jobs are no longer tightly regulated.

How is it possible to organize this new proletariat? How can this growing sector of the working class advance toward class consciousness, under conditions of the transnationalization of capital? How can it link up with the more traditional sectors of the working class?

Conclusion

Just as capital is a global system, the world of labor and its challenges are also increasingly transnationalized. As yet, there has not arisen an international response on the part of the working class. It keeps itself predominantly within its national structures, which pose enormous limitations on workers' action. As the space and time of production are reconfigured globally, there has been a process of both re-territorialization and de-territorialization. New industrial regions emerge and many disappear, at the same time that more and more factories become globalized.[22]

The center of present-day social confrontation is given by the contradiction between *total social capital* and the *totality of*

---

21. Lyophilization, or 'freeze-drying', is a dehydration process that works by freezing perishable material. The lyophilization metaphor is used to evoke the elimination of living labor that occurs during the restructuring of production. See Juan J. Castillo, *Sociologia del Trabajo*, Madrid: CIS, 1996, and 'A la Búsqueda del Trabajo Perdido', in *Complejidad y Teoria Social*, eds. A. Pérez-Agote and I. Yucera, Madrid: CIS, 1996.

22. See Antunes, *The Meanings of Work*, 93–95.

labor.[23] Therefore, just as capital makes use of its globalized mechanisms and international organs, so also must workers' struggle become – in the spirit of the IWA – increasingly international. On this terrain, as we know, capital is well ahead of labor in its level of solidarity and class-action. Yet it often happens that the success or failure of a strike in one or more countries depends upon the solidarity and action of workers in productive units of the same company elsewhere.

Existing international labor organizations nearly always have a traditional bureaucratic and institutionalized structure that leaves them incapable of offering an alternative social vision opposed to the logic of capital. They tend to assume a defensive stance or one that is subordinate to the logic of internationalization of capital, opposing merely some of its most dire consequences. The conflict between native (territorialized) and immigrant (de-territorialized) workers reflects the process of economic transnationalization, to which the labor movement has been unable to provide a satisfactory response.

In this way, besides the cleavages that exist between secure and precarious workers, men and women, young and old people, native and immigrant, black and white, skilled and unskilled, 'included' and 'excluded,' and many other examples to be found with the national space, the stratification and fragmentation of labor are also accentuated by the growing internationalization of capital. This broader, more complex and fragmented world of labor is manifested: (1) within particular groups or sectors of work; (2) between different groups of workers within the same national community; (3) between different national bodies of labor, pitted against one another by international capitalist competition; (4) between the labor force of advanced capitalist countries – relative beneficiaries of the global capitalist division of labor – and the relatively more exploited labor force of the 'Third World'; and (5) between employed workers and the unemployed, including those that are increasingly victims of the 'second industrial revolution'.[24]

The precarious workers struggle, as did workers during the Industrial Revolution, for basic workers' rights. The Fordist workers try to resist the complete destruction of their rights. These two basic poles of the same working class face a future in which their prospects are bound together. The former – the "disorganized" – seek a complete end to precarization and dream of a better world. The

23. See István Mészáros, *Beyond Capital: Towards a Theory of Transition*, London: Merlin Press, 1995.
24. Ibid., 929.

latter – the "organized" – want to avoid being degraded to the status of the world's newly precarious.

Given that the destructive logic of capital is seemingly multiple but in essence unitary, if these vital poles of labor don't ally themselves organically, they will suffer the tragedy of greater precarization and complete dehumanization. If, on the other hand, they forge ties of solidarity, of common class-affiliation, and of a *new mode of being*, defining and planning their actions, they may have greater power than any other social force to demolish the social metabolism of capital and thereby begin delineating a *new way of life*.

We should recall, in closing, this decisive observation of the IWA, made even stronger now by the globalizations of capital and of labor:

> One element of success they possess — numbers; but numbers weigh in the balance only if united by combination and led by knowledge. Past experience has shown how disregard of that bond of brotherhood which ought to exist between the workmen of different countries, and incite them to stand firmly by each other in all their struggles for emancipation, will be chastised by the common discomfiture of their incoherent efforts. This thought prompted the workingmen of different countries assembled on September 28, 1864, in public meeting at St. Martin's Hall, to found the International Association.[25]

The experience of the IWA, which for a long time appeared to have been buried, is being resurrected 150 years later.

Translated by Daila Fanny and Victor Wallis

---

25. Marx, "Inaugural Address," MECW, vol. 20, 12.

The Strength of Our Collective Voice: Views of Labor Leaders from around the World

Babak Amini

The International Workingmen's Association (IWA) was a ground-breaking effort to give power to the most exploited, a voice to the voiceless, and collective cohesion to the most fractured. It was due to its uncompromising dedication to the working class that the IWA caught the attention of workers around the world. The spirit of internationalism, courage to face their most ruthless enemies, piercing insights into the complex issues of the time, and astonishingly creative proposals to overcome them are among the most enduring legacies of the IWA.

In recent years, we have seen a deepening crisis in capitalism brought about by the financial meltdown of 2008, ongoing environmental catastrophe, growing dislocations and flow of migration due to regional and international wars, and increasing economic inequality. In the midst of these undeniable factors, many have turned toward genuine alternatives to the existing political and economic paradigm. It has become increasingly critical now for trade unions to be at the forefront of the social movements that have been erupting globally, especially during the last few years.

Hence the importance we give to the voices of the trade union leaders in this collection. We need the perspective of those who work tirelessly to protect the rights of the labor against neoliberal onslaught in the form of draconian austerity measures unleashed on the poor and the working class.

The following interview with prominent trade union leaders and workers' movement activists from various countries is done in the spirit of the internationalism of the IWA. Its aim is to emphasize the commonality among national working-class struggles while at

143

the same time highlighting the differences that need to be understood and negotiated.

This interview would have been impossible without the comradely help of Marcello Musto, Ricardo Antunes, Patrick Bond, Gilbert Achcar, Mimmo Moccia, Omar El Shafei, and Hyun Ok Park. I sincerely thank them for their invaluable support throughout the process.

EFITU (Egyptian Federation of Trade Unions) is a national organization independent of government, political parties, corporations, and civil society organizations. EFITU is a product of the 2011 Egyptian uprising that toppled Hosni Mubarak and triggered an ongoing revolutionary process. EFITU aims at organizing public and private sector workers, retirees, and the unemployed, to ensure their well-being by raising standards in the areas of healthcare, education, insurance, and pensions.

Fatma Ramadan is an Egyptian trade unionist, labor researcher and socialist, who has been deeply involved in organizations – including the Coordination Committee for Trade Union Rights and Freedoms – founded during the decade preceding the 2011 uprising. As a founding member of EFITU, she is coordinator of its Committee for Solidarity with Strikes and Sit-ins, which has been playing a militant role at the national level despite the post-2011 shift to the right on the part of the EFITU leadership. She currently heads the Right to Work Unit at the Egyptian Initiative for Personal Rights (EIPR), a prominent human rights organization.

FIOM (the Italian federation of metalworkers), established in 1901, is a member of the Italian General Confederation of Labor (CGIL) at the national level, the European Metalworkers Federations (FEM) at the continental level, and the International Federation of Metalworkers Unions (FISM) at the international level. FIOM has gone through a fascinating and inspiring history of resistance, labor militancy, and structural evolution. FIOM openly opposed the war in 1914 and fought to keep Italy neutral. After leading a successful campaign in 1919 to reduce working hours to eight hours per day and 48 hours per week, it triumphantly confronted the employers' counterattack in 1920 by leading sit-ins of 400,000 metalworkers and 100,000 workers from other sectors. The defeat of the employers' organization led to wage increases, six days of paid holidays, improved overtime and nighttime working condition, etc. During WW2, union members took part in anti-Nazi and anti-Fascist armed resistance. In 1946, the FIOM was turned into the federation of blue and white collar metalworkers. Having experienced defeat and serious membership decline in the 1950s due to the difficult political climate, FIOM regained its strength beginning with the revolutionary events of 1968. Its victories included reduction in working hours to 40 hours per week without wage cuts and recognition of the right to hold meetings in the factory during working hours. The worldwide emergence of neoliberalism took its toll on FIOM in 1980 when Fiat (the largest Italian manufacturer) announced the dismissal of 14,469 workers and defeated a subsequent 35-day strike. Italy saw a fundamental industrial restructuring in the late 1980s which led to a rapid growth of small and medium-size enterprises with low occupational safety standards, the disappearance of industrial zones around big cities, and ultimately a sharp decline in union membership. Since 1993, FIOM has continued to bargain at both the national and the company level.

Maurizio Landini started working as an apprentice welder in a cooperative at the age of 15. He eventually became Secretary General of FIOM. He was elected to the National Secretariat of the metalworkers' union CGIL in 2005, and participated in negotiations for renewal of the metalworkers' contract in 2009.

KPTU (the Korean Federation of Public Services and Transportation Workers' Unions) is an industrial federation of unions organizing in the public, social service, and transport sectors. The KPTU is affiliated to the Korean Confederation of Trade Unions (KCTU), a democratic national center in South Korea, and the global union federation of Public Services International (PSI). Currently, KPTU has over 146,000 members including utilities and public institution workers (e.g. in rail, subway, public transportation, social insurance, energy and safety), airline and airport workers, cargo truck, bus, taxi and other transport workers, care workers, cleaning and other property service workers, etc. During the last several years, KPTU and other affiliated unions have been confronting the Korean government's efforts to undermine collective bargaining agreements guaranteeing union activities, decent working conditions, and the right to strike in the public sector (through its broad and vague definition of essential services). This is accompanied by government attempts to privatize utilities and public transport. In the mid-2000s, KPTU and its affiliates succeeded in staving off the direct sale of public institutions to private capital by organizing several powerful strikes. They are currently fighting for collective bargaining agreements for education support workers and other precarious public sector workers (who now make up roughly 20 percent of the public sector workforce).

Wol-San Liem has been Director of International Affairs for the KPTU since September 2012. Between 2006 and 2012, she worked for the Research Institute for Alternative Workers' Movements (RIAWM) and the Migrants' Trade Union (MTU) in South Korea. She received her PhD in History from New York University in 2010.

MST (Brazil's Landless Workers Movement – Movimento dos Trabalhadores Rurais Sem Terra) was founded in 1984 after a period of isolated struggles at the end of 1970s by rural workers who were driven off their lands by mechanization, extensive use of pesticides, and increasing control by large multinational agribusiness companies. MST claims the right to occupy what it deems to be unproductive rural land in accordance with Article 184 of the Brazilian constitution which requires the government to "expropriate for the purpose of agrarian reform, rural property that is not performing its social function."

Progressively expanding its scope and influence in Brazilian society, the MST started with land reform through occupation of lands by rural workers, later turning its attention to the urban population through fighting for production of healthy, GMO-free, pesticide-free food for all, and eventually making itself one of the most militant social movements in Brazil by calling for fundamental policy changes and "Agrarian Reform for Social Justice and Popular Sovereignty." Given the inherently transnational nature of large corporations in agriculture, the MST sees its mission extending beyond the national borders of Brazil as it seeks to build international solidarity through the Via Campesina peasant movement.

As one of the most significant social movements in Latin America, the MST now has over 1.5 million members in 23 out of 26 states in Brazil and has organized more than 2,500 land occupations, with about 370,000 families settled on 7.5 million hectares of occupied land. MST has also been outstandingly active in providing education to tens of thousands of landless workers and children.

The interview was conducted in March 2014 with two militant leaders of the MST: **Kelli Mafort**, a member of the national leadership, and **Gilmar Mauro**, a member of the National Coordinating Council.

NUMSA (The National Union of Metalworkers of South Africa) is the largest metal workers' trade union in South Africa, with more than 338,000 members. It was formed in 1987 by the merger of four different unions, some of which had formed in 1960s and 70s. In its militant struggle to improve working conditions, it has achieved substantial gains, including centralized bargaining to protect workers from low wages, exploitation, and poor benefits. Thanks to its uncompromising commitment to the working class and smart political choices, its membership has grown to about 50 percent of the workforce in the metal industry. In addition, NUMSA has sought to unite metal workers across race, ethnic, and gender lines. This is particularly important for South African society as it tries to resurrect itself from the social consequences of the apartheid era.

Trade union politics in South Africa is in the midst of important new developments. NUMSA, as the largest affiliate of the Congress of South African Trade Unions (COSATU), has begun to withdraw its support for the African National Congress (ANC), and has called for COSATU to break from its tripartite coalition with the ANC and the South African Communist Party – a coalition that has been the main basis for the ANC's hold on national power. NUMSA has called for a new socialist political direction for South Africa.

NUMSA faces numerous challenges in the future with regard to flexible and short-term contract labor, underpaid labor especially in the motor, retail, metal and engineering sectors, and loss of its quality staff members due to their drift toward the private sector or the government for higher wages.

Irvin Jim, General Secretary of NUMSA, was an anti-apartheid activist in the late 1980s and joined the workforce in a rubber factory in 1990s. He soon became a union activist and later a shop steward (union representative). He became the youngest NUMSA activist in the central committee and, in 2008, was elected General Secretary of NUMSA.

WFTU (the World Federation of Trade Unions) was founded in 1945 in Paris, at the first World Trade Union Congress, representing 67 million workers from 55 countries and 20 international organizations. The basic objectives of this congress were quite similar to those of the UN Charter, which calls for a peaceful world free of social injustice. However, rather than speaking in the name of "we the peoples of the United Nations," WFTU speaks on behalf of "we the working people of the world." One of the main clauses in the WFTU constitution is "to combat war and the causes of war and work for a stable and enduring peace." WFTU saw "the speedy and complete eradication of fascism" as one of its primary tasks. To this end, it supported antifascist national liberation movements around the world. It also supported the labor movements and organizations in newly independent countries.

The composition of WFTU has seen significant change during the past six decades, reflecting the great changes in world politics. However, it has always maintained the core idea of emancipation of the working people by fighting against all forms of exploitation and oppression, through education, organization, and mobilization of the working class in national and international networks of solidarity. As an international labor organization, WFTU maintains its independence from governments, political parties, or private employers.

H. Mahadeva, Deputy General Secretary of WFTU, was born in 1941 in India, in the Kanyakumari district, joined the Air Force and studied technology at the Air Force Flying College in Jodhpour. There, he joined the union and later was transferred to Bangalore where he got deeply involved in trade union movement. He helped a number of unions in private and public sector industries all over the south of India. He later moved to the national level and became Deputy General Secretary of All Indian Trade Union Congress (AITUC) and then to the WFTU where he is now the Deputy General Secretary in charge of the Asia-Pacific Region.

1. *This year marks the 150th anniversary of the International Working-men's Association (IWA) which was founded in London on September 28, 1864. Despite a rather short lifespan (1864–76) and modest membership, the IWA caught the attention of workers around the world because it represented the common struggles of the proletariat. As a trade union activist, what do you see as the most enduring legacies of the IWA?*

Fatma Ramadan: The IWA was the product of a rapid rise in European workers' movements. The 1860s witnessed rapid strides of trade unionism in Britain and France and the emergence of the first mass workers' political organization in Germany, the General German Workers' Association. A new spirit of international solidarity began to emerge within labor movements. The IWA emerged as a political and organizational expression of this spirit of proletarian internationalism. During its life, the IWA took positions on a number of issues such as working hours, working conditions, and the horrors of child labor.

As a trade union activist, it seems to me that the most enduring legacy of the IWA lies in the convergence of workers' struggles for reform with an internationalist revolutionary perspective. This merger of the struggle for reforms with a vision of international revolution urgently needs to be revived today in our age of crisis-ridden senile capitalism. The internationalism of the IWA is all the more relevant in the age of capitalist globalization.

Wol-San Liem: The preamble to the General Rules of the IWA states that "the emancipation of the working classes must be conquered by the working classes themselves" and that "emancipation of labor is neither a local nor a national, but a social problem, embracing all countries in which modern society exists." I believe that the most important and enduring legacies of IWA are their strong belief that workers must become a self-determined political force across national boundaries, and trying to put this principle into practice by creating a committed mass base. In addition, the IWA established many fundamental principles that remain with us in the labor movement – shortening of the workday, abolition of child labor, etc.

There are several challenges to the realization of IWA aspirations. First, the discussion of political principles and a vision of an alternative society are becoming increasingly rare in most labor movements. This is definitely true in South Korea, although there is still a larger group of unionists who maintain a commitment to such debates than in a place like the United States.

Secondly, concepts such as "class emancipation" or "internationalism" are often abstract ideals that lack concrete application and practical guidelines. When the IWA existed, the concept of a workers' internationalism was both an ideal and a practical issue. To maintain and make use of this legacy, we need to develop a practical internationalism that includes concrete goals and means for workers' organizing collective action on a global scale.

Maurizio Landini: Since 1864, we have had 150 years full of important events that changed the life of humankind. Historic tragedies, wars and dictatorships, popular revolutions, fights for freedom, civil and political rights, workers and women's emancipation, fundamental human rights such as health, school, working conditions, etc. They were difficult and complex years, but crucial on the path to democracy and working-class participation in the political life in many countries. I think the most important IWA contribution has been to recognize that the fight against injustice and inequality must be waged at a global level. Fraternity, solidarity, and equality are values without borders. So, I think the original idea of IWA was bringing all those national organizations, parties, and unions together to found an international association. Nowadays, national states can no longer confront the power of multinational corporations. Big money has all the economic and political power in its hands. So, the only solution is: think globally, work globally, and fight globally. This is the core lesson of IWA: *Workers of the World Unite!*

> **2.** *We live in the age of austerity; neoliberal policies have waged a war against the working class, the poor, and the most vulnerable, to channel the public wealth into fewer and fewer hands. What do you see as the role of trade unions in reversing this move toward increasing austerity, and cutting down on social security and public spending?*

Fatma Ramadan: A widening of the narrow conception of trade unions as reformist entities whose struggle is limited to improvement of wages and working condition is necessary if trade unions are to wage an effective struggle against intensified austerity. By increasing precarity through factory closures, mass layoffs, job cuts in the public sector, and limiting the social safety net and public spending, employers and states have been hugely weakening the capacity of trade unions to organize. In Egypt, for instance, the Unified Labor Law of 2003 aimed at facilitating temporary work, layoffs, and privatization. Workers' resistance to the law was carried out mostly through informal organizational ventures, as trade unions had been incorporated since the 1950s as an arm of the authoritarian state rather than an organ of workers' struggle. This informal resistance was part of the rising struggle that eventually led to the revolutionary situation that erupted in Egypt (and much of the Arab World) in 2011.

Trade unions have a double motivation to fight such policies, which are detrimental to both workers' standards of living and the capacity of trade unions to organize. Effective resistance to austerity, however, requires a wider conception of trade unionism in yet another sense. For both resistance against these policies and also the capacity of trade unions to organize, unions need not only to develop a wider vision for society as a whole (contesting general state policies), but also to link themselves to non-workplace social movements. This is necessary in order to create the mass mobilization needed to reverse the trend and effectively challenge the status quo.

Wol-San Liem: As an officer in an industrial union federation that represents public sector workers, I believe the role of public sector unions in fighting austerity and budget cuts to the public sector is vital. In Korea, we talk about our role in strengthening the public character of vital services like public transport, energy, water, healthcare, education, etc. In the international labor movement, we talk about defending "quality public services." The concepts are pretty much the same – that is, access to public services and social welfare are democratic rights belonging to all people – and it is our job, as public service providers, to defend these rights against cuts and privatization. This requires that we make it clear that the attack on the public sector, usually accompanied by attacks on public sector unions, is an attack on democracy – both the democratic rights to quality public services and the democratic rights of workers to freedom of association, and collective bargaining and action.

In Korea, we are currently engaged in a heated battle against privatization of the railway, gas and electricity, healthcare, and a range of other public services. We carry on this fight in close partnership with other social forces who are rightly concerned about dwindling access and rising prices. Our strategies involve everything from working with opposition party legislators to putting forth anti-privatization bills, to protest and strike action. These fights have to go on. Of course, however, we will never achieve full public accountability under the current capitalist system. So a long-term vision and strategy is needed.

H. Mahadevan: In the name of "humanizing" globalization, the employers, financial institutions such as the IMF (International Monetary Fund), the World Bank and the WTO (World Trade Organization) offer and impose a path of capitalist reconstruction and continue to preach There Is No Alternative (TINA). The world of labor, with the sole perspective of altering the system which has made inequalities between continents, between countries, and within countries to grow to dangerous proportions, should therefore reject these policies and act in favor of a true alternative, for a better world free of exploitation, frustrations and humiliations and proving There Are Alternatives (TAA) including Socialism Is The Alternative (SITA).

Trade unionism should prepare itself to become an efficient counterbalance in the face of the aggressive and costly policies of neoliberalism, which eliminate the historic achievements of the workers, destroying systems of social protection, healthcare, education, retirement, pensions, and the environment. If one of the purposes of the labor movement is to close the gap between rich and poor or to create greater social equality, inevitably the question is whether these could ever be achieved under capitalism or whether the working class should plan methods for challenging capitalist institutions including the fundamentally exploitative character of the wage

151

relation. *We, trade unions, therefore, need to define and act on an Agenda that has the potential to change people's lives.*

Maurizio Landini: Since the emergence of the neoliberal ideology 40 years ago, unions around the world have been the target of capitalist attack on workers' living standards and wages. Capital needs to defeat the unions in order to weaken their collective bargaining capacity and to pit workers against one another. This can be seen in the fact that the unionization rate is very low, compared to its peak in 1970s. Big companies have a powerful weapon: in search of better conditions for maximizing profit, they can move their plants elsewhere in the world. Blackmail is commonly practiced and, in order not to lose their jobs, the workers often agree to sacrifice their working conditions to increasingly lower standards. The question is how to break this vicious cycle. I think there is only one way to deal with it: by going back to our roots. This does not mean we should return to the past. Past is past and things will never be the same. Rather, we have to return to our past *values*. The labor movement had dreamed of breaking down all borders to unite the workers of the world. That has not happened because international labor organizations are still too weak to deal with the new global powers. So my answer is: unite, unite, unite!

3. *In the midst of growing unemployment, with 27 million newly unemployed since the 2008 economic crisis, bringing the global number of unemployed to 200 million, how are the trade unions planning to connect to this sector of the population who see themselves outside of the workers' movement?*

MST: The consequences of neoliberalism can be seen in the fragmentation of various categories of workers, the declining number of previously significant industries and emergence of new sectors, the reduction of formal employment, and increased numbers of workers in the service sector, all at the expense of the working conditions and living conditions of an ever increasing portion of the working class. Precarious work coupled with structural unemployment in a jobless society, has been a hallmark of our time.

This situation has significantly impacted the social and the political mechanisms. Apart from the obvious effects of unemployment, trade unions are most affected by the quantitative reduction of the industrial working class and its fragmentation within industry itself. Now, unions represent a small portion of the working class, since most workers are not formally under contracts. With unemployment, informality, bureaucratic blackmailing, and internal organizational problems, the number of trade union members has significantly declined.

The feeling of inferiority imposed by bourgeois ideology on the unemployed is based on the idea that unemployment is related to persons' inability to work, or to their not being qualified for the available jobs. Thus, workers feel both fear and guilt for being unemployed, thinking that they cannot get jobs because they are "incompetent," too old, too young, inexperienced, illiterate, semi-literate, unskilled, etc. We must then rescue the workers' self-esteem and direct their indignation at the ruling classes. We must recognize that the world of labor has undergone drastic changes over the last century, challenging us to identify new social subjects who struggle to resist capitalism today.

In the case of MST, the rural unemployed, among others, have always been part of its social base. However, the reconfiguration of the world of labor has caused the urban unemployed to fight for agrarian reform. This introduces an interesting change in the political trajectory of MST regarding the idea of the centrality of work in social relations and the realization that agriculture, like any other work activity, can be learned and done by any human being.

Moreover, the urban unemployed workers called for another commitment by MST, namely, to push the fight beyond the struggle for land. People are joining MST not necessarily because of its demand for land reform, but for its strength and militancy. MST fights for *urban reform* which hinges on *agrarian reform* (the MST's central goal).

Maurizio Landini: The 2008 global financial crisis did not happen by accident. It was the result of many years of financial deregulation, small government, and unfettered globalization. It followed the Washington Consensus ideology: unbounded enrichment of those at the top would produce wellbeing for all others. On the contrary, it has produced the 1 percent whose income and wealth have increased substantially. The remaining 99 percent become poorer year after year. What should be done? Obviously, the problem is a political one. We need a fundamental political change. It is not true that 27 million new unemployed – 200 million total unemployed – are the result of natural evolution of the market. They are the direct result of certain political choices. You change the policy and unemployment will fall.

Unions can get in touch and mobilize the unemployed through a global movement. We have already become multi-ethnic national unions, even in countries such as Italy which previously did not have much immigration. Now we need an international union, uniting workers employed in different companies across the world, whose focus also includes the unemployed and their needs. In recent years, we had important social movements, but now we need a more stable on-the-ground organization. ITUC (International Trade Union Confederation) and Global Union at the world level and ETUC (European Trade Union Confederation) at the European level have already engaged in this project, but they need more power. And this has to be delegated by national unions. The latter should give up part of their sovereignty. This is not an easy historical process at all: it requires political will and feelings of solidarity that globalization has tarnished.

Irvin Jim: Given the immense wealth in the world, which is unjustly concentrated in very few hands under capitalism, we have enough to provide for the entire world population. To overthrow this unjust system, there is a need to roll back the neoliberal agenda. This struggle must be waged internationally by the trade unions. Many people have argued that we can give capitalism a human face through structural reform. However, capitalism has no solution for the problems that confront humanity. During economic boom, capitalism makes a profit just as it does during economic crises and downturns by destroying the workers. What it does not compromise is its sole objective, which is maximization of profit. We know that if we allow capitalism, it extends its greedy hands wherever possible.

Regarding the unemployed, we must say, the working class is not just people who work; the unemployed are also part of the working class! Why do you think somebody who is not working cannot be mobilized and organized? The frustration that the unemployed have to endure every day in the search for jobs is a continuation of the exploitation of the working class. Some people stop looking for jobs not because they do not want to work but because they are forced out of the job market. One of the things that NUMSA has been championing is to focus on both shop-floor struggles and community struggles, since it is important to have a dynamic link between the unemployed at the community level and those who work on campaigns and social movements.

H. Mahadevan: The WFTU, in its Presidential Council meeting on 14–15 February 2014, held in Rome, resolved that the trade unions in all countries will organize strikes, demonstrations, and rallies confronting the crucial problem of *unemployment,* and demanding rights for the unemployed. Unemployment is an issue that can unite workers all over the world. The mobilizations will demand stable jobs for all, and elimination of the causes that generate unemployment. They will also seek ways to fight for the survival of the unemployed.

Over the past several years, because of the economic and social crisis, the phenomenon of non-unionization has worsened. The negative media campaigns, the repression and murder of trade union leaders, and the questioning of the right to unionize, to strike, and to demonstrate have produced a particularly harmful atmosphere. We should respond effectively and in a united manner to the anti-union offensive. All these issues demand answers from the trade union movement and are valid for any country, continent, and society.

Trade unionism should build a solid alliance with the peasant movement in order to put an end to the plundering and for the recovery of their lands and means of production, necessary for the defense of their culture, responding to their domestic needs and contributing to real reforms. A common struggle of workers and peasants is required in order to achieve democratic agrarian reforms that would place the land in the hands of those who till it. Trade unions, both internationally and nationally, should be the organizational framework for the younger generations, immigrant workers, the unemployed, and those excluded from collective bargaining, in particular the millions of workers in the informal sector.

4. *In the context of soaring power of multinational corporations with their significant ability to absorb temporary financial downturns and to relocate cross-nationally in response to labor militancy in one country, how can the labor unions, which typically operate on a national basis, respond effectively?*

Fatma Ramadan: Here the internationalist legacy of the IWA is most relevant and invaluable. Trade unions need to consciously develop ties of solidarity across national borders. An important step in this direction for unions is to prioritize the defense of migrant workers, who increasingly constitute a significant portion of the super-exploited and oppressed in much of the world. This, once again, requires a kind of radical democratic trade unionism challenging the racism of the capitalist system. If there is solidarity between workers of different ethnicities and national backgrounds within and across countries, then workers can effectively resist capital's attempts to curb labor militancy by relocating. There are many examples of partially successful struggles along these lines in recent years. This question is crucially important in the current Arab revolutionary process, as migrant workers constitute a massive oppressed majority of the workforce in

155

the heart of regional capitalism and of reactionary politics in the Gulf region.

Wol-San Liem: In my answer to the first question, I referred to the need for a "practical internationalism." For me, practical internationalism means organizing campaigns and collective actions of workers who are connected to one another not by national borders, but by the production and supply chains of multinational corporations. Such campaigns would organize workers into a transnational struggle, if not a multinational union, and hopefully also into an internationalist consciousness. Some efforts that point in this direction are already underway, but we need a much greater commitment from national union leaderships to not only short-term solidarity actions, but also long-term organizing projects which require research, and human and financial resources.

Unfortunately, the majority of union leaderships are not inclined to make such a commitment. They argue that such a strategy will not help increase membership and bargaining power in the near future. Thus, careful consideration has to go into choosing targets and partner-unions in other countries to work with.

Irvin Jim: The first thing to note is that that there is an ongoing struggle between the working class and the capitalist class with their intricate system of multinationals and transnational corporations which are basically on a crusade to maximize their profit by all means necessary. Because of the absence of responsible governments, militant trade unions, and working-class political parties, these corporations are able to control transnational capital mobility. The flow of capital is determined by where profit can be maximized with the least resistance. Therefore, when we say we must promote union collaboration, we do not want to just act as a counterweight against capital; we need to be able to challenge the multinationals and their agenda with militancy and uncompromising persistence. We know that they can terminate any meaningful and progressive competition, and can determine or undermine legitimately elected governments. It is not possible to challenge this global nature of capitalism without creating a global network of solidarity between trade unions in addition to raising the level of consciousness of workers. We must organize workers to appreciate that it is not enough to just have a union in one country if that union is not linked to other unions all over the world. There lies the crucial role of international solidarity.

5. *The idea of transnational organization of workers to create a global
    network of solidarity was first materialized in the IWA. One
    hundred and fifty years later, globalization has been one of the
    most effective tools used by the capitalist class to crush workers'
    movements. How feasible and effective have been attempts to build
    relationships of solidarity between various trade unions across the
    globe?*

Wol-San Liem: The most concerted efforts to build international
relationships among unions are the international trade union organizations, which have been operating in many cases for over a hundred
years. My union is part of Public Services International (PSI) and the
International Transport Workers' Federation (ITF). These organizations belong to the non-Communist family of Global Union Federations (GUFs). There is also a family of parallel organizations made
up primarily of unions associated with Communist parties.

I believe the GUFs play a very important role in the international
labor movement, by providing a structure and resources that unions
can use to connect to one another, share information about common
issues, and be represented on the international stage. The GUFs also
initiate some important projects, for instance in the areas of trade
union rights, occupational health and safety, etc. But the GUFs are
often bogged down by an emphasis on meetings rather than long-
term struggles, and have limited mobilizing capacity.

In the area of bilateral relationships, it is not hard to find examples
of meaningful solidarity. Australian and US unions have recently
cooperated to organize US truck drivers employed by the Australian
transnational transport corporation Toll. International solidarity
actions, which put pressure on Philippine Airlines, helped the Philippines Airlines workers win their two-year long struggle for reinstate-
ment last year. My union federation's rail affiliate received a great
deal of solidarity from rail unions in other countries during its
23-day strike against privatization last year, and is beginning to
build longer-term relationships with some of these unions. But, these
sorts of efforts are infrequent and usually peripheral to unions' main
goals and daily work. A reorientation towards building international
relationships is needed.

MST: The political perspective of agribusiness has directly impacted
the social movements for democratization of access to land and the
implementation of land reform worldwide. These impacts affect the
peasants, landless rural workers, occupiers, indigenous communities,

local fishermen, those affected by dams, small farmers, mining communities, and rural waged employees, as well as the proletariat of agribusiness in general.

Capital has adopted disastrous approaches to the environment, labor, and peasant lives. This condition has an international dimension and hence must be confronted in that context. The international link between peasants has been given by Via Campesina, with operations on all continents and a presence in over seventy countries. Via Campesina Brazil brings together social movements such as MST, MAB (Movement of People Affected by Dams), MMC (Movement of Rural Women), and MPA (Movement of Small Farmers).

Via Campesina advocates an agricultural and water program that prioritizes food sovereignty to stimulate production of healthy food, diversification of agriculture, and agrarian reform (with broad democratization of land ownership). It also struggles against the privatization of land, forests, water, and all natural resources.

Spearheaded by Via Campesina, actions of International Women's Day have been one of the most inspiring examples of struggle and confrontation with capital. These political actions fundamentally denounce the existing model of capital, the state, and the government. The focus of the struggles has been transnational corporations such as Monsanto, Aracruz, Vale, ADM, Bunge, Cargill, Stora Enzo, Raizen, Cutrale, Syngenta, etc.

6. *What is the labor movement's vision for addressing the devastating effects of global climate change, which is predicted to cause massive displacement and food shortages in large parts of the world in the coming decades?*

Maurizio Landini: Climate change, along with globalization problems, is the other pillar of the strategic shift for the social and political left. Environmental stress, raw materials over-exploitation, energy issues and carbon emissions, rising temperature, melting glaciers and rising sea levels, increase in extreme weather events: those are all aspects of a problem which can no longer be deferred. It is essential for us to manage the conflict between the defense of today's conditions and the conquest of a sustainable future.

Facing the problem of how to stop environmental exploitation, we have to ask ourselves: won't emphasis on the production of vehicles for individual rather than public transportation ultimately lead to high fuel consumption? Should we make more mega-SUVs, or more trains and railways? Moreover, shouldn't we push for locally produced goods rather than producing where there is the highest return on investment? And, above all, do we have to continue to fuel a demand for individual consumptions, often excessive and unnecessary, at the cost of lower quality?

It is clear that the real solution lies not just in the sum of many individual investment and consumption choices, but in striving for fairer and more balanced economic growth planning. There should also be more social control over economic organization. We need a fairer distribution of income between shareholders and stakeholders: rebalancing this is essential to achieve not only greater social justice but also a more sustainable, healthy, and balanced economic system.

Irvin Jim: For us in the South, it is a considerable challenge because even though we recognize that global warming, caused by fossil fuels, is a problem, we cannot abruptly change our entire economy into a green economy, when in fact we need jobs in South Africa. Green or brown, a job is a job in terms of the wages. Regarding the issue of fossil fuel, we must take the approach of having energy mix to ensure that we have a diversity of production and access. But there is a glaring challenge of access to the technology which is currently made and controlled by the North. So, I think we should always ask, "to what extent" should we swing towards the "green process"? Also, we should consider which nation-states and multinational corporations benefit from the new green technology. So, there are issues of democratization, of power relations between the North and South which, in my view, concern the working class in both North and South. Of course, the current unsustainable situation demands that we make a transition; we now know that we are facing an imminent threat caused fundamentally by the essence of capitalism which is greed. Green jobs and the transition to a green economy should be part of our political discussions.

Fatma Ramadan: Climate change is a huge threat to the survival of the human race. It is a dramatic indication of what is at stake in our current economic, political, cultural and civilizational crisis. Left-leaning social movements and activists have played a great role in raising consciousness about the organic link between capitalist accumulation and climate deterioration. This consciousness is yet to be embodied in mass resistance to climate change.

The labor movement should be at the forefront of such a mass movement. Again, this requires broadening the conception of traditional trade unionism. The nascent trade unions in Egypt have yet to formulate any vision on this question, despite the fact that Egypt is one of the countries particularly threatened by massive devastation if current trends of climate change continue unchallenged. Militant trade unions in the country should raise consciousness about the question. In this, they crucially need to interact with more established and experienced trade unions abroad.

Succeeding in mobilizing around climate change and its effect has a potential for building anti-capitalist global networks of resisting, and hence can revive militant trade unionism in a spirit akin to that of the IWA. It should be a priority for the radical left.

7. *Many believe that capitalism is rapidly reaching its limits. The militant global struggle for higher standards of living and wages, and the undeniable effects of global climate change have crippled the ability of capitalism to externalize costs to increase surplus value. How do you see the future of capitalism and what will be the role of trade unions in a potentially revolutionary period?*

MST: It is necessary to examine the limits of capital in the context of its structural crisis which unleashes a voracious need for expansion and domination of new regions. In Brazil, the multinational corporations have marched ahead overwhelmingly, destroying any obstacle including institutional, legal, and political resistance from the people who live in those areas, such as the indigenous peoples, peasants, and traditional fishermen. This significantly impacts the MST's struggle for land and consequently requires the movement to rethink its agrarian program. This process of reflection and debate was synthesized in the People's Agrarian Reform Program which was the focus of the MST's Sixth Congress, held in February 2014.

To move toward the defeat of capitalism, we need to link specific social demands with a broader revolutionary political project. Hence, it is essential to have the organizational tools to help the working class ensure its leadership.

It is important to reflect on the limitations of the classic organizational forms. During the state welfare era in the core countries, the working class was organized through two main instruments – trade unions and political parties – which fought for rights that were granted by the state in the form of public policy, labor legislation, and social security.

Little by little, the achievements of the class, which were the result of numerous struggles, were assimilated or taken away by the capitalist system. Currently, these achievements are being systematically removed. The popular movements in various parts of the world are evidence of this. The organizational instruments strengthened during the welfare state era are no longer appropriate to face this change in the objectives of the struggle. In the words of Istvan Meszaros, they are defensive instruments unable to organize the resumption of offensive struggle. This imposes the need for the class to forge political and organizational tools needed to pursue their revolutionary project, whether through building new instruments or redefining existing ones.

Fatma Ramadan: Capitalism today is a genuinely morbid system. It is threatening the very survival of the human race. Our world is one of crisis, exploitation, and oppression. It is also a world of resistance, struggle and revolution. The experience of the Arab revolutionary process over the last three years, however, shows that revolutionary triumph is far from inevitable.

In revolutionary times such as ours, trade unions are crucial. They can only realize their potential if they develop a vision for a radical alternative to the current social order. The defeats suffered by popular movements over the last decades and the current extreme weakness of the left put strong limitations on the possibilities of radicalization. Gramsci's words are as relevant as ever: "the crisis consists precisely in the fact that the old is dying and the new cannot be born; in this interregnum a great variety of morbid symptoms appear." We live in exciting yet difficult times in which the responsibility of the global left, despite its current weakness, is huge. If the left wants to take such responsibility, it needs to forge organic links to militant trade unionism, putting forward a genuinely democratic and emancipatory vision for a world free of exploitation and oppression. In this, the lessons of the great struggles of the last decade, with their potential and limitations, will prove crucial.

8. *What is the biggest challenge for the labor movement in the next decade?*

Fatma Ramadan: I would say that the biggest challenge for labor movement is to focus on a much wider social movement of the oppressed. This does not mean, as we are commonly told, abandoning a class perspective. To the contrary, a deepening of class politics is required. This entails that the organized labor movement has to adapt to what Bolivian militant trade unionists during their heroic battles of the last decade have called "the new world of work," a world in which workers are increasingly fragmented and casualized. The legacy of recent struggles, especially in Latin America, shows that such fragmentation is not an insurmountable obstacle to organization and militant struggle. A dynamic social movement, unionism from below, blending the social and the political, the workplace and the neighborhood, in a spirit of radical, participatory, pluralistic democracy is a must if people are to believe that another world is possible.

Maurizio Landini: Truthfully, I don't know if capitalism is rapidly reaching its limits. Certainly it is becoming more difficult to outsource costs and to increase surplus value. The inherent instability of finance capitalism and the huge shadow financial system pose quite unusual challenges. The underlying problem is that the government, essentially working on a national basis, is no longer able to control and guide the behavior of giant corporations. These are pervasive and greedy creatures. Is this a potentially revolutionary period? I honestly don't know. Modern history, however, shows that when situations became untenable and social anger bursts, it often triggers dangerous – anti-democratic and authoritarian – adventures. Therefore, I think the next 10 years' biggest challenge for the unions is to solve the problem of inequality.

Whole generations in the western world are at risk of being worse off than their parents. What should be done? I think the unions must focus specifically on their members and must not allow the elite political parties to affect their priorities. I do not believe in self-sufficiency of unions but I firmly believe in their autonomy and independence. The union represents workers – employed and unemployed – and it has to remain closely linked to them. The union has to focus on working-class problems, without shyness or hesitation. It has to become more radical, in opposition to the radical nature of dominant neoliberal ideology. I embrace this task, and I will work for a union which has the strength and determination to build the future, through full restoration of its bargaining authority and its representativeness. The future is on our shoulders and is our responsibility.

Wol-San Liem: From a practical perspective, the labor movement needs to recognize that we have increasingly lost our political and social power vis-à-vis capital and right-wing political forces over the last several decades.

First, union membership is dropping across the globe. Low density means weakened bargaining power, and less political and social influence. If we do not figure out how to organize unorganized workers – many of them precarious, migrant and/or women – we will not have a labor movement to speak of in the next 10 or 20 years. Organizing new demographics of workers who are employed in strategically important sectors of the global economy is one of our most urgent tasks.

Second, we have not developed effective strategies for challenging transnational corporations, which can easily shift production sites to or find suppliers in other countries, while we remain organized on a primarily single-country, single-company/workplace basis. The development of strategies for communicating, bargaining, and acting collectively on cross-sectoral, industrial, regional, and global levels is essential to changing the power imbalance.

Finally, we need to (re)start thinking about, discussing, debating, and developing workers – the working class – as a political force. I personally do not think this necessarily means the creation of workers' political parties (although it probably will in some contexts). For me, the development of workers' political power means that unions and/or workers' organizations are making conscious efforts towards leading social and political change, beginning to contemplate what an alternative society and political economy would look like, and, in the long-run, building a movement to achieve that vision. In the end, unless we can move in this direction our efforts to build power through organizing or strengthening international solidarity can only be partially successful.

H. Mahadevan: The challenge for class-based and democratic trade unionism is to build bridges among the different class-based unions that fight against the capitalist system and to overcome historic divisions and misunderstandings among unions that have a common vision, with the aim of giving the most coordinated responses possible. It is necessary to create a stable coordination among the trade unions that have a radical critique of the capitalist order and the current neoliberal model.

Trade unions should work towards *financial independence and autonomy from administrations and public institutions.* Trade unions must be financed fundamentally by their members, so that they can put forward their own demands and not be controlled by the blackmail of public institutions.

The WFTU, in the Asia-Pacific Trade Union Conference held in Port Dickson (Malaysia) during October 2013, decided to campaign for a Common Charter of Demands including: full employment for all, aiming towards eradication of poverty, with need-based salary and wages and with full security including statutory pension for all; to stop sub-contracting, outsourcing, and off-loading; to stop environmental degradation in the name of development and to protect natural resources for the benefit of humanity; to protect sovereign rights of nations as against imperialistic hegemony and market-driven policies under WTO, World Bank, and IMF dictates; to ensure women's empowerment through progressive policies and to extend maternity benefits to all working women; to provide equal wage for equal work without gender bias; to ensure working rights and social security for all migrant workers, as per the UN charter; to abolish 'bonded labor' and guarantee alternate employment; and to ensure protection of migrant workers by governments.

Irvin Jim: I think neoliberalism has given rise to a form of capitalism that has become globally dominant. In our fight against this hegemonic form of global capitalism, we must pressure different nation-states with the notion that manufacturing matters. We must fight for job creation. What is the point of telling young people to go to school and learn when, after graduation, they cannot work in their specialization and have to work in precarious jobs? We must build a society that produces, that defends the existing manufacturing capabilities, and that marches toward industrialization not for the purpose of capital accumulation and greed, as is the case in capitalism, but to achieve equal distribution and meet human needs, as is the core socialist aspiration.

MST: The current situation is very different from what revolutionaries faced at the beginning and middle of the last century. The neoliberal phase of capitalism poses great challenges for revolutionaries today, mainly related to complex changes in the technical conditions of production, international schemes of domination, changes in information flows and circulation systems, social differentiation within the proletariat itself, massive numbers of ghettos in the suburbs, etc. Therefore, among many other challenges, we emphasize the understanding and stimulation of new types of action and new mechanisms of mass participation that are being incubated either in the simple struggle for survival, or in the course of building political movements.

Creating the new form of power, namely *People's Power*, means creating new social and political relations. They cannot be extracted from the current state of affairs; rather they must emerge from an on-the-ground process. If Marx is right to say that we are as we do, what we do today must be a revolutionary action. If we want freedom, our actions have to be libertarian.

A significant part of the left worldwide presupposes that the state, under the control of a party, will be the main agent, the "engineer," of change toward social justice. As a result, the prevailing view is that these changes will be made in a top-down fashion. According to this logic, the role of labor movements and the mass of voters is to put the "engineers" in the right place for using the instruments of the state, making the people mere passive receivers of social benefits or the source of electoral support rather than the active source of power.

When popular participation is reduced to mere electoral support, what the leftist administrations can achieve is often negligible and it sometimes results in setbacks when the left loses elections to the right-wing parties. Although we do not oppose taking part in elections in principle, the view that one can obtain structural change through the election of an individual, without a solid popular support, is a mistake.

We cannot stress enough that every organizational structure is, or should be, an instrument in the service of change whose protagonists cannot be replaced in this process, that is, the organization has to be in the service of the strategic project.

Our central challenge will be to relocate the socialist struggle as a human need and not just as a utopia or as a mystical cultural value. The radical essence of our struggle will reflect the depth of our human need, but the society we want to build must reflect the unlimited scope of our dreams.

The German War on American Workers: Deutsche Telekom in the United States*

Tony Daley

For the last 25 years, income and wealth in the US have shifted to the wealthiest Americans. Workers' wages have stagnated while productivity (output per hour of work) has increased by 25 percent. In real terms, median weekly earnings between January 2004 and third quarter 2013 were *down* 1 percent.[1] This divergent trend between real wages and productivity means that working people are not reaping the gains of economic growth in the US.

The national minimum wage is worth 23 percent less in real terms than what it was in 1968.[2] The official poverty rate has grown to 15 percent of all Americans, with 46.5 million people living in poverty.[3] Meanwhile, the top executives of large US companies enjoy bountiful pay packages. The Economic Policy Institute found that the annual compensation of top CEOs has risen 835 percent since 1978 while private sector pay has risen 5 percent.[4]

* An earlier version of this article appeared in *International Union Rights*, Vol. 20, Issue 4 (2013). The author, a Research Economist at the Communications Workers of America, is grateful to the editors of IUR for permission to publish this expanded and updated version. Much of the information presented here is based on the author's direct experience of fifteen years as a union staff-member. The views expressed here are those of the author and do not necessarily reflect those of CWA.

1. US Bureau of Labor Statistics, November 1, 2013. Available at: http://www.bls.gov/news.release/pdf/wkyeng.pdf. See also Lawrence Mishel and Heidi Shierholz, "A Decade of Flat Wages: The Key Barrier to Shared Prosperity and a Rising Middle Class," Economic Policy Institute, August 21, 2013.
2. Sylvia A. Allegretto and Steven C. Pitts, "To Work With Dignity: The Unfinished March Toward a Decent Minimum Wage," Economic Policy Institute, August 26, 2013
3. US Bureau of the Census, "Income, Poverty, and Health Insurance Coverage in the United States: 2012," Washington, DC, September 2013. Available at: http://www.census.gov/prod/2013pubs/p60-245.pdf
4. Lawrence Mishel, "The CEO-to-Worker Compensation Ratio in 2012 of 273 Was Far Above That of the Late 1990s and 14 Times the Ratio of 20.1 in 1965," Economic Policy Institute, Economic Snapshot, September 24, 2013.

Economists point to many different reasons behind the growing inequality in the US. In general, government has permitted market forces to reward a small minority at the expense of the overwhelming majority of wage earners. Public policy has shifted income and wealth to the top percentiles through regressive tax policies that have lowered taxes on the wealthy and reduced transfer payments to the poor.[5]

The assault on labor unions drives this inequality. The pervasive use of union avoidance consultants has discouraged workers from exercising their rights. The percentage of workers covered by a collective bargaining agreement has shrunk to under 7 percent in the private sector.[6] The labor movement's political force is incapable of moderating the zealotry of the Right.

The National Labor Relations Act of 1935, subsequently amended, is the foundation for American labor law. Its preamble states that it is henceforth public policy to encourage "the practice and procedure of collective bargaining by protecting the exercise by workers of full freedom of association." Unfortunately, political leaders have presided over the weakening of the NLRA. Employers have learned to game the rules, and the lack of political action to balance the playing field has gutted the legislation of its effectiveness. When employers threaten to close a facility during organizing drives (which they do over half the time) or fire worker activists (which they do one-third of the time), the right of workers to organize a union is an empty right.[7] Sanctions hardly dissuade law-breakers: employers routinely file for delays in the face of complaints from the National Labor Relations Board (NLRB). If they are found in violation of the NLRA, employers are liable only for lost wages of a fired worker – minus any income earned after the dismissal. Most typically, employers settle complaints they are about to lose for a lesser penalty.

As foreign companies have invested in the US, they too have adopted the anti-union practices of US companies – in part because of the apparent cost advantages of low-road industrial relations afforded by weak labor law, and in part because of an unwillingness to contradict the behavior of US managers.[8]

---

5. Joseph E. Stiglitz, *The Price of Inequality: How Today's Divided Society Endangers Our Future*. New York: Norton, 2012, Chapter 4.
6. BLS, private sector coverage from the Bureau of the Census, Current Population Survey, 2012.
7. Kate Bronfenbrenner, "No Holds Barred: The Intensification of Employer Opposition to Organizing," Economic Policy Institute and American Rights at Work Education Fund, May 20, 2009. Available at: http://www.epi.org/publication/bp235/
8. Harold Wilensky, *American Political Economy in Global Perspective*. Cambridge and New York: Cambridge University Press, 2012.

Deutsche Telekom (DT) is that kind of company. Its track record of worker abuse shows the extent to which it conspires with other companies in undermining and disregarding US labor rights. DT's weak excuses that its subsidiary T-Mobile obeys the law are belied by a pattern of increasingly abusive behavior at the workplace and a recent broad indictment by the NLRB. Not surprisingly, the assault on worker rights has degraded work at T-Mobile. As DT's largest shareholder, the German government has a responsibility to hold the company accountable for its violations of international labor rights.

The choices under US labor law

US labor law is premised upon exclusive representation; a work unit can have only one employee representative. The law requires, however, that a majority of workers must choose a labor union and they must do so independently of influence from the employer. The law offers wide latitude in determining such a majority: the employer may accept individual statements of support from a majority of the workers, or the NLRB may supervise an election. Under current law, the first is voluntary for the employer while the second is mandatory. Meanwhile, the company must not campaign for a union.

The company, though, may campaign *against* the union. This gives management an inherent advantage since US unions have no guaranteed access to work premises. Instead, union representatives must meet with workers off-site and outside work hours. Inside the facility, workers may marshal arguments for collective representation, but only during non-work time. In contrast, the employer is free to use work time to argue that employees should reject a union at the workplace.[9]

US companies display a range of behaviors along issues of freedom of association. AT&T, the largest telecom company in the US, accepts union authorization cards as a measure of support and it uses a third party (American Arbitration Association) to verify totals. When workers start signing up for representation, the company remains neutral and even trains lower level managers to abstain from comment. As a result, the Communications Workers of America (CWA) represents 132,000 workers at AT&T of which 44,000 work for AT&T Mobility, the wireless provider.

---

9. See Lance Compa, *Free Speech and Freedom of Association: Finding the Balance*, ITUC Position Paper, June 2013. Available at: http://www.ituc-csi.org/IMG/pdf/free_speech_and_freedom_of_association_final.pdf

Within the same industry, T-Mobile US (TMUS) represents the other extreme. Controlled by the German telecom giant DT, TMUS takes the position that it can only recognize a majority of workers wanting a union if an election takes place.[10] It also argues that employees need the "facts" before they can make an informed choice in an election. It is unabashed in communicating the message that the company does not want employee representation, taking full advantage of the law's provisions in terms of employer speech. Employees are forced to listen to managers harangue the labor movement in general and CWA in particular. Meanwhile, managers can silence union supporters within the workplace. Elections are plagued with consistent employer badgering of employees to vote against "third parties."

When pressed on worker rights, DT claims that it respects the law of countries in which it operates. This is not entirely true, as the company has faced numerous complaints from the NLRB (see below). It argues that it cannot import German-style codetermination to foreign subsidiaries and that there is no single model of labor relations. DT further says it can only recognize a union representing a majority of workers in the US if there is an election. It must retain its "free speech" rights to communicate actively and repeatedly to workers that it opposes organizing and union recognition.[11]

Corporate speech – in contrast to either employee speech (which is severely restricted) or the speech of low-level managers (who must speak with one voice) – is the wedge used by DT to intervene lawfully in the decision of workers to choose an employee representative. DT has been in the forefront of the industry suggesting that companies even have an obligation, not just to exercise their speech rights, but to use those rights to oppose workers attempting to organize. In its response to the Human Rights Watch report on the behavior of multinational companies in the US (which included considerable material on DT), the International Organization of Employers wrote a paper asserting that a company has "an obligation not to stand by idly."[12] The

10. TMUS is a company controlled, according to New York Stock Exchange standards, by Deutsche Telekom which owns 67% of TMUS and appoints seven out of 11 directors.

11. Letter from Dietmar Frings, Deutsche Telekom Senior Vice President Employment Policies and Relations, to Rosa Pavanelli, General Secretary, Public Services International, February 8, 2013.

12. International Organization of Employers, A Response by the International Organisation of Employers to the Human Rights Watch Report – "A Strange Case: Violations of Workers' Freedom of Association in the United States by European

report benefited from the technical guidance of DT's US attorneys from the law firm of Littler Mendelson. DT has also circulated the report to stakeholders.

Deutsche Telekom in the US

DT entered the US market in 2001 by acquiring VoiceStream Communications. For years, the company (re-named T-Mobile USA in 2002) was a cash cow for German investors, returning a steady stream of dividends back to the home office. Under-investment in 3G technology by DT, however, allowed industry leaders AT&T and Verizon to widen their lead over T-Mobile. AT&T attempted to purchase the company in 2011 but US regulators scuttled the acquisition because of anti-trust concerns. The uncertainty around the deal, though, brought lower margins and customer turnover. The company lost branded contract customers for seven consecutive quarters until second quarter 2013.[13] In May 2013, DT combined its T-Mobile USA assets with the small wireless carrier MetroPCS to create TMUS, a public company listed on the New York Stock Exchange – of which DT now owns 67 percent of the shares.

The 2013 merger with MetroPCS promises to degrade the overall situation for workers at T-Mobile. MetroPCS served exclusively prepaid customers – those who do not buy long-term contracts. Prepaid customers – disproportionately low-income and seniors – tend to be more price conscious than other wireless customers, and therefore bring less revenue to the company. The company may now be positioned to compete favorably in the prepay niche, but that position will likely bring lower revenues per customer and put downward pressures on costs with workers being the largest cost item.

Nonetheless, T-Mobile has shaken up the wireless market by eliminating two-year plans, ending some early termination fees, and providing free international roaming. Consequently, a price war has broken out among the carriers at least for the short term. TMUS has increased customers in the last year by roughly 2.5 million and projections point upward for the short term. A number of analysts, however, suggest that grabbing customers comes at a high cost that may not be sustainable in the long run.[14]

Multinational Corporations," Geneva, Switzerland, May 2011. Available at: http://www.uschamber.com/sites/default/files/comments/IOE_HRW_Response.pdf

13. Engadget, April 4, 2013.
14. http://ipcarrier.blogspot.com/2014/04/can-sprint-and-t-mobile-us-survive.html

Union hostility at T-Mobile

When DT made the initial offer for VoiceStream in 2000, the CEO of DT, Ron Sommer, had a phone conversation with then-president of CWA Morton Bahr in which Sommer promised Bahr that if CWA supported the acquisition, DT would not interfere with workers' attempts to organize local unions. As a result, CWA argued in favor of the acquisition in meetings with Clinton White House officials, in testimony before Congress, through lobbying Members of Congress who were seeking to limit foreign ownership, and through support at the Federal Communications Commission. Both the Department of Justice and the FCC approved the merger, and it closed in spring 2001.

Immediately after the deal closed, technicians at VoiceStream in the state of Connecticut sought to organize a local union. VoiceStream management brought in attorneys known for their union-avoidance work and ran an anti-union campaign to dissuade workers from organizing. Among the tactics encouraged were threatening workers with loss of employment in the event of a strike, interrogating workers about the union, and issuing dire warnings of the consequences of voting for the union.[15] In the representation election, the workers chose not to be represented. The fact that DT now owned VoiceStream did not change management's anti-union practices.

In 2004, workers at T-Mobile USA (DT changed the name in 2002) discovered a 150-page training manual for managers that showed systematically how to push workers to reject organizing local unions. The author of the manual wrote, "Preserving the union free privilege is an honor."[16] Among the many reasons the manual gives for "resisting the union" are the extra costs of paying workers better wages and benefits, the suggestion that unions create an adversarial climate, and the possibility of a strike. While pointing out that in several states union membership is not mandatory, it also laments the fact that non-members do not get to vote on contracts (correct statement) and suggests the union would not defend non-members (incorrect statement: unions have a legal responsibility to enforce the contract for members and non-members).

Although T-Mobile management later claimed to stop using this particular manual – while developing other materials that conveyed the same message – the actions at worksites have been consistently

---

15. National Labor Relations Board Settlement Agreement, Case No. 34-CA-9800, December 3, 2001.
16. William R. Adams, *For Your Information*, 6th ed., Adams, Nash, Haskell & Sheridan (law firm), 1983, p. 8.

in opposition to workers freely choosing to exercise their rights of Freedom of Association. In particular, trainers show every new employee a slide show denigrating the union; one slide states: "we are better off communicating directly with each other, rather than through a third party, like the CWA."[17] The company also recommends: "your supervisor or HR is available for any questions you have about the union."[18] The company also ensures that managers toe the line: a 2005 job advertisement for human resource managers included the requirement of "maintaining a productive and union-free environment."

Executing the union avoidance policy has meant monitoring worker attempts to organize. In Allentown, Pennsylvania, security guards routinely videotaped license plates of workers who talked to union organizers outside workplace parking lots.[19] A 2008 memo from a manager of retail stores to subordinates in Oregon demanded that she be informed of all contact with unions.[20] In 2011, managers in Frisco, Texas, were seen using binoculars to spy on conversations between workers and union organizers.

Whenever workers attempt to form local unions, management holds "captive audience" meetings. Typically, these meetings cover various aspects of work, and then devote time to dissuade workers from joining the union. There are numerous instances when managers claim workers will be forced to pay dues considerably in excess of CWA dues. Other arguments include references to the union as a "third party" that will interfere with management–employee relationships. Union activists are frequently referred to as "union bosses."

During a representation election in Connecticut in July 2011 (the same unit that sought election in 2001), T-Mobile USA flew top executives from corporate headquarters in Bellevue, Washington, to meet one-on-one with workers to encourage them to vote against the union. A strong majority when the election was requested evaporated to a slim one-vote majority, and the unit was barely certified. Later that summer, technicians in upstate New York withdrew an election petition because management had chiseled strong support into a minority. In December 2011, top executives again met one-on-one with

17. "New Employee Orientation," 2012, slide 13.
18. "New Employee Orientation," 2012, slide 14.
19. National Labor Relations Board Settlement Agreement, Case 4-CA-34590.
20. The NLRB forced the company to post a notice that it would not require employees to report union contacts. National Labor Relations Board Settlement Agreement, Case 36-CA-10359.

technicians on Long Island to encourage them to vote against the union, and pro-union workers lost the election.

In both the upstate New York and Long Island cases, various levels of management descended on the unit for mandatory meetings with workers in which management disparaged the union, labeled it a "third party," and made inaccurate claims about the cost of union dues. Managers claimed that the union was spreading many false-hoods, and workers were encouraged to go to the company for the "facts." Management claimed that once the union became the official bargaining agent, the slate would be wiped clean, collective bargaining would start from scratch, and, while workers might gain benefits, they might also very well lose them. Managers sent each worker a person-alized email communication that tallied prospective dues. In the Long Island case, a union activist was singled out for wanting to be a "union boss," and the regional manager stated he was not trustworthy.

The captive audience meetings were the most brutal for a small group of retail workers at a New York MetroPCS store who filed for an election in July 2013. Seven of the nine workers at the store were subjected to a total of 30 meetings in the basement, even after the workers signed a petition requesting the meetings cease because of the effect on morale. One worker stated he was forced to attend five meetings that lasted on average two hours over the course of two weeks. Local supervisors, regional managers, and even the Vice Presi-dent from Human Resources flew in from the west coast headquarters to denigrate the labor movement, make insinuations about CWA, and dissuade workers from voting for the union. Even CEO John Legere showed up at the store during this effort. Nevertheless, on September 25, the workers voted 7–1 for representation.

A worsening climate

TMUS has begun using selective terminations to cut down organiz-ing drives. A top performer at the Wichita call center was disciplined and eventually fired for wearing a union T-shirt and for publicly sup-porting the union. Two union supporters were fired in Albuquerque for their pro-union stances. Other union leaders at both the Wichita and Albuquerque call centers have been formally disciplined for their union work. The message is clear to worker-organizers: if you build a union, you could lose your job.

The NLRB has taken notice. In late March 2014, it consolidated several of its complaints against T-Mobile – the labor law equivalent of an indictment – into one national complaint. It charged TMUS US with the three illegal terminations and with the disciplining of two other workers in Wichita, Kansas and Albuquerque, New Mexico as well as having harassed and intimidated workers in retaliation for their union activity. The NLRB also accused TMUS of subjecting workers to overly broad rules – in the code of conduct and employee handbook and elsewhere – thereby preventing them from discussing the terms and conditions of employment.[21]

The indictment represents a government response to repeat offenses and also to the escalation of anti-union hostility by TMUS. The NLRB previously issued numerous worksite-specific complaints that TMUS interfered with legally protected activity. Complaints typically resulted in "settlements" by which the company promised not to engage in similar behavior. Instead of keeping these promises, however, TMUS committed the same offenses at other workplaces. The company then intensified its overall campaign leading to the firing and suspension of visible union supporters.

The NLRB determined that TMUS is engaging in a centrally directed campaign to prevent employees from obtaining union representation. Evidence from the first day of the Wichita trial in February 2014 showed that managers reported any union activity to corporate headquarters in Bellevue, Washington, which coordinates company response.[22] The corporate response includes counter points to union literature as well as supplemental management training. The sheer number of these "Third Party Activity" reports suggests a company-wide strategy to asphyxiate any sort of collective action.

The degradation of work

Scant union representation at T-Mobile – only two bargaining units totaling 25 workers in a company with 40,000 employees – enables first-line managers to act as they see fit to increase productivity. CWA's conversations with T-Mobile workers around the country detail worker abuse, humiliation, and extraordinary job-induced

21. National Labor Relations Board, Region 14, "Order Further Consolidating Cases, Second Consolidated Complaint and Notice of Hearing [Cases 28-CA-I067S8, 28-CA-117479, 14-CA-106906, 2-CA-115949], March 31, 2014. For brief media coverage, see Jeff Sistrunk, "NLRB Consolidates Anti-Union Cases against T-Mobile," *Law 360*, April 9, 2014.
22. "Third Party Activity Report," August 24, 2012, introduced into evidence. NLRB and CWA v. T-Mobile USA (Case Nos. 14-CA-104731, 14-CA-105502, 14-CA-106124, and 14-CA-106906), February 4, 2014.

stress. What we have found at T-Mobile is not unique, but is nonetheless shocking.

Call center coaches blast loud music to "motivate" workers. Managers shake workers' chairs and tell them to work faster. In the face of this antagonism, the customer service representative is expected to maintain a pleasant and courteous tone with the often-irate customers who call.

Some managers use humiliation to spur productivity. A call center worker in Chattanooga, Tennessee, was forced to wear a dunce cap because she did not meet her performance standard. The hat was then passed around to others in her pod when their metrics dropped. In Albuquerque, a group manager at the call center required coaches to wear a backpack shaped like a monkey if their team scores declined. Workers were then encourage to "get the monkey [of low scores] off the back" of the team.

Meanwhile, the performance standards that workers must meet are changed on a regular basis. At times workers are forced to sell a certain value of extra services (even as they attempt to troubleshoot customers' technical or service issues). At other times it has been the rate at which customer problems are resolved with one call only. Or it might be the length of the call handling time.

In general, call center workers are expected to be on the phone with customers 96 percent of the time while spending a short amount of time (380 seconds for General Care) with each customer. This means pregnant workers must clock out – effectively lowering their income – before using the bathroom to avoid lowering their metrics.[23] Such metrics affect one's overall standing at the workplace which determines the bidding queue for semi-annual shift bids. Lower standing means unfavorable schedules, presenting real problems for parents of small children or those who care for the elderly. CWA has documented numerous instances of workers quitting because of bad schedules.

It is not surprising that call center workers, in particular, suffer a high level of job-induced stress. "From a scale from one through 10," recounted a call center worker from the now-closed Brownsville facility, the stress level "was an 11."[24] At another call center, a former worker lamented, "I would leave work and take that frustration and anger home with me."[25] At a third shuttered call center, an ex-employee reported:

23. http://www.momsrising.org/blog/why-i-believe-in-paid-sick-leave-2/
24. Interview with Xavier Solis, former employee, T-Mobile, Brownsville, Texas, November, 2012.
25. Interview with an anonymous former employee, Fort Lauderdale, Florida, November 2012.

There were times where it got pretty stressful. I actually had to seek treatment for high blood pressure, stress-related tension in the muscles. I had to see a therapist for that – just for massages. I had to take high blood pressure medicine. And so it was pretty stressful.[26]

A former worker from the Wichita call center reported:

I don't know how many times you go into the bathroom and somebody is puking. And it's because they're stressed. They can't get their numbers.[27]

Several T-Mobile employees have reported that the stress had serious medical implications. A woman who worked in the call center in Lenexa, Kansas (since closed), reported:

I remember leaving [training] and I thought I was having a heart attack. I came home and told my husband I need to go: 'You need to take me to the emergency room. I think I'm having a heart attack.' Blood pressure was sky-high and it was just the stress from making the numbers and having a coach who stood over you.[28]

One worker from yet another closed facility in Frisco, Texas, bluntly summed up the feelings of many T-Mobile workers: "I was working in a mill, in a slave mill."

The global response

The DT labor practices in the US have not gone unnoticed around the world. The International Trade Union Confederation (ITUC) has pushed DT to alter its union hostility in its "We Expect Better" campaign. ITUC General Secretary Sharan Burrow highlighted a distinguished panel of local, national, and international leaders who listened to worker stories in South Carolina in February 2013.[29] Secretary Burrow pushes organizing rights in general and TMUS organizing rights in particular in every possible venue.

UNI Global Union has been in the forefront of an effort to encourage DT to sign a global framework agreement that would include organizing rights in the US. UNI almost succeeded in reaching an agreement in 2006 but when DT changed leadership (both CEO and Global HR Director), the company changed tack, resisting an

---

26. Interview with Jerry Smith, former employee, Frisco, Texas, November 2012.
27. Interview with Pam Smith, former employee, Wichita, Kansas, July 15, 2012.
28. Interview with Katherine Ramzy, former employee, Lenexa, Kansas, November, 2012.
29. See CWA, TU, ver.di, "Standing up for Good Jobs in Charleston: T-Mobile Workers Speak Out," May 2013.

agreement that would rein in its US managers. UNI has met with DT executives over the years to reach a resolution. It has also encouraged affiliates within DT to push organizing rights. UNI General Secretary Philip Jennings has met with union activists in the US and verified the cards of a majority – that eventually evaporated into a minority – of workers before the Long Island election.

The core of the global response has involved ver.di, the large German services union, which represents over 100,000 DT workers in Germany. Since 2001, ver.di and its predecessor unions have supported efforts to bring labor-management practices in the US into conformity with both its practice in Germany and the company's policies as expressed in its "Social Charter." Likewise, it worked with CWA and UNI to achieve a global framework agreement.

In 2008, CWA and ver.di formed TU, a joint organization to represent T-Mobile USA workers. Within TU, CWA organizes workers and meets with community and political leaders in the US while ver.di pushes the German management of DT and meets with German political leaders. Both CWA and ver.di participate in bargaining. Over 1,000 workers have signed TU membership cards.

To facilitate a close working relationship between CWA and ver.di, the two unions coordinate actions, meet on a regular basis, and provide materials in both languages. CWA has hired bilingual staff. Ver.di has arranged for TU activists to speak at DT shareholder meetings. In May 2013, TU activists testified before the Bundestag about working conditions and met with both national and local political leaders. CWA President Larry Cohen addressed the ver.di congress in 2011 and spoke to strikers at DT in 2012. CWA activists provided solidarity messages during the ver.di strikes.

CWA and ver.di have sought to educate every single DT employee in Germany about working conditions and union hostility in the US. They have developed worksite-to-worksite partnerships that involve regular contact through phone calls, e-mail communications, and site visits. DT worksite leaders, typically works councilors, use vacation time to visit the US, talk with T-Mobile workers, participate in organizing activities, and meet with community and political leaders.

Partners then return to Germany and recount those conversations in a variety of ways – ver.di national publications, worksite newsletters, and works council meetings. Works councilors and ver.di national leaders have addressed worker assemblies – mandatory all-employee meetings under German Codetermination – to present the T-Mobile story. Regular telephone calls and an active German social media presence keep concerned observers current.

Ver.di has also engaged in individual actions in Germany to publicize the plight of T-Mobile workers. DT is a sponsor of the Bayern München football club, and ver.di members have protested in front of the gates to games. In a DT meeting with small and medium sized companies in September 2013, ver.di members stood in silent protest. Later, Berlin activist Nadine Jüngling debated then-CEO René Obermann about the situation in the US, telling him, "I have been to South Carolina, I have met those workers, I know what I am talking about. You are out of touch."

Employees now own a different narrative when the company tries to explain away the US problem. DT recognizes that the US subsidiary is creating legitimacy issues in Germany. Tomas Lenk, head of the Berlin call center's works council, recounted the exchange at a worker assembly in Hannover in fall 2013. After hearing that TMUS workers frequently must clock out to use the bathroom, a worker complained that her first-line supervisor had given her only 10 minutes of bathroom time outside of statutory breaks. A manager popped up to say he personally would resolve the problem.

The partnership program helps organizing in Germany. Ver.di members recognize that the company's practices in the US could easily be re-imported to Germany.

German accountability

The German government has a direct responsibility for the continued assault on worker rights in the US. It owns 31.7 percent of DT, making it the largest single shareholder in the company. DT's behavior should be a matter of international concern for the German government: through its unwillingness to end the union hostility of DT and other German companies, the German government contributes to the growth of social inequality.

Furthermore, DT has flouted US law twice in the last two years. In 2012, T-Mobile announced the closure of seven call centers and the displacement of 3300 workers. Workers reported that much of the call volume was going to overseas vendors. CWA applied to the US Department of Labor (DoL) for enhanced benefits for those workers. Trade Adjustment Assistance provides two years of unemployment compensation, training vouchers, and subsidized health care coverage. CWA provided evidence from workers at the vendors in the Philippines and Central America proving that some of the work had been offshored. Throughout the process, even when directly questioned by the DoL, T-Mobile declared the work was not being sent overseas.[30] The company not only sought to deprive its former employees of their rightful benefits, it openly deceived the US government.

In 2013, the US State Department gave DT the opportunity to resolve its US labor conflict. CWA, ver.di, and UNI Global Union filed a complaint in July 2011 under the OECD Guidelines for Multinational Enterprises, alleging that T-Mobile had "engaged in a pattern of conduct designed to undermine and frustrate employees' efforts to choose union representation freely and to deny employees their rights to collective bargaining." The US National Contact Point (housed in the State Department) found that there was a basis for mediation between the company and the unions. DT withdrew from the process after having expressed doubts about the impartiality of the Federal Mediation and Conciliation Service (FMCS), a US government agency that has existed since the 1940s.

According to the UN Guiding Principles on Business and Human Rights adopted in 2011, businesses have a responsibility to respect human rights "over and above legal compliance with national laws and regulations." It is not enough for DT to excuse the behavior of TMUS by claiming (incorrectly, as we saw above) that it "obeys the law."

Rather, the company must have a due diligence process to report possible abuses, and must remedy the reported violations. DT does engage in Corporate Social Responsibility reporting. However, the only mention of US labor issues in recent CSR reports is a mention of a collective bargaining agreement with the Connecticut technicians, not the allegations of union-busting.[31] The absence of any reporting on Freedom of Association issues in the US suggests either a failure at due diligence or a lack of transparency. Companies have a responsibility to remedy problems they uncover. The withdrawal from the OECD process suggests that the company is not interested in remediation.

Under the UN Guiding Principles, governments have a duty to respect human rights beyond their territorial borders, especially if they are key stakeholders in a company. Unlike Corporate Social Responsibility guidelines, the UN Guiding Principles are not voluntary: governments have a mandate to respect and enforce the rule of human rights law.

---

30. A Freedom of Information Act Request to the DoL showed that the company answered that the work had not been sent offshore.
31. http://www.cr-report.telekom.com/site13/employees/hr-responsibility#atn-1383-4350,atn-1383-4348

THE INTERNATIONAL AFTER 150 YEARS

The German government has the responsibility under the UN Guiding Principles to "investigate, punish and redress private actors' abuse." In late 2012, members of the Bundestag called on the government to account for the behavior of T-Mobile in the US. In its March 2013 response, the government tepidly urged the companies in which it owned shares to participate in the UN Global Compact and the OECD Guidelines, both voluntary processes. It claimed that it did not enjoy any "direct right of intervention" in the affairs of German companies. DT's withdrawal from the OECD case made a mockery of German voluntarism.

DT's abuse of workers in the US and its disrespect for US and international law tarnish Germany's reputation as a country of strong social partnership. It is time for the Merkel government to shed its reluctance to intervene in the affairs of German companies and exercise its responsibilities under international law.

Implications

The German war on T-Mobile workers is only a slight exaggeration. Other European and Japanese transnational companies have also been known to sink to the lowest levels of US labor law. The Volkswagen case – in which the company was willing to install a works council at the Chattanooga assembly plant – was an exception. The German management team at DT, backed by the management members of the Supervisory Board, acquiesced to the anti-labor actions of T-Mobile management.

Such hostility to unions has contributed to the inequality of American society. The absence of significant union presence at T-Mobile has enabled the company to drive down wages so that a significant number of full-time employees qualify for government assistance.[32] The company responds that its wages and benefits are competitive with those of other wireless carriers. While starting wages are comparable, there is no salary progression to reward seniority and no negotiated pay increases, so worker pay stagnates. New workers frequently make more than workers with five years or more of seniority. The freeze on pay announced in 2013 would not have been possible with a collective bargaining agreement.

The war on workers within T-Mobile may not even be a cost-saver for the company. At least partly because of the brutality of

---

32. Read the profile of a Wichita call center worker and the comparison of her pay with that of her CEO: Available at: http://www.aflcio.org/Corporate-Watch/Paywatch-2014

management, T-Mobile experiences an employee turnover that exceeds 100 percent annually in some call centers.[33] Thus, on top of labor costs for those employees engaged in productive work, the company pays high training costs and employs workers with little experience.

Unfortunately, there is little indication that DT will back away from its blanket support for T-Mobile's anti-worker actions. Despite the innovation of the CWA/ver.di partnerships, DT has not ended the destructive anti-worker behavior of its controlled entity. Likewise, the bad press that DT has received because of the behavior of T-Mobile has not diminished its support for its subsidiary.[34]

The intransigence of DT has wider implications. The continuous assault by T-Mobile management on worker rights has not gone unnoticed by socially responsible investors. These are not gadfly activists. Most of the European pension funds take corporate social responsibility seriously and base investment decisions at least in part on CSR records. The firings, the disciplining, and the NLRB complaints undercut the credentials that DT has fought hard to build.

It may take increasingly aggressive worker actions to move either DT or T-Mobile to change anti-worker management. Whatever those actions, they will clash with the model of social dialogue built by German companies. Put another way, the union hostility practiced abroad by German transnationals has the potential to undermine the German model. Such worker actions may eventually affect the business model of T-Mobile. As we saw above, the company sees future growth in the prepaid segment and among price-sensitive consumers. Growing support for the workers among student and low-income communities alone has the potential to erode key markets for T-Mobile.[35]

DT intransigence may be driven by its desire to sell its US assets, calculating that a non-union asset would fetch a higher price. The company may not find an easy exit, however. The most likely purchaser is Sprint, and both the Department of Justice and the FCC have

---

33. CWA, "Standing up for Good Jobs in Charleston: T-Mobile Workers Speak Out," May 2013.

34. "Brutaler Psychoterror," *Der Spiegel*, November 22, 2012. Available at: http://www. spiegel.de/international/business/union-campaign-takes-on-t-mobile-usa-working-conditions-a-868525.html. See also the eight-minute exposé of DT on the Monitor program aired by the German TV Channel ARD in September 2011. Available at: http://www.youtube.com/watch?feature=player_embedded&v=pjp037P7dkE

35. For the student campaign at T-Mobile, see United Students Against Sweatshops, Justice for T-Mobile Workers: Available at: http://usas.org/campaigns/tmobile/. Ministers from African-American churches have spoken out forcefully about the treatment of T-Mobile workers in several call center communities, including Charleston, SC, and Nashville, TN.

given pretty clear indications that they will not allow Sprint to purchase T-Mobile. Therefore, the company will likely be in the US
market for the foreseeable future.

The struggle for worker rights at T-Mobile promises to be a long
one. What will break the current deadlock is uncertain. The struggles
at T-Mobile, like the struggles at other non-union companies, are
part of a larger fight over democracy. T-Mobile workers will need to
work with other progressive forces not just on their own campaign
but on a wider campaign to take on corporate power and restore our
democracy.

Barriers and Openings to a New Socialist Internationalism: South African Histories, Strategies and Narratives

*Patrick Bond**

Introduction: pre-1994 South African internationalism

The 1864 meeting of the International Workingmen's Association (IWA) brought the universality of proletarian ideas and representatives into focus. At St Martin's Hall in London, delegates converged from France, Italy, Ireland, Poland and Germany. From a South African vantage point in 2014, there have been extraordinary moments, like that one, to look back upon, in the interests of inspiring a renewed bottom-up popular-internationalist optimism for these global times. After a brief review of parallel historical moments, this article's second section considers some of the terrain upon which renewed, radical transnational civil society has recently emerged: anti-racism and reparations for apartheid profiteering; political solidarity (Zimbabwe, Swaziland, Palestine and Burma); "global governance"; environmental management; and economic policy. The single most explicit barrier, as discussed in the third section, is persistent working-class xenophobia, with its distinctive roots in divide-and-conquer capitalism. The article concludes by reflecting on new opportunities for socialist internationalism that flow logically from the historic roots and contemporary fruits of cross-border struggle, especially now that AIDS treatment advocacy and grassroots water decommodification strategies have taken society in positive directions, and a genuine socialist impulse is rising from metalworkers and allied "United Front" community and environmental activists.

To foreground those opportunities, consider two of the central problems acknowledged even in mainstream society as the most vital issues of our time: climate change and economic volatility. Respectively,

*This paper was presented to the Gyeongsang National University Institute for Social Scivpence, supported by a grant from the National Research Foundation of Korea.

54 and 52 percent of those people the Pew Research Center surveyed in 2013 list these as the two most pressing threats, ahead of the favored threats of world elites (Islamic extremism, Iranian and North Korean nuclear capabilities, etc).[1] For socialist internationalists, this is a confirmation that campaigns bubbling in the world social movements these past few years are now well situated to shift from a war of position to a war of movement. The question asked in this article, is whether in this new context, leftist cadres are ready to mobilize far more effectively than they have to date in their local and national settings, and to quickly upgrade their tentative internationalism to conjoin the economy and climate in a way that forces open a simple question: will capitalism fatally soil our world nest, or can a socialist movement arise with the required balance to address the system at all scales, avoiding localistic and nationalist cul-de-sacs? While we cannot answer that at this stage, the concluding section considers the power relationships and strategic options unveiled when South Africans successfully seek solidarity, e.g. in cases of AIDS treatment and water decommodification.

At present, we may be forgiven for retaining optimism of both will and intellect. South Africa is a site with impressive particularities, extremely high levels of social protest, and an exceptionally bright future for the left. It is a society blessed by what was perhaps the world's most vibrant anti-corporate internationalism, during the anti-apartheid sanctions campaign. So although atypical, it is interesting to consider aspects of socialist internationalism that are becoming more visible, especially in terms of economic and environmental justice. If socialist internationalism cannot thrive in South Africa, and if tendencies to xenophobia cannot be squelched in the process, then it is hard to imagine success in any other site.

First, however, we might recognise a few seminal moments of transnational unity (even of the lowest common denominator) of the sort characterized by the First International at that London IWA meeting. Such flashbacks would perhaps begin with an event a further 60 years back, the 1804 Haitian revolution, and then interrogate early nineteenth century anti-slavery campaigning (although bearing in mind the 2007 debunking of Charles Wilberforce on the bicentenary of his prohibition law). From the early twentieth century onwards, tremendous efforts were made to forge racial solidarity across vast

---

1. Pew Research, "Climate Change and Financial Instability Seen as Top Global Threats," Washington, 13 June 2013. Available at: http://www.pewglobal.org/2013/06/24/climate-change-and-financial-instability-seen-as-top-global-threats/

geographic distances, such as the earliest recorded African liberation conference, organized in London by Trinidadian lawyer Henry Sylvester-Williams in 1900 (three years before he moved to Cape Town). Subsequent efforts to build African diasporic unity were made by Marcus Garvey, George Padmore and W.E.B. Du Bois, and also lesser-known stalwarts like Anna Julia Cooper and Anna Jones in New York, and Charlotte Manye Maxeke in South Africa.

A full history would also do more justice to influences of both imported and exported strategies and narratives. These include, first, Mahatma Gandhi's *Satyagraha,* initially practiced at scale in 1913 in what is now KwaZulu-Natal Province (at Newcastle) midway between his 1894–1914 homes in Durban and Johannesburg. Gandhi was soon deported and took the approach back to India, with extraordinary results three decades later. Second, there was the simultaneous rise of the African National Congress (ANC) thanks in part to John Dube's elite education gained at an Ohio liberal arts college, Oberlin. Dube lived just a mile from Gandhi for many years and founded the ANC in 1912 (although Gandhi did not understand the merits of alliance with Africans at that stage). Fifty years later came the Black Consciousness philosophy developed by Steve Biko, which also emanated from Durban just at the time the city's port witnessed the revival of the country's modern labor movement.

In between, South African liberation activists were inspired by the (partially-successful) 1950s to 1970s decolonization movements across the continent, especially armed uprisings in Guinea-Bissau (led by Amilcar Cabral), Angola (Agustinho Neto) and Mozambique (Samora Machel) that were successful against Portugal in 1975 (after its own fascist government was replaced in a coup) and against the Rhodesian regime (led by Robert Mugabe and Joshua Nkomo) in 1980. The ANC and PanAfricanist Congress had initiated low-level guerrilla warfare aimed at minor economic infrastructure in 1960, though in retrospect, this mainly amounted to occasional symbolic "armed propaganda" attacks and they may have contributed less than they caused internal harm, e.g. a demobilization of the masses, a militarist culture, infiltration by apartheid spies, and within South Africa, more severe "anti-terrorist" clampdowns. Black South Africans and their allies also enthusiastically watched the US civil rights and Black Power movements emerge through that decade, and Martin Luther King repaid the solidarity with joint United Nations sanctions, campaigning alongside ANC leader and fellow Nobel Peace laureate Albert Luthuli in 1966. Ongoing awareness about neo-colonialism resulted from the liberation movements' era of exile (1962–90), with recent South African leaders like Thabo Mbeki continuing (to this day) to cite what Frantz Fanon considered the widespread "false decolonization" then underway in Africa, as he predicted so accurately in 1961 in his last work, *The Wretched of the Earth*.[2]

The figure of Nelson Mandela as a carrier and amplifier of these traditions is obvious; even after his death he remains the most potent reminder of the liberation struggle. Fierce debate continues today in South Africa about his role in the Communist Party during the early 1960s, as well as about the varied contributions to the SA struggle from African allies, the USSR and China. Most importantly, Cuban intervention against apartheid's army in the Battle of Cuito Cuanavale, Angola, in 1988 was a turning point in regional power relations, along with the West's victory in the Cold War. Together they justified white retreats on the military and political fronts. The prestige that the exiled ANC could claim amongst mass constituencies around the world (from Third World liberation movements to Scandinavian social democrats) set the stage for Mandela's return in 1990 to the "international community." However, with power relations at their most adverse during the early 1990s, Mandela gazed upwards at Western power *not* as the anti-imperialist fighter whom in 1962 the CIA helped imprison for 27 years by alerting the police to block a road near Durban, but instead as a reconciler able to make peace with both local racists and the world capitalist elite in preparation for his 1994–99 presidency. Tragically but truthfully, that reconciliation has been labelled, by his former comrade and later SA Intelligence Minister Ronnie Kasrils, the "Faustian Pact" in which Mandela conceded that international capital would play a formidable role in the country's 1990s transition from racial to class apartheid, including worsening the society's world-leading inequality, doubling unemployment, and deeply damaging local and regional ecologies.[3]

Given the short-term success of Mandela's false decolonization and the continuing electoral popularity of the ANC, the medium-term imperative of South Africa's working class is to struggle for local, regional and global justice *against* his political-economic legacy. That legacy includes his corruption-riddled party, given that it now appears impossible – to all but staunch SACP loyalists – to reform (as the interview in this volume with Irvin Jim demonstrates). In considering a "foreign policy bottom up" for the period ahead, the

---

2. Frantz Fanon, *The Wretched of the Earth* (New York: Grove Press, 2005).
3. Ronnie Kasrils, *Armed and Dangerous* (Johannesburg: Jacana Media, 4th Edn Foreword, 2013).

vagaries of past South African internationalisms do play a role, even if marginal. Lessons do need to be learned by anyone with a class-conscious project who would attempt to link national liberation to anti-imperial sentiments, as "Third Worldist" analysts are wont to do, often at the risk of excessive romanticism. Indeed there is even a current of thinking on the left that suggests that the new BRICS bloc – led by a neoliberalized Brazilian president once dedicated to building a genuine labor party, aggressive Russian nationalists, the Indian Hindu-centric elite, the raw-capitalist Chinese Communist Party and the Moscow-trained leaders of South Africa – can become *anti*-imperialist,[4] notwithstanding overwhelming evidence that it is in fact *sub*-imperialist.[5]

To understand the dynamics of these emerging-power circuitries may require us to recover IWA argumentation prioritizing class unity across borders. But conditions in South Africa also immediately require that the IWA be augmented by the insights Rosa Luxemburg provided in her 1913 book *The Accumulation of Capital*. Much of her empirical material was secondary literature about the world's periphery, including the Belgian Congo (now Democratic Republic of the Congo), the German colony of Namibia, and South Africa. Drawing on this background information, Luxemburg's theory of imperialism put at its center the tension between capitalism and non-capitalist social relations, from which a more sophisticated socialist internationalism must subsequently proceed:

> Accumulation of capital periodically bursts out in crises and spurs capital on to a continual extension of the market. Capital cannot accumulate without the aid of non-capitalist relations, nor ... can it tolerate their continued existence side by side with itself. Only the continuous and progressive disintegration of non-capitalist relations makes accumulation of capital possible. ... Historically, the accumulation of capital is a kind of metabolism between capitalist economy and those pre-capitalist methods of production without which it cannot go on and which, in this light, it corrodes and assimilates. Non-capitalist relations provide a fertile soil for capitalism; more strictly: capital feeds on the ruins of such relations...[6]

---

4. Rhadika Desai, "The Brics are building a challenge to western economic supremacy, *The Guardian*, 2 April 2013; Pepe Esposito, "Brazil, Russia, India, China and South Africa: BRICS go over the Wall," *Asia Times*, 27 March 2013; Glen Ford, "Throwing BRICS at the US Empire," *Black Agenda Report*, 28 March 2013

5. See, Patrick Bond, "Sub-imperialism as Lubricant of Neoliberalism: South African 'deputy sheriff' duty within Brics," *Third World Quarterly*, 34 (2), 2013, 251–270.

6. Rosa Luxemburg, *The Accumulation of Capital* (New York: Monthly Review Press, 1968), Chapter 29.

That same dilemma confronts anyone working on the internationalist class struggle front today: under conditions of capitalist crisis – one response to which is a "continual extension" of globalization – how can the parasitical relationship of capitalism to the non-capitalist spheres be brought into socialist framing with the requisite respect needed for alliance-formation that will be capable of pushing society beyond capitalism?

Again, for historical precedent, South Africa is rich in examples, with early indicators of cross-border class-struggle relevance not limited to the communist, socialist and anarchist ideologies (including working-class institutions from British Fabian traditions) that were imported through white settler-colonial routes. In addition, a home-grown process of regional labor organizing among black workers known as the Industrial and Commercial Union (ICU) took root during the 1920s, after its launch in Cape Town. This location reflected the unprecedented strength of dockworkers whose 1919 strike shook South Africa, but the ICU soon gained members across Southern Africa. The union rose to 100,000 members in 1929 before fading when its charismatic leader, Clements Kadalie, was forced out through infighting. At that point, a Third Internationalist commitment to conjoining "communist" and nationalist struggles began, after South Africa's first (whites-only) communist party had notoriously endorsed racist job-protection formulations during a 1922 mineworkers strike. The relations between the Soviet Union and South African forces remained strong – though of dubious merit in terms of broader inter-nationalism – until ruined by perestroika in the late 1980s and the USSR's crash in 1991. Further left, starting in the late 1920s, Trotsky's brief correspondence with his South African allies in the late 1930s confirmed a small but persistent current of revolutionary socialist thinking and activism.

Most importantly though, from the late 1950s South Africa bene-fitted from an anti-racist internationalism that chose a formidable global campaigning approach with strong anti-capitalist content: boy-cotts, divestment and sanctions (BDS). The campaign targeted firms active in South Africa, with the argument that capitalists making super-profits from apartheid (especially thanks to the migrant labor system) were immoral, that the taxes they paid to Pretoria fuelled oppression, and that even though the firms' South African workers would be adversely affected by BDS, those workers and their organiz-ations mainly supported this non-violent strategy. When anti-apart-heid BDS peaked in mid-1985, by all accounts it contributed substantially to South Africa's economic crash. For it was not only the renewed militancy of poor and working-class people in South Africa during the 1980s that ended white political power, it was the weakening of a central pillar of the system's support: international economic legitimacy and the profitability of racism to multinational corporations. The strength to wedge a fatal split between these corporations (especially banks) and their local English-speaking capitalist allies in Johannesburg and Cape Town on the one hand, and the white government in Pretoria on the other, was a vital contribution of international solidarity.[7]

It is not surprising that BDS is being applied today to Israel and to fossil fuel corporations with repeated reference to South African victories. This history stands contemporary activists in strong stead, as Irvin Jim's interview in this volume makes clear:

> We need to be able to challenge the multinationals and their agenda with militancy and uncompromising persistence. ... It is not possible to challenge this global nature of capitalism without creating a global network of solidarity between trade unions in addition to raising the level of consciousness of workers.[8]

But the dire state of the main global labor networks – i.e. the sad choice between a corporatist International Trade Union Confederation and a semi-fossilized World Federation of Trade Unions – requires the largest and most militant South African union, Jim's National Union of Metalworkers of SA (Numsa) and their new United Front allies, to now consider an internationalism that unites *through and beyond* class solidarity. Numsa will come under even more intense attack from the ANC, SACP and Cosatu [Congress of SA Trade Unions] in 2014–15 as their leaders scope out a potential political party for poor and working people. In this context, a full-fledged emancipation for South Africa will traverse not only local sites of oppression, but also various terrains already mapped out by transnational radical civil society networks, in which South Africans have regularly played a lead role. It will also entail a stronger resistance to xenophobia, patriarchy and nascent ethnicist ills that weaken the South African working class. Finally, it will tackle the two biggest issues – the melting

---

7. Connie Fields, "Have you Heard from Johannesburg: The Bottom Line," film. Available at: http://www.clarityfilms.org/haveyouheardfromjohannesburg/episodes.php; Patrick Bond, *Elite Transition: From Apartheid to Neoliberalism in South Africa* (London: Pluto Press, 3rd edn, 2014); John Saul and Patrick Bond, *South Africa – The Present as History* (Oxford: James Currey, 2014).
8. Irvin Jim interview in *Socialism & Democracy*, "The Strength of Our Collective Voice: Views of Labor Leaders from around the World," this issue.

climate and melting world finance – with the requisite capacity to link issues in the most visionary eco-socialist way possible. The last two decades of nascent internationalism in South Africa, including solidarity on the AIDS medicines and water-justice fronts, guide us at least some of the way.

Contemporary internationalisms

There are at least a half-dozen moments of revealing international solidarity politics that erupted from a tense post-apartheid society. Various measures of this tension might be cited. For example, in September 2012, the World Economic Forum's *Global Competitiveness Report* rated the South African working class as the world's leader in adverse employee–employer relations (in a survey done even prior to the August 2012 Marikana massacre and subsequent wildcat strike wave). This was an impressive ratcheting up of class struggle over the prior year, when the SA workforce ranked only 7th out of the 144 countries surveyed. In September 2013 the SA workers again won the label of most militant proletariat in 148 countries surveyed by the World Economic Forum, far ahead of second-place Venezuela.[9] Communities were also world leaders when it came to the rate of protest, with police measuring 1882 "violent" protests in the year 2012–13. According to the minister of police in September 2013, "Over the past four years, a total of 46,180 protests were attended to and all were successfully stabilized, with 14,843 arrests effected."[10] It is telling that he included as a "success" the August 2012 police intervention at the Marikana platinum mine owned by Lonmin, which included a well-documented premeditated massacre of 34 workers, the planting of weapons on dead victims, and torture of at least 44 survivors.[11]

Given the extreme degree of class struggle these data represent, the possibility of labor internationalism is enticing, especially considering

---

9. World Economic Forum, *Global Competitiveness Report 2013–14*, September 2013. Available at: http://www.weforum.org/reports/global-competitiveness-report-2013-2014

10. Nathi Mthethwa, "Remarks by the Minister of Police at the release of the SA Police Services 2012/2013 National Crime Statistics," Pretoria, September 2013. Available at: http://politicsweb.co.za/politicsweb/view/politicsweb/en/page71656?oid=405740&sn=Detail&pid=71656

11. Patrick Bond, "Marikana's meaning for crisis management: An instance of South Africa's Resource Curse," in Ulrike Schuerkens (Ed), *Global Management, Local Resistance* (London: Routledge, 2014). For a gender solidarity perspective on Marikana and other anti-extractivist struggles in the Southern African region, see the Women in Mining project website: http://www.womin.org.za

that millions of working-class people across the world participated in sanctions campaigns against South Africa during the 1960s to the 1990s. One reflection of that legacy was the choice of South Africa to host the 2001 United Nations World Conference Against Racism (WCAR). The official WCAR talk-shop itself was considered an historic defeat for those insisting on advancing social justice. Demands made by anti-racism activists – namely, reparations for slavery, colonialism, apartheid and neocolonialism, and a more profound censure of Zionist neo-apart-heid oppression of Palestinians – failed to move the UN meeting, or even gain the host's support. Neither South African President Mbeki nor UN Secretary General Kofi Annan deigned to meet the more than 10,000 demonstrators (led by internationalist poet Dennis Brutus and the first official Mandela biographer, Fatima Meer) who marched to within a few meters of the Durban International Convention Centre entrance on 31 August 2001. Los Angeles community leader Eric Mann remarked on the "leverage and impact of the march, but also the bitter-ness of the exchanges between its leaders and the South African govern-ment" in part because of "the Durban Social Forum coalition's critique of neoliberalism, in particular, the privatization of public services such as water, and its support for the demands of the landless movement."[12]

On subsequent days, the streets came alive with campaigns for reparations and Palestinian liberation, supported with great vigor by groups as diverse as Jubilee South affiliates, South Africa's large Muslim community and thousands of international anti-racism acti-vists. The NGO parallel summit also generated a progressive resol-ution, and when it was rejected by UN Human Rights Commissioner Mary Robinson, she was booed as she left the hall. All of this increased pressure on the official delegates who issued vaguely progressive sen-timents inside the WCAR, which in turn led to the US and Israeli gov-ernments storming out. But WCAR rejected the demand from NGOs and some African state leaders that payment be made by the North to compensate for centuries of colonial plunder, whose effects continue contributing to vastly imbalanced economies, societies and inter-national power relations. The EU's chief negotiator, Belgian foreign minister Louis Michel, justified his own country's history in the Demo-cratic Republic of the Congo at a press conference: "Colonialism could not be considered a crime against humanity, for at the time it was a sign of economical good health."[13] Mbeki and his foreign minister,

12. Eric Mann, *Dispatches from Durban* (Los Angeles: Frontline Books, 2002), 127.
13. Ben Cashdan, *Globalization and Africa: Whose Side are We On?* (video; Johannesburg, Seipone Productions, 2002).

Nkosazana Dlamini-Zuma, refused to support reparations activists, saying merely that more donor aid was needed.[14]

Frustrated by the failure of the WCAR to advance their agenda, leaders of Jubilee South Africa, the Khulumani apartheid-victims group and other faith-based activists turned to the US and Swiss courts. Civil cases for billions of dollars in damages were filed on behalf of apartheid victims against large multinational corporations which made profits from South African investments and loans.[15] The Bush regime and corporate lobbies pleaded with US courts to nullify an interpretation of the Alien Tort Claims Act that made apartheid-reparations suits possible.[16] In April 2003, in the wake of Archbishop Desmond Tutu's final Truth and Reconciliation Commission (TRC) report which recommended a reparations payment by businesses which benefited from apartheid, Mbeki announced that it was "completely unacceptable that matters that are central to the future of our country should be adjudicated in foreign courts which bear no responsibility for the well-being of our country." Further efforts by the Reparations Task Force and Cape Town's Anglican Archbishop Njongonkulu Ndungane prior to the lawsuits failed to generate even a civil discussion about the corporations' profiteering from the apartheid crime against humanity.[17] In July 2003, Mbeki and justice minister Penuell Maduna – later a lawyer for the same firms – went to even greater lengths to defend apartheid-era profits, arguing in a nine-page brief to a US court, that by "permitting the litigation," the New York judge would discourage "much–needed foreign investment and delay the achievement of the government's goals. Indeed, the litigation could have a destabilizing effect on the South African economy ..."[18] As a friend of the court on behalf of the claimants (alongside Tutu), Nobel laureate Joseph Stiglitz replied that the comments by Mbeki and Maduna had "no basis."[19]

---

14. *Business Day*, 7 September 2001.
15. Patrick Bond, *Talk Left, Walk Right* (Pietermaritzburg: University of KwaZulu-Natal Press, 2006).
16. *Business Day*, 17 June 2003.
17. *Financial Times*, 19 May 2003.
18. *Sunday Independent*, 25 July 2003. Replying to this logic a month later, prize-winning Indian author Arundhati Roy told BBC radio, "In what ought to have been an international scandal, this same government officially asked the judge in a US court case to rule against forcing companies to pay reparations for the role they played during apartheid. Its reasoning was that reparations – in other words justice – will discourage foreign investment. So South Africa's poorest must pay apartheid's debts so that those who amassed profit by exploiting black people can profit more?" (BBC, 24 August 2003.)
19. *Sunday Independent*, 9 August 2003.

Attacking the reparations movement appeared to be a critical priority for world elites, both because of the billions of dollars in apartheid profits under contestation and also because later, there arose a "climate debt" demand for reparations based on the Global North's excess consumption of greenhouse gases (in 2009, the US State Department's negotiator at the UN climate summit, Todd Stern, decisively rejected any "culpability or liability" for US climate debt to victims of extreme weather events, droughts, floods, rising sea levels and other damage). Recognizing the far-reaching implications of the Jubilee and Khulumani campaigns, in November 2002 Clinton-era US deputy treasury secretary Stuart Eizenstat, a supporter of reparations claims against pro-Nazi corporations, provided "talking points" to help capital fight the Alien Tort Claims Act. Eizenstat worried that if South African reparations activists "can galvanise public opinion and generate political support... they may achieve some success despite legal infirmities."[20] Working explicitly against the prospect of reparations activists winning public support, in August 2003, Africa's richest man, Nicky Oppenheimer, renamed the Rhodes Building in Cape Town alongside Mandela, when opening a new foundation, "Mandela Rhodes." Mandela used the occasion to attack the reparations lawsuits as "outside interference" and then remarked (without apparent irony), "I am sure that Cecil John Rhodes would have given his approval to this effort to make the South African economy of the early twenty-first century appropriate and fit for its time."[21] Quite.

A few weeks earlier the *New Left Review* had published an interview with Soweto community leader Trevor Ngwane, who did not mince words: "Without detracting from those twenty-seven years in jail – what that cost him, what he stood for – Mandela has been the real sell-out, the biggest betrayer of his people."[22] Ngwane referred

20. *New African*, July 2003.
21. *Sowetan*, 26 August 2003. In 2007, after an early court defeat that threw the case out, the plaintiffs' appeal in the US courts was victorious, leading Mbeki to again back US corporations, claiming the judges implied "that US courts are better placed to judge the pace and degree of South Africa's national reconciliation. I can't understand why any South African would want to be brought under such judicial imperialism." The answer was obvious: justice was not being done to apartheid's victims at home. Even though the Alien Tort Claims Act came under repeated attack by corporations and conservative judges, the case continued in mid-2014; see Michael Osborne, "Apartheid lawsuit passes another hurdle," *Business Day*, 5 May 2014.
22. Trevor Ngwane, "Sparks in the Township," *New Left Review*, July–August, 2003. Ngwane noted: "The ANC was granted formal, administrative power, while the wealth of the country was retained in the hands of the white capitalist elite,

not only to the deal with the International Monetary Fund in December 1993 that Kasrils also identified as seminal; there were at least a dozen other such instances, which included joining the World Trade Organization on disadvantageous terms, adopting World Bank policy advice to raise interest rates to record highs, repaying the foreign banks which financed apartheid, lifting the main exchange controls, cutting corporate taxes dramatically, privatising crucial state assets, adopting a home-grown structural adjustment policy, and in many other ways serving the interests of multinational corporations and local elites.[23]

On the other hand, the lasting memory of Mandela struggling for – and never compromising on – the 'one person, one vote' minimalist democratic demand will continue to inspire internationalist solidarity in coming decades. Civil society forces remained loyal in general, but on dozens of important policy debates took issue with Mandela's government. Nevertheless, in the wake of his disappointing 1994–99 presidency, there were two other major opportunities to generate progressive global-scale pressure through Mandela's prestige. One was in 2003, when Washington went to war in Iraq because, as Mandela put it, "All Bush wants is Iraqi oil." In February of that year, Mandela said, "Bush, who cannot think properly, is now wanting to plunge the world into a holocaust. If there is a country which has committed unspeakable atrocities, it is the United States of America. ... They don't care for human beings."[24] One year later, however, Mandela retracted this statement. When the Iraq War began in March 2003, South African activists protested strongly against both George W. Bush and the state's Denel Corporation, which was selling arms to the Bush/Blair regimes for use in Iraq. To be sure, one section of the anti-war movement, with ANC, Cosatu, SA Communist Party and some church membership, did not raise or support the critique of Denel, and that was one reason for a split anti-war movement, with the left mobilizing much larger numbers of protesters in various demonstrations in 2003.

The second opportunity related to AIDS treatment, which Mandela endorsed *after* it had become an extremely important wedge issue

Oppenheimer and company. Mandela's role was decisive in stabilizing the new dispensation; by all accounts, a daring gamble on the part of the bourgeoisie."

23. These agents had paid sufficient tributes to Mandela that his wife Winnie claimed he had a $10 million asset base accumulated from 1990–96. See *Jet*, "Nelson and Winnie Mandela divorce," 8 April 1996.

24. John Murphy, "Mandela slams Bush on Iraq," *CBS News*, 3 February 2003. Available at: http://www.cbsnews.com/2100-500257_162-538607.html

between at least five million HIV+South Africans and global capital ("Big Pharma") and its allies in the World Trade Organization and US government. Still, that belated endorsement was extremely important in hastening the delegitimization of Mbeki's AIDS-denialist stance. There are many explanations for his posture, which has been held responsible by Harvard Public Health School researchers for more than 330,000 unnecessary deaths. They include Mbeki's apparent fear of – or fibbery about – an alleged CIA plot on behalf of Big Pharma.[25] Regardless of motives, Mbeki's move postponed generalized access to AIDS medicines, which was the goal of Big Pharma since those in Africa needing treatment couldn't afford to pay the huge monopolity-prices for it. It was only the combination of internal and external pressure against extraordinary odds that overwhelmed the AIDS activists' opponents.

Another example of vibrant internationalist sentiment is the rise of global grassroots environmentalism. A year after the first big protest against the United Nations at the Durban WCAR, the UN World Summit on Sustainable Development ("Rio+10") was held in Johannesburg. It quickly became another site of struggle, mainly against "neoliberalized nature." On 31 August 2002, 30,000 demonstrators, including many thousands visiting from abroad, marched 12 kilometers from an impoverished township to the main convention center, decrying the UN's capitulation to corporations.[26] Environmental campaigning with global linkages had begun in South Africa during the 1990s, because the post-apartheid government's ecological stewardship proved even worse than apartheid's. In nearly every category of threats to ecology – natural and social – this abysmal record is well documented by the government's own statistics.[27] Some of the internationalist networks that emerged to fight state and capital

---

25. According to the then editor of the *Mail & Guardian* newspaper in a report never rebutted, President Thabo Mbeki believes the CIA is part of a conspiracy to promote the view that HIV causes AIDS. Mbeki also thinks that the CIA is working covertly alongside the big US pharmaceutical manufacturers to undermine him because, by questioning the link between HIV and AIDS, he is thought to pose a risk to the profits of drug companies making anti-retroviral treatments. Mbeki fingered the CIA in his address to African National Congress MPs at a caucus meeting in Parliament. Howard Barrell, "Mbeki Fingers CIA in AIDS Conspiracy," *Mail&Guardian*, 6 October 2000. Available at: http://www.nelsonmandela.org/omalley/index.php/site/q/03lv03445/04lv04206/05lv04302/06lv04303/07lv04308.htm

26. Bond, *Talk Left Walk Right*, Chapter Seven.

27. See Patrick Bond, *Unsustainable South Africa* (London: Merlin Press, 2002) and *Politics of Climate Justice* (Pietermaritzburg: University of KwaZulu-Natal Press, 2012).

focused specifically upon hazardous chemicals (Thor mercury), occupational safety and health (especially asbestosis), nuclear energy, incineration, timber plantations and the petroleum industry. In Durban, by the mid-2000s, some of the strongest civil society linkages and solidarity relations were being forged by communities struggling with oil (South Durban Community Environmental Alliance and groundWork, e.g. with Nigerian and Ecuadoran anti-petroleum activists) and other toxins, and fighting carbon trading (Durban Group for Climate Justice). Two South Durban activists won the coveted Goldman Environmental Prize (Bobby Peek in 1998 and Desmond D'Sa in 2014), as did an anti-fracking campaigner (Jonathan Deal from Treasure the Karoo Action Group in 2013).

In one of the most impressive solidaristic cases of environmental and social justice, the group Abahlali baseMjondolo ("movement of shackdwellers," with many thousands of followers, mostly in Durban) won repeated international support – including demonstrations at South African diplomatic missions abroad – when their marches and protests were regularly banned or repressed, their shacks forcibly removed, or their activists murdered. Many of the grievances related to a degraded home environment where water, sanitation and electricity were lacking.[28]

After some minor victories, however, this activism faded, as did many of the major urban social movements from the early 2000s.[29] Then in 2014, the Abahlali project appeared to be distracted from a liberatory politics when the organization endorsed the electoral campaign of the white-dominated, neoliberal opposition party, the Democratic Alliance (DA). As Abahlali's president S'bu Zikode put it, "This decision is not one that is based on ideology. Poor people do not eat ideology, nor do they live in houses that are made out of ideology."[30] Since the DA would not have influence over housing in Durban, the reasons for this apparently emanated from Abahlali's concern for their community leaders' security, in the wake of a series of attacks on the movement, and their desire for

---

28. See Ashwin Desai, *We are the Poors* (New York: Monthly Review Press, 2002), described by Naomi Klein as "one of the best books yet on globalization and resistance."
29. Patrick Bond, Ashwin Desai and Trevor Ngwane, "Uneven and combined Marxism within South Africa's urban social movements," in C. Barker, L. Cox, J. Krinsky and A. Nilsen (Eds), *Marxism and Social Movements* (London: Routledge, 2013), 233–255.
30. Sibusiso Tshabalala, "Why Abahlali endorsed the DA: S'bu Zikode speaks to *GroundUp*," *GroundUp*, 5 May 2014. Available at: http://groundup.org.za/content/why-abahlali-endorsed-da-sbu-zikode-speaks-groundup

political support.[31] Although there are very intense debates about what kind of international solidarity has been generated in this case, with one Durban critic of social movements charging romanticization of Abahlali to the extent even of "censorship" of local strategic disputes (by a Harvard journal, allegedly engineered by a well-known progressive anthropologist),[32] the innovative impact of Abahlali's networking cannot be disputed. Abahlali at its peak gained the solidarity of an extraordinary mix of middle-class social-movement aficionados and academics[33] on the one hand, with working-class "Right to the City" activists in several major urban centers on the other. Bridging such divides, the award-winning film *Dear Mandela* brought the movement's 2005–12 accomplishments to much wider audiences.[34]

Other revealing moments showed how the spirit of solidarity could wax, wane and wander, especially when ideological processes became confusing. The Landless People's Movement (LPM), for example, received exceptional solidaristic support from the global peasant-support network Via Campesina (VC) during the early 2000s, because, as Peter Rosset reported in 2005, VC's technical staff felt that, "There are situations with young, inexperienced organizations in the VC, like the case of the LPM in South Africa, and others. Can the VC play some sort of mentoring and training role? If we don't, it is likely that such organizations will be captured by donors or NGOs." The then lead LPM organizer, Mangaliso Kubheka, listed the merits of internationalism, specifically citing VC activists who came from Brazil's Movement of Landless Workers:

> We cannot trust the government, the NGOs, or the donors not to have their own agendas. Through the VC we have been exposed to other social movements, and we have learned a lot about how to fight for our rights. We have also learned about what to do with land once you have it. We have received a lot of encouragement from the VC, encouragement in the fight for land

31. These included the June 2013 assassination of a high-profile Cato Manor Abahlali activist (Nkululeko Gwala), and the local ANC's attack on Abahlali's Kennedy Road settlement in September 2009. See Raymond Suttner, "The Abahlali/DA pact: difficult situations require difficult decisions," *Polity*, 5 May 2014. Available at: http://www.polity.org.za/article/the-abahlalida-pact-difficult-situations-require-difficult-decisions-2014-05-05

32. Heinrich Bohmke, "The social movement hustle" (2013). Available at: http://heinrichbohmke.com/2013/05/comaroff/

33. See, e.g. Nigel Gibson, "Zabalaza, Unfinished Struggles against Apartheid: The Shackdwellers' Movement in Durban," *Socialism and Democracy*, 21 (3), 2007, 60–96.

34. Christopher Nizza and Dara Kell, *Dear Mandela* (2012). Available at: http://www.dearmandela.com/

and for food sovereignty. . . . The international VC who were there helped a lot in mediating our internal problems. Also at the World Summit on Sustainable Development [in August 2002], the VC gave us courage, and encouraged us to do our march even though the government was threatening us. It was critical that the government see that the LPM had international support. It is crucial that we have international partners, because the South African government is terrified of being exposed if they do something bad. For example, they fear international solidarity actions when they arrest LPM leaders. . . . We desperately need more visits to the LPM by international leaders of the VC. This has two purposes: one is to show a public face of international support for the LPM, and the other to give us advice on internal organizational issues.[35]

This was all true, yet no amount of advice and solidarity could halt the LPM's ideological and institutional collapse, partly because of institutional shortcomings (including the classical problem of rural patriarchy), partly because of adverse relations with land-reform NGOs, and partly because of state repression and divide-and-conquer politics which peaked in 2002. According to Berkeley-based scholar activist Zach Levenson, as recently as 2010, ideological degeneration and hype were also factors.[36]

Within South Africa, solidarity links to three other liberation campaigns were also fraught with ideological contradictions between a predatory post-apartheid state and progressive civil society: Zimbabwe, Swaziland and Palestine. The latter advanced furthest and fastest, in part because it suited the ANC to remind its constituents of the long struggle for freedom it shared with the Palestine Liberation Organisation. However, while through 2013, Pretoria led the world on enforced labelling of products from the illegally-Occupied West Bank territories, hence discouraging their consumption through moral suasion, there continued a great many diplomatic and economic relationships with the Israeli regime that the local BDS movement insisted be broken, to no avail.[37] One example was the regular appearance of Israeli ships in the Durban harbor – though once in early 2009, just after 1400 Gazans were killed by Israeli forces in a single month, the SA Transport and Allied Workers Union (Satawu) refused to unload a ship in protest (instead, scabs did the job that day, and

---

35. Peter Rosset, "Participatory Evaluation of La Via Campesina," Center for the Study of the Americas, San Cristóbal de las Casas, Chiapas Mexico, 2005 Available at: http://www.norad.no/en/tools-and-publications/publications/publication?key=117349.

36. Zachary Levenson, "Social Movements in South Africa," *International Viewpoint*, 5 September 2012. Available at: http://www.internationalviewpoint.org/spip.php?article2730.

37. See http://www.bdssouthafrica.com/

sadly, the much-applauded Satawu action was not repeated). The strengths of BDS against Israel included two university showdowns in which local activists defeated Zionist pressure.[38]

The Zimbabwe and Swazi democracy movements received periodic boosts from supporters (including Cosatu) in the main South African cities. But the two movements' own lack of internal coherence – e.g. failure to specify their desire for symbolic, smart or serious financial sanctions, or border blockades – represented a missed opportunity as their struggles for justice ebbed and flowed. There were two suggestive processes from the South African labor movement. First, Cosatu periodically blockaded the SA–Swazi border post, though this never proceeded beyond an occasional irritation, and the ties between Pretoria and Swaziland's King Mswati remained tight (even personal in Zuma's case, for his notorious nephew Khulubuse married one of Mswati's daughters in 2013).[39] Second, recall the inspiring refusal by Satawu (and then Mozambican, Namibian and even Angolan) workers to unload bullets and weapons from a Chinese frigate destined for Robert Mugabe's repressive armed forces at a critical juncture during the 2008 national election.[40]

These examples notwithstanding, South African labor internationalism was uneven. During the late 1990s and early 2000s, some sections of Cosatu – especially textile workers whose leadership often adopted a corporatist approach to unionism – also mistakenly endorsed the failed, protectionist "Social Clause" concept within the framework of World Trade Organization reform.[41] They were also prone to occasionally issue myopic global governance proposals that coincided with processes in the International Labour Organization. Generally, however, Cosatu maintained a progressive internationalist approach, finding common cause with oppressed peoples, and along with the SA Communist Party regularly offered strong moral support to the Cuban, Bolivian and Venezuelan governments. The overall problem for

38. Patrick Bond, "From Apartheid South Africa to Palestine", *Counterpunch*, 13 October 2010. Available at: http://www.counterpunch.org/2010/10/13/from-apartheid-south-africa-to-palestine/ and Patrick Bond and Muhammed Desai, "The Academic Boycott of Israel," 24 May 2012. Available at: http://www.counterpunch.org/2012/05/24/the-academic-boycott-of-israel-2/

39. See, e.g. Cosatu Press Statements, "Swaziland border blockade," 4 April 2006. Available at: http://www.cosatu.org.za/show.php?ID=747

40. Nicole Fritz, "People Power: How Civil Society Blocked an Arms Shipment for Zimbabwe," SA Institute for International Affairs, Occasional Paper 39, Governance and APRM Programme, Johannesburg (2009).

41. Patrick Bond, *Against Global Apartheid* (London: Zed Books, 2003).

Cosatu remained its alliance with the ANC government, as shown in a 2007 conference on internationalism in which state officials postured about progressive foreign policy initiatives, all evidence to the contrary notwithstanding. By late 2013, the alliance appeared to suffer what might become a fatal stress, insofar as the largest trade union, the National Union of Metalworkers of SA (Numsa), whose 340,000 members numbered roughly a quarter of Cosatu, refused to endorse the ANC because of its persistent neoliberalism and corruption. Numsa's internationalism was one of its greatest strengths.[42]

These are just examples – not a comprehensive list – of how, dating to the end of formal apartheid, "foreign policy bottom-up" was established by progressive South Africans under difficult conditions, in which "talk left walk right" rhetoric from the ANC often distracts attention. But difficult class politics require mediation. For example, one class vector that unites many of the cases above is the *middle-class basis* for many of the initial appeals to internationalist solidarity, as staff in NGOs (and to some extent universities) fired up the internet ether to make connections that, in turn, related many of the base movements to each other in sectoral gatherings. This was most visible, from 2001 and nearly every year thereafter, at the World Social Forum, a venue which itself came under increasing critique because of its middle-class orientation. *But precisely that power and capacity require serious scrutiny so that they are not misused.* And in terms of barriers to progressive solidarity, a second class-contradiction represented one of the most unfortunate tendencies within the South African working class: its penchant for xenophobic responses to socio-economic challenges.

Defeating – or defeated by? – working-class xenophobia

In May 2008, it was evident that South Africa's prolific community and labor protests could as easily be directed against fellow residents and workers – especially if they hailed from outside South Africa – as against the deeper-rooted sources of problems such as unemployment, housing shortages and excessive (often cut-throat) internecine commercial competition within the townships. Along with rising domestic violence and the AIDS pandemic, the xenophobia wave was

---

42. See Irvin Jim interview, this issue; and Patrick Bond, "South Africa's Resource Curses and Growing Social Resistance," *Monthly Review*, 65 (11), 2014. Available at: http://monthlyreview.org/2014/04/01/south-africas-resource-curses-growing -social-resistance

perhaps the most obvious manifestation of a tearing social fabric. As in Zimbabwe during its 1990s period of failing neoliberal economic management, South African nationalists, especially the black upper and middle class, are ascendant.[43]

There remain deep economic problems rooted in the apartheid-era economy, such as the migrant labor system.[44] Because of the liberalization of both trade and finance, and especially because of the decision by the Mandela and Mbeki governments to allow the largest corporations to delist their Johannesburg Stock Exchange financial headquarters in favor of London, the current account deficit grew to a dangerously high level by May 2008 (-9 percent), compared to the ability of the economy to generate foreign exchange. Interest rates were raised more than 10 percent as a neoliberal defence mechanism. In the process, much more foreign debt was taken on, and employers had greater recourse to hiring cheaper immigrant workers. Although overall corporate profits were up more than 7 percent against worker wages – the wage share fell from 56 to 49 percent – since the low-point of the late 1980s, a decisive problem remained for those anticipating a labor-intensive growth trajectory: manufacturing profits had fallen dramatically since the early 1980s in relation to financial and speculative profits. South Africa's export advantages remained in a few areas difficult to maintain, such as auto components, coal, and base metals (the latter required vast electricity subsidies to aluminium smelters). Low fixed investment rates persisted, especially by private sector investors, in part because of excess idle capacity in existing plant and equipment. That mainly explained the very low level of Foreign Direct Investment, contrasting with dangerously high inflows of liquid portfolio capital attracted by South Africa's high real interest rate. The repeated currency crashes passed along high price inflation in petroleum and food, generating yet more social unrest.

This economic context set the stage for the nightmare that played out in May-June 2008, when repeated upsurges of xenophobia over several weeks caused at least 64 deaths (mostly of immigrants) and the displacement of at least 70,000 people, mainly in the metropolitan areas of Johannesburg and Cape Town. The state's failure to assess the threat to immigrants has been the subject of extensive discussion.

---

43. Gill Hart, "The Provocations of Neoliberalism: Contesting the Nation and Liberation after Apartheid", *Antipode*, 40 (4), 2008. See also Gill Hart, *Rethinking the South African Crisis* (Pietermaritzburg: University of KwaZulu-Natal Press, 2013).
44. Baruti Amisi, Patrick Bond, Nokuthula Cele and Trevor Ngwane, "Xenophobia and Civil Society: Durban's Structured Social Divisions," *Politikon*, 38 (1), 2011.

When these tendencies in the society were formally drawn to Mbeki's attention in the December 2007 African Peer Review Mechanism report – "xenophobia against other Africans is currently on the rise and must be nipped in the bud" – Mbeki replied that this was "simply not true".[45] But not only had there been multiple reports in prior months about the murders of shopkeepers from Somalia in Western and Eastern Cape townships, as well as police brutality and abuse at the Lindela repatriation centre outsourced by Home Affairs. In addition, a 2006 FutureFact survey asked South Africans if they agreed with this statement: "Most of the problems in South Africa are caused by illegal immigrants or foreigners." The depressing results:

> ... 67 percent agreed, a substantial increase on a few years ago, when the figure was 47 percent. And it is reflected among all population sectors of the country. FutureFact also put this statement to respondents: "Immigrants are a threat to jobs for South Africans and should not be allowed into South Africa" – with which 69 percent agreed.[46]

When the violence began in mid-May 2008, the immediate reaction from the state, academics and NGOs was the call for more civic "education," usually about human rights, the plight of refugees, or the role that neighbouring societies played in hosting South African exiles during apartheid. However, beyond platitudes, civic education would not be sufficient to address genuine grievances, as the government's Human Sciences Research Council found:

> South African citizens literally feel "besieged" by a range of socio-economic challenges. This feeling is particularly acute for men of working age who are struggling to find employment or make a living and feel most directly threatened by the migration of large numbers of "working men" from other parts of the continent.[47]

There are various ways in which the structural tensions translate into violence against immigrants:

- lack of jobs, as formal sector employment dropped by a million after 1994, and declining wage levels as a result of immigrant willingness to work for low pay on a casualized basis;

45. SA Press Association, "Mbeki Critical of Crime Issues in APRM Report", Pretoria, 6 December 2007.
46. *Mail&Guardian* online, "What we feel, warts and all", 12 July 2008. Available at: http://www.mg.co.za/article/2008-07-12-what-we-feel-warts-and-all
47. Human Sciences Research Council, "Citizenship, Violence and Xenophobia in South Africa: Perceptions from South African Communities," Democracy and Governance Programme, Pretoria (2008).

- immigrant tenacity in finding informal economic opportunities even when these are illegal, such as street trading of fruits, vegetables, cigarettes, toys and other small commodities;
- housing pressures whereby immigrants drive up rentals of a multi-occupant dwelling unit beyond the ability of locals to afford;
- surname identity theft (including fake marriages to South Africans who only learn much later); and
- increases in local crime blamed on immigrants.

Behind some of this tension is the recent expansion of the migrant labor system. In 1994, the choice was made *not* to rid South Africa's economy of migrancy, which could have been accomplished by improving wages, maintaining much higher employment, turning single-sex migrant hostels into decent family homes, and compelling the extension of formal employment benefits (health insurance, housing, pensions) to black workers and their families, as is the case with higher-income white workers. Today, hostels remain but with the rise in unemployment, the buildings are often full of unemployed men, and these were the source of many xenophobic attacks.

Although South Africa's racially-defined geographical areas formerly known as Bantustans have disappeared, the economic logic of drawing inexpensive labor from distant sites is even more extreme now that it no longer is stigmatized by apartheid connotations. Instead of hailing mainly from within South Africa, the most desperate migrant workers in the major cities are often from Zimbabwe, Malawi, Mozambique and Zambia, countries partially deindustrialized by South African business expansion since 1994. Others are refugees from the eastern region of the Democratic Republic of the Congo, where South African and other multinational corporations actively colluded with war lords to generate illicit precious-metals and mineral outflows, at the expense of several million deaths.

Additional structural factors in the regional labor market – especially sites where immigrant workers predominate – also contribute to stress in everyday life: the HIV/AIDS pandemic (especially along trucking routes); the prevalence of child labor; ongoing farm labor-tenant exploitation; low skill levels and inadequate training; rising privatization pressures and controversies over other public sector restructuring measures; sweatshop conditions in many factories; and a new two-tier wage system aiming to fragment South Africa's already highly-flexible labor market. Contrary to popular belief, even the Organization for Economic Cooperation and Development and the IMF consider South African workers to be the fourth least protected (in terms of job security) in the industrial world, after those in the US, Canada and Britain.[48] In one frank admission of self-interest regarding immigrant workers, First National Bank chief economist Cees Bruggemann told *Business Report*, "They keep the cost of labor down. ... Their income gets spent here because they do not send the money back to their countries."[49] If many immigrants don't send back remittances (because their wages are low and the cost of living has soared), that in turn reminds us of how apartheid drew cheap labor from Bantustans: for many years women were coerced into supplying unpaid services – child-rearing, healthcare and eldercare for retirees – so as to reproduce fit male workers for the mines, factories and plantations.

And in turn, the need for civil society to think beyond the immediate grievances and find international solidaristic relationships remains. On 24 May 2008, Johannesburg civil society mobilized several thousand people – local supporters and immigrants alike – to march through Hillbrow in solidarity with immigrants. Various other initiatives in townships across South Africa showed that communities could welcome immigrants back, and live in harmony. The provision of resources by churches, NGOs and concerned citizens was impressive, even while the state backtracked from responsibilities, and in some cases including Durban, actively oppressed fearful immigrants who remained homeless and unable to return to communities.

The state's role often flagrantly contributed to the problems. As just one example, in June 2012, a riot at the main immigrant detention center west of Johannesburg, Lindela (privatized to a notorious corporation, Bosasa, a company created by the ANC Women's League), revealed how the South African Department of Home Affairs held people "at the centre for longer than the 120 days stipulated in the Immigration Act. The conditions under which refugees at the centre on Gauteng's West Rand are held have been a cause of concern for NGOs and refugee organizations for several years."[50] In 2006, Boassa (the firm running Lindela) had been condemned by Parliament's Public Accounts Committee for its annual $7.5 million "rip off" profit, as well as for deaths in detention, but was nevertheless reappointed. Bosasa guards "treat us like animals," according to refugee complaints, and several respected NGOs – Lawyers for Human

48. International Monetary Fund, "Article IV Statement: South Africa" (Washington, DC: International Monetary Fund, 2010).
49. Lyse Comins, "African immigrants add value to local economy," *Business Report*, 22 May 2008.
50. Chandre Prince, "Lindela 'hell' ignored: Home Affairs accused of turning blind eye to reports of abuse of refugees," *The Times*, 8 June 2012.

Rights, Section 27, Passop and Médecins sans Frontières – repeatedly complained about lack of healthcare at Lindela and Cape Town's Maitland Refugee Centre. But when asked to address the grievances, two Home Affairs spokespeople "said they were too busy to attend to the query because they were writing a speech for the minister, Nkosazana Dlamini-Zuma."[51]

At that very moment, Dlamini-Zuma was campaigning across Africa to become the African Union Commission chairperson, attempting to unseat the Francophone incumbent Jean Ping of Mali. There were widespread allegations not only that her candidacy was ironic in view of Home Affairs xenophobia, but that South Africa was practicing subimperial ambitions in an underhanded way, drawing complaints from countries which normally would not have supported a candidate from one of the four most powerful African countries (Egypt, Kenya, Nigeria and South Africa) to be the African Union commission leader, as a matter of retaining regional balances. To overcome the opposition, according to the leading South African newspaper, at that very time, "Pretoria stands accused of buying support for its candidate for African Union commission chief."[52]

Conclusion: The next socialist internationalism

A much more robust socialist-internationalist ideology is a necessary though insufficient condition for overcoming the kinds of debilitating limitations described here. In what was surely its greatest accomplishment, the 1864 IWA established a clear sense of genuine debates within the world's organized working class, even if after 1868 the classical differences between socialists (Marx) and anarcho-syndicalists (Bakunin) drove an ideological wedge through the movement. At least the contending political standpoints were set out in a clear manner; in future internationals, these were honed into statements of socialism that reflected the balance of forces of their day: "Workers of the world unite!" in the First International; reformist parliamentary social democracy and labor party formation during the Second International (1889–1916); the Comintern Third International (1919–43) centered on the Soviet Union's national interests and early versions of Third World nationalism ("Workers and oppressed peoples of the world unite!"); and the Trotskyist Fourth International

51. Mckeed Kotlolo, Graeme Hosken and Philani Nombembe, "Riot puts spotlight on 'violation' of refugees: Home Affairs branded xenophobic," *The Times*, 5 June 2012.
52. Sean Christie, "Vote lobbying lands SA in hot water," *Mail & Guardian*, 1 June 2012.

(1938–63) which was all too purist and sectarian. A Fifth International was promised by Hugo Chávez in 2007, but there appears no prospect of that project's revival following his 2013 death.[53] All fell short of creating a broader left-internationalist politics in their time, partly because of the organizational and intellectual cultures they had forged. But for all their faults, the foundational principles, analyses and practices of the Internationals were doubtless global in vision and *socialist*.

In contrast, Frantz Fanon lamented in 1961, "For my part, the deeper I enter into the culture and political circles the surer I am that the great danger that threatens Africa is the absence of ideology."[54] The same can be said of many failures of the left in post-1994 South Africa. So to conclude, in a period since the 1960s in which the New Left introduced a permanent concern for gender, race, nation, different-abledness and the natural environment, what are the more optimistic assessments we can provide from South Africa? Is there a near-term future which features the ideological maturity and richer class analysis and practice required to overcome xenophobia and build bridges across borders? Four final examples illustrate the terrain, the more hopeful prospects, the daunting challenges, and at least some of the dangers ahead as we seek a new socialist internationalism: campaigns for free AIDS medicines and against water privatization which have been successful, and for climate justice and international financial sanity which have not been yet, but must be in future, as well as modes of solidarity we need to generate, and bad habits of North-to-South scholar-to-activist condescension (and worse) to avoid.

First, the 1999–2004 solidarity among health activists won by the Treatment Action Campaign (TAC) was an extraordinary accomplishment, representing the most favorable internationalist politics since apartheid's demise. When TAC began its work in late 1998, an annual course of anti-retrovirals (ARVs) cost $15,000, restricting access to a tiny minority. Pretoria's 1997 Medicines Act provided for compulsory licensing of patented drugs, but that law was immediately confronted by the US State Department's "full court press" (the formal description to the US Congress), in large part to protect intellectual property rights generally, and specifically to prevent the emergence of a parallel inexpensive supply of AIDS medicines that would undermine lucrative

53.   Luis Bilbao, "Hugo Chavez, Internationalism and Revolution," *Links*, 19 March 2013. Available at: http://links.org.au/node/3264
54.   Fanon, *The Wretched of the Earth*, 186.

Western markets.[55] US Vice-President Al Gore directly pressured Mandela and Mbeki in 1998–99, demanding they revoke the law. But in July 1999, Gore launched his 2000 presidential election bid, a campaign generously funded by big pharmaceutical corporations (which in a prior election cycle provided $2.3 million to the Democratic Party) and so TAC's allies in the AIDS Coalition to Unleash Power (ACTUP) began to protest at Gore's early campaign events. The demonstrations ultimately threatened to cost Gore far more in adverse publicity than he was raising in Big Pharma contributions, so after two months of persistent ACTUP protest, he changed sides and withdrew his opposition to the Medicines Act, as did Bill Clinton a few weeks later at the World Trade Organization's Seattle Summit. Big Pharma did not give up, and filed a 1999 lawsuit against the constitutionality of the Medicines Act, counterproductively entitled "Pharmaceutical Manufacturers Association v. Nelson Mandela" (which even *Wall Street Journal* editorialists found offensive). By April 2001, additional protests by Médecins sans Frontières, Oxfam and other TAC solidarity groups at Big Pharma member offices in the world's major cities compelled the withdrawal of the lawsuit. By late 2001, the Doha Agenda of the WTO adopted explicit language permitting overriding of Trade Related Intellectual Property Rights for medical emergencies. As a result, once Mbeki's position was defeated by TAC within internal ANC political processes two years later, local generic medicines manufacturers lowered costs substantially through voluntary licensing of the major AIDS drugs. By 2013 more than two million people were receiving AIDS medicines for free at public clinics, and South Africa's life expectancy soared to 61 from a low of 52 in 2004. However, the narrowness of the solidarity and the campaign's strategy must also be remarked upon, for the main criticism levelled against TAC during this period was that in order to achieve these objectives, it had to continually revert back to a modus operandi "within the box" of a single issue, never daring to connect-the-dots to areas that would have been logical as accompanying campaigns, such as demanding free electricity (to rid homes of dirty energy like paraffin, coal and wood) or free water. Without clean energy and water, the spread of respiratory and water-borne diseases take millions of patients quickly from HIV+ to full-blown AIDS.[56]

---

55. Nicoli Nattrass, *The Moral Economy of AIDS in South Africa* (Cambridge: Cambridge University Press 2004); Patrick Bond, "What is it to be radical, in neoliberal-nationalist South Africa?," *Review of Radical Political Economy*, September 2011.

56. This changed only in 2008 with the xenophobia crisis when TAC's Khayelitsha activism became multi-sectoral, and subsequently several TAC leaders branched out

Second, water is indeed a useful lens to view movement-society relations, because another international campaign involved South Africans at the very height of world concern about household water privatization. In Johannesburg, one of the world's highest-profile "water wars" commenced in early 2000, at precisely the same moment the "Coalition for the Defense of Water and Life" in Cochabamba, Bolivia overturned a privatization project of the World Bank and Bechtel Corporation. Leaders of both movements – Oscar Olivera and Trevor Ngwane – met at the World Bank protest in April 2000 to compare notes on analysis, strategies, tactics and alliances; after high-profile roles in that demonstration, both then featured in well-circulated films about their struggles.[57] In July 2000 at the University of the Witwatersrand Urban Futures Conference, the Johannesburg region's Anti-Privatization Forum burst onto the scene, with its core support from Soweto, and adopted an explicitly socialist program. In the process, South Africans like Ngwane helped to turn the world water wars into ongoing tribunals against commodification, and then into debates about whether human rights narratives should be adopted internationally. While there are certainly arguments in favor of deploying "rights talk,"[58] in the case of *Mazibuko versus Johannesburg Water*, South Africa's Constitutional Court ruled in October 2009 against Soweto plaintiffs organized by Ngwane, and in favor of the neoliberal policies imposed by French water privatizer Suez when it managed Johannesburg Water from 2001-05. Although Suez was compelled to leave Johannesburg before it applied for a 25-year extension on its contract, the damage was done: water was supplied via prepayment meters and in much lower quantities than the minimal needed (the ANC's 1994 *Reconstruction and Development Programme* promised at least 50 liters per person per day). In *Mazibuko*, activists used every argument on behalf of greater water provision, but

---

into new NGOs such as Section 27 and Ndifuna Ukwazi which had broader self-mandates.

57. Olivera's struggle was portrayed in *Blue Gold: World Water Wars; Even the Rain;* and *One Water*. Ngwane starred in *Two Trevors go to Washington*.

58. The case in favor of "rights talk" was that it resonated with the Constitutional accomplishments of South Africa's progressive forces, because winning what are typically regarded as the world's most advanced socio-economic rights provisions in the 1996 document proved an important step in TAC's campaign. Indeed, in July 2002 a Constitutional Court judgement forced the Mbeki regime to begin providing the mother-to-child HIV-prevention medicine Nevirapine. However all other Constitutional Court judgments on socio-economic rights before and after were either affirmative in a defensive way (e.g. striking down shack-clearance legislation in KwaZulu-Natal province) or negative for plaintiffs.

although the first two judgements in the High Court and Supreme Court backed the Sowetans, the final court judgment confirmed Johannesburg's policies, illustrating the danger of appealing to rights. After losing, many activists reverted to their preferred method of water access: illegal reconnections of the water pipes after state disconnection, following the logic of a popular slogan of the time: *Destroy the meter, enjoy free water.*[59]

The reason the water case is important in solidarity terms is that it set out the limited parameters of both local constitutionalism and liberal internationalism. The Universal Declaration of Human Rights asserted in 1948 that all individuals have certain basic entitlements to political, social, or economic goods, including even employment. These were generally ignored, but against the background of commodified water policies spreading across the world, a new global movement arose after 2000 asserting that water is essential to human life. After the Cochabamba, Soweto and similar struggles, social conflict surrounding water began to be framed in terms of the right to water. In a sense, the success of the Third International – even after it faded towards the end of World War II – was in establishing a pole against which liberal internationalism had to stand. The UN General Assembly's July 2010 reassertion of "the right to safe and clean drinking water and sanitation as a human right that is essential for the full enjoyment of life and all human rights" was probably the high point, and in 2012 at the Rio+20 UN environment summit, further backsliding occurred, led by the United States and its allies.[60] What can be learned from the South African cases is that evoking socio-economic entitlements can, in some circumstances, provide activists with the moral standing required to combat large systems of power, especially national states. Defensive and occasional offensive victories can be won. But at the same time, the rights narrative takes activists out of their normal habitat of social mobilization, and into what can become a counterproductive space. Rights talk, according to critics, tends to:

- promote individualist strategies based on private/familial scales instead of public/political processes;
- be consumption-oriented, without linkages to production and ecology;

---

59. *Mazibuko & Others v. City of Johannesburg & Others*, South African Constitutional Court 28, Johannesburg (2009); Patrick Bond, "Water rights, commons and advocacy narratives," *South African Journal of Human Rights*, 29 (1), June, 2013, 126–144.
60. Patrick Bond, "Values versus Prices at the Rio Earth Summit," *Links*, 19 June 2012. Available at: http://links.org.au/node/2915

- be "framed not to resist but to legitimise neoliberalism" (as Daria Roithmayr argues);
- leave in place society's class structure, which "bleeds off any real move to dismantle these processes through redistribution and reparations" (Roithmayr);
- adopt a technicist discourse which alienates the mass base and society in general;
- make mass-based organisations the "client," and one that is increasingly "domesticated" (according to Tshepo Madlingozi), with some activists even told to halt protests during litigation so as not to anger judges;
- be "watered down" in South Africa, made less potent thanks to Constitutional clauses of "progressive realisation," "reasonable" measures, "within available resources";
- lead activists up legal alleyways that distract them from a more transformative route to politics;
- be self-defeating because simply for class reasons, judges are among society's most conservative elites; and
- never satisfyingly deliver the goods – not when the overall objective of the ruling elite is often to create scarcity.[61]

There is a different approach: an eco-socialist narrative, for example, of "the Commons." The difference is not merely that water is demanded as an individualized consumption norm in one (rights) and is "shared" in the other (commons). Other contrasts between the political cultures of rights and of commons are explicitly analysed by Karen Bakker, who insists rights advocates suffer a "widespread failure to adequately distinguish between different elements of neoliberal reform processes, an analytical sloppiness that diminishes our ability to correctly characterize the aims and trajectories of neoliberal projects of resource management reform."[62] Rights narratives also artificially split political economy from political ecology, because the social and natural interrelationships of a struggle tend to be fragmented. It is here, again, that the critical ideological conflicts between liberal internationalism (the budding world human rights regime) and socialist internationalism are playing out, just as did earlier dialectics in the IWA.

---

61. See, e.g. Daria Roithmayr, "Lessons From Mazibuko: Shifting From Rights to the Commons," 3 *Constitutional Court Review* 317, 2010.
62. Karen Bakker, "The 'Commons' versus the 'Commodity'': Alter-Globalization, Anti-Privatization and the Human Right to Water in the Global South," *Antipode*, 39 (3), 2007, 430–455.

The third case in which South Africa serves us with solidaristic lessons is climate justice. While space does not permit a full evaluation of how eco-socialist currents have belatedly risen to contest a fossil-addicted energy system, and how Durban's December 2011 hosting of the UN Conference of the Parties 17 revealed market failures, state failures and civil society failures, these are predictable enough. The balance of forces never improved much, after the Durban Group for Climate Justice emerged in October 2004 based on solidarity between activists and allied researchers across the world fighting carbon trading – the bankers' strategy to commodify the air and sell the right to pollute.[63] Still, along the way the largest World Bank loan ever – $3.75 billion for the largest coal-fired power plant under construction anywhere on earth, Eskom's Medupi station (whose greenhouse gases exceed the national totals of 115 individual countries) – was nearly foiled by an impressive solidarity campaign catalysed by groundWork, the South Durban Community Environmental Alliance, and Earthlife Africa in April 2010.[64] A similar campaign began in late 2013 to impose financial sanctions on the carbon-intensive parastatal agency Transnet to derail its $25 billion port-petrochemical expansion, attracting the surprisingly positive attention of *The Economist* and *Guardian* once D'Sa won the Goldman Environmental Prize in April 2014.[65] But international solidarity to move South Durban forward will necessarily move from the defensive to the offensive, with "transition town" assistance coming from climate justice activists to not only reverse the plans of state and capital, but ensure an alternative low-carbon and labor-intensive development strategy that meets the South Durban Basin's basic needs for housing, services, transport and even urban agriculture.[66]

Fourth, the necessity of resisting climate change coincides precisely with the need to reboot the world financial system, since so many of the

63. I set these lessons out in Patrick Bond (Ed), *Durban's Climate Gamble: Trading Carbon, Betting the Earth* (Pretoria: University of South Africa Press 2011), and Patrick Bond, "Durban's Conference of Polluters, Market Failure and Critic Failure," *ephemera*, 12 (1/2), March 2012. Available at: http://www.ephemerajournal.org/contribution/durban%E2%80%99s-conference-polluters-market-failure-and-critic-failure

64. Bond, *Politics of Climate Justice*, Chapter Six.

65. *The Economist*, "South African campaigner wins environmental prize," 28 April 2014; John Vidal, "South Africa's 'cancer alley' residents face new threat from port development," *The Guardian*, 28 April 2014; SDCEA, "Port-petrochemical expansion threatens South Durban," 2013. Available at: https://www.youtube.com/watch?v=taFtYFmFXEE.

66. Alternative Information and Development Centre, "Million Climate Jobs," Available at: http://climatejobs.org.za/index.php/research.

forces of capitalist crisis and financialization that generate "false solutions" within an ostensible "green economy" (e.g. bogus strategies like carbon trading) are also driving overconsumption and overproduction through overindebtedness.[67] In reply, the leading force in South Africa in the wake of Jubilee South Africa's early 2000s collapse is Numsa, which has established itself as one of the world's greatest labor voices for renewable energy, and in addition has the country's most advanced critique of free capital flows, with a strong record of advocacy for the reimposition of exchange controls.[68] Only with a radically different scale of financial policy can the minimally sensible regulation of economics take place, as even John Maynard Keynes himself suggested in 1933: "Ideas, knowledge, science, hospitality, travel – these are the things which should of their nature be international. But let goods be homespun whenever it is reasonably and conveniently possible, and, above all, let finance be primarily national."[69]

It is here that we see the South African post-apartheid left beginning to transcend the single-issue constraints of TAC and the rights-commons divide observable in the water sector, and ratchet up the pressure on climate politics and against internationalized finance. It is here that not only *decommodification*, but also *deglobalization of capital* must be considered vital to expanding access to basic needs like medicines and water, and in South Africa this has occurred thus far even though power relations were terribly adverse at first. They turned much more favorable because of the *globalization of popular solidarity*. Even if this formula was the opposite of the South African government's typical stance – which leaned towards the globalization of capital and, with respect to globalized people, harsher immigration controls bordering on xenophobia, plus repression against visiting protesters at major events – there was continuity in people's support for black South Africans facing threats to their lives, from the era of racial apartheid to the era of class apartheid.

---

67. Patrick Bond, "Global Economic Volatility and Slap-Dash Repairs to the International Financial Architecture," in M. Vernengo, G. Epstein and T. Schlesinger (Eds), *Banking, Monetary Policy and the Political Economy of Financial Regulation* (Cheltenham: Edward Elgar, 2014).

68. Patrick Bond and Azwell Banda, "South African Workers Tackle Neoliberalism," *Against the Current*, November-December 2009, and Samantha Ashman and Nicolas Pons-Vignon, "Political Rupture in South Africa and the National Union of Metalworkers," *Global Research*, February 2014. Available at: http://www.globalresearch.ca/political-rupture-in-south-africa-and-the-national-union-of-metalworkers-numsa-new-start-for-socialist-politics-in-south-africa/5368480

69. John Maynard Keynes, "National Self-Sufficiency," *The Yale Review*, 22 (4), 1933, 755-769.

To achieve this conception of a foreign-policy bottom up, requires balance among what Peter Waterman has described as the six versions of solidarity: "Identity, Substitution, Complementarity, Reciprocity, Affinity and Restitution. Each of these has its own part of the meaning of international solidarity; each is only part of the meaning, and by itself can only be a limited and impoverished understanding of such."[70] But the solidarity between the Global North and Global South that lies ahead should also take note of the many problems repeatedly encountered among solidaristic scholars and social movements in South Africa. These, in my view, boil down to ten "sins" that are often committed, and indeed that problems recorded in the pages above testify to:

- *gatekeeping* (or worse, *hijacking*): in which a researcher takes ownership of a movement, its interpretation and even access;
- *substitutionism*: replacing (not augmenting) the local understanding with the researcher's understanding or vision;
- *ventriloquism*: replacing local phrasing with a researcher's own words (in press releases, articles, statements of demands, etc.);
- *careerism* through *parasitism*: exploiting information gained, without reporting back or turning benefits back to the base;
- *technicism* or *legalism*: sometimes necessary to contest the enemy's technicism, but sometimes incapable of comprehending realities, usually causing premature deradicalization;
- *divisiveness*: favoring or profiling certain factions or individuals, often in a sectarian way;
- *hucksterism*: romanticizing and overstating the importance of the movement/struggle;
- *score-settling*: importing researchers' petty internecine rivalries, and causing degeneracy in movement politics as ego-clashing replaces open, honest debate;
- *failure of analytical nerve*: inability (often due to fear) to draw out the fully liberatory potentials of the movement and its struggles; and even

---

70. Waterman explains: *Identity* is expressed by the slogan "Workers of the World Unite!", implying one long-term general interest; *Substitution* is exemplified by development cooperation, or 'standing in' for the poor, exploited and powerless; *Complementarity* is the solidarity of "differential contribution" to a common interest or aim (which could be between workers, or North-South); *Reciprocity* is the exchange of similar quantities or qualities over time; *Affinity* suggests personal identity/friendship between, say, eco-feminists, socialists (of a particular hue), and even stamp-collectors; *Restitution* is recognition and compensation for past wrongs. See Peter Waterman, *Globalisation, Social Movements and the New Internationalisms* (London: Cassell, 1998), Chapter One.

- *betrayal*: turning against the movement, giving information to its enemies, or accepting the validity of unwarranted enemy arguments.

This, then, is simultaneously the most hopeful and sobering set of lessons from internationalism following apartheid. The challenge is for the next South African left to tackle. Undoubtedly the strongest component of South African democratic eco-socialism in the 2015–19 period, before the next general election, is the metalworker breakaway union as it attempts to forge solidarity with local community, social and environmental activists. To do so, the "United Front" that is being built must be at once sufficiently concrete to carry forward the "Movement Towards Socialism" declared by the metalworkers in late 2013 *on the ground* (in spite of long-standing class and political differences between workers and the mass of unemployed, not to mention women who suffer South Africa's extreme versions of patriarchy) and sufficiently internationalist to generate the next round of solidarity with South African radicals. In the past, like Marx's mates in the IWA, South Africans have taught the world an enormous amount about the potential for transformative power deployed from below. In the future, similar lessons beckon us all back to a form of socialist solidarity that is still very much work in progress here, and everywhere.

Book Review

Marcello Musto, ed., *Workers Unite! The International 150 Years Later* (London: Bloomsbury, 2014)

What is most distinctive about this book is that, instead of being about "Marx and the International," it is about the International Workingmen's Association (IWA) itself – though fully recognizing the important role that Marx played within it. This makes it a rarity. More importantly, it is a unique anthology of documents from the International as a whole, including reports and resolutions from the Paris bookbinders, the Central Section of Working Women of Geneva, and other little-known or unknown authors – to say nothing of several by Mikhail Bakunin.

Marxists have tended to approach the First International as something of a sidebar to Marx's career. Both the Second and Third Internationals claimed to be directly and fundamentally Marxist, and Lenin's *State and Revolution* provided an especially powerful link between what Marx wrote about the Paris Commune – on behalf of the First International – and the Bolshevik politics of revolution. The solidification of this link in "official" Marxism during the Stalinist era effectively cast the retrospective reading of Marx – particularly his political writing in the era of the International – through a Bolshevik lens. Subsequently, neither anti-Communists nor Leninists of any stripe have had reason to challenge this view.

The perspective of this book, however, is fundamentally different. The centrality of Marx's role within the International is, of course, not in question. Indeed, as Musto observes from the start, Marx was the "political soul" of the General Council (GC) of the IWA, writing all of its main resolutions and all but one of the reports of its Congresses. Yet Marx had no role in the decision to found the International; he was never able to take for granted that his views would carry the day in debates; and much of his "leadership" included taking responsibility for day-to-day matters (even to the extent of ensuring that adequate office supplies were on hand).

Perhaps because of the importance of retaining paper copies of all sorts of transactions at the time, and certainly due to the conscientious efforts of the IWA itself to make its work known through the publication of significant addresses and the resolutions of its Congresses, a very large quantity of material relating to the organization has been preserved. Some of this material, such as Marx's *Inaugural Address*, his *Value, Price and Profit*, and *The Civil War in France*, has been widely available ever since its publication by the International itself, or subsequently in the late nineteenth or early twentieth century in connection with the Second International. In commemoration of the 100th anniversary of the International, finally, there was a significant effort by Progress Publishers in Moscow to make the rest of the material (at least insofar as it conformed with its view of the IWA) available in limited editions intended for libraries and specialists.

But there has been no previous anthology from the documents of the First International (which in total amount to more than 7000 pages) intended for the general reader. Moreover, most of the previously published documents that were in French – including the proceedings of the Congresses – have never been translated into English. And the orientation not only of the Moscow-based publications, but also of Marxists generally, meant that the documents – indeed even the existence – of a Bakuninist International following upon the great split in 1872 did not receive appropriate recognition. In its efforts to overcome all these limitations, this book marks a crucial breakthrough.

All the most significant documents, including the major pieces by Marx that have long been widely available, are reproduced in the book. Yet, whereas those pieces have previously for the most part been presented in the context of collections of Marx's political writings, here they are presented in their more immediate historical context as contributions to the collective formulation of political positions taken by the International as a whole. In addition to the previously disseminated addresses and resolutions, there are excerpts from the minutes of the GC and Congresses, including synopses of speeches by Marx, Bakunin, and many other participants. Importantly, the selection of such excerpts has not been made with a view towards highlighting the importance of Marx (which, of course, is also not denied), but to reveal the sometimes intense debates that were pursued, and the real importance of contributions from a variety of other participants, some of whom are barely known to history.

The Introduction and notes provide a clear and concise historical context for each of the documents, and accounts of their prior publication. Especially notable is the attention given not just to the positions taken by the GC, but also to those taken by local sections and federations on the major issues of the day. The independence of thought that can be seen in the history of these sections, and in the positions they articulated, is a revelation. We encounter not only the views of

Marx and his most notable antagonists, but also those of committed socialists who fell into neither camp.

For example, there is the position taken by the Central Section of Working Women of Geneva in 1872. Their mandated resolution for the Hague Congress included two fundamentally important points that they had developed independently:

> Considering first: that the working woman's needs are equal to those of the working man and that the pay for her work is much less, the central Section of Working Women requests the Congress to include in its resolutions that henceforth agreements reached between employers and strikers of a trade in which women are employed will stipulate the same advantage for them as for men ...
>
> Considering, secondly: that the more different groups of opinion there are on the ways of achieving the same aim, the emancipation of labour, the easier it is to generalize the working class movement without losing any of the forces (even the most widely diverging) to concur in the final result; that it is advisable to leave to individuals, within the principles of the International, the right to group according to their tastes and their opinions.
>
> Consequently: the Working Women of the Central Section demand: that the General Council shall not have the power to reject any section, whatever particular purpose it proposes, whatever its principles, provided that purpose and principles are not capable of harming those of the International Working Men's Association and are compatible with the General Rules.

This is an important call for a broad conception of the mission of the International. It tended to be favourable to the position of Bakunin within it, but was not itself Bakuninist, and seems to have genuinely favoured the widest possible range of views compatible with the International. At the same time, it conceived this position in conjunction with advancing the interests of women workers. It is very much to the Musto's credit that he presents this position for us to consider.

The thematic selection and arrangement of documents encourages us to appreciate the International as a vitally democratic association. It opens with the founding documents of the International. It then continues, in accord with the actual development of debates, with sections on "Labour", "Trade Unions and Strikes", the "Cooperative Movement and Credit", "Inheritance", "Collective Ownership and the State", "Education", the Paris Commune, a broad range of international issues, and crucial issues of working-class political action and organization. The selections broadly reflect the ideas within the International as a whole, including not only those that are well known, but also less well-known positions put forward by Marx and his main opponents as well as ideas emanating from local sections and individual members.

Under "Labour", for example, there is an excerpt from the report of the committee on labour and capital that was presented to the Lausanne Congress of 1867. The report's authors were a Parisian bookbinder, a Swiss artisan, a Parisian weaver, a mechanic from Lyon, and a Parisian bronze worker. The excerpt focuses upon the effects of machinery, and in brief compass addresses both its great promise and the enormous problems it brings:

> The Committee acknowledges that, of all the means used to date, machinery is the most powerful to achieve the outcome we seek, namely the betterment of the material conditions of the working class; yet, to arrive at this end, it is of the utmost urgency that labour take hold of the means of production. . . . With the invention of machinery, the division of labour becomes necessary. . . . Unfortunately, in this way, all noble ambition in man has been annihilated and his liberty completely nullified as he passes into the condition of a machine, henceforth the property of the one who employs him and holds him in a state of complete dependence.

Also included in this section is a synopsis of an intervention by Marx on the subject of machinery at the 1868 GC meeting. As one might expect, the author of *Capital* made a number of important points, but the prior contribution from the committee of industrial workers stands up well even in direct comparison with Marx's comments. It is enlightening to see not only that the workers were up to the task, but that they recognized the importance of this issue and undertook to address it within the broader mandate of their committee. Workers' reports to other congresses make a similarly strong impression. All these reports were originally in French, and none has previously been translated into English.

One finds the same sorts of valuable documents in each section of the anthology. Under "Trade Unions and Strikes", there are texts from two articles that Marx wrote at the request of the GC (he was in fact nearly always called upon to present the public face of the International, though at his suggestion all public statements were always signed by all members of the GC). These articles, on the need to oppose strikebreakers and on the Belgian government's vicious massacre of workers, are not widely known, and they reflect an important aspect of Marx's ideas and political commitment. The remaining eight documents, however, are from reports and resolutions prepared by others, primarily workers, for the annual congresses, six of which have never previously appeared in English.

The real concerns of the members of the International, and the serious debates that they had over many basic issues of socialism, the advancement of class interests, and forms of political practice, emerge clearly from these documents. It is not only that there were important political differences from the start, and other, even more profound, differences that came to the fore over the life of the International. What is even more striking is the extent to which many of the positions being put forward, familiar to so many today, were being articulated more or less for the first time. Here is a record of the working class initially feeling its way through the issues that have since become central to socialism, trade unionism, anarchism, and social democratic reform.

Musto, in the Introduction, gives an excellent account of each of the major periods of the International, from a balanced but critical perspective. He is attentive to all the positions that co-existed within the IWA, treating each fairly and without partisanship. His acknowledgement of the important role played by Bakunin and his supporters is rare from someone who is so clearly himself a Marxist. Indeed, he goes further, to give serious consideration to the "autonomist" IWA established by the Bakuninists, which lasted for five years after the 1872 Hague Congress expelled Bakunin. Moreover, Musto treats this organization as part of the history of the IWA, rather than conceiving the International as having come to an end with the removal of the GC to New York. Such an approach could never have been taken by anyone associated with the Communist Parties of old. Even the "centralist" IWA, which survived in New York from 1872 to 1876, is incorporated as a part of the overall history. Documents from both these organizations which survived after the end of the London GC are included.

Musto also challenges the figures that have been put forward regarding the membership of the IWA, which has been hugely inflated by friend and foe alike. Tracking down numbers from the most reliable sources, he arrives at figures that are only one-half to as little as one-twentieth of previous estimates. This scrupulous attention to historical accuracy is evident throughout the book, as is Musto's even-handedness. One can be confident that his account of the IWA's struggles – and of the ideas of its central protagonists – is reliable.

Notes provide information for each of the excerpts and their authors. The bibliography lists all the reports from the congresses and conferences that were published by the IWA at the time, as well as the collections of original documents that were primarily published in the 1960s and 1970s. There is also a comprehensive listing of the major secondary works, not only in English, but also in French, German, Italian and Spanish. Finally, included as an appendix are the lyrics to the workers' anthem, *The Internationale*.

219

The last time that the First International received much attention was in 1964, in conjunction with its 100th anniversary. Much of what has been written in the past reflected political and academic positions associated with the Cold War, and the world has of course changed enormously since the mid-1960s. Not only is this anthology unique (one would have to access more than 10 volumes, several in French, and none readily available outside research libraries, to read the material otherwise); it has been put together with present-day concerns in mind, as men and women from 150 years ago speak to us today in all their diversity.

What do they say? We can read, from 1867, the assertion that work is the main expression of human destiny in the modern age, displacing the role of religion, and that it is for this reason that women should have every right to fully and freely engage in the world of work – with maternity leave among the means to make this feasible. We read calls from the workers of one nation to those of another to respect an ongoing strike – a call which is successful and leads to victory. We read Bakunin arguing, despite his opposition to the state in every form, that the state should outlaw inheritance, with Marx responding that this is surely to put the cart before the horse, and that what needs to be abolished is the power of capital, after which inheritance is hardly an issue at all. We read Marx discussing the strengths and weaknesses of the systems of public education in some American states, asserting the importance of the American war against slavery as ushering in a new era of the rights of labour, and maintaining the crucial novelty of the International itself as an organization founded by workers and built through their own efforts to become a force for them "to emancipate themselves". We read the American General Secretary in New York putting forward the view that "When, upon its birth, bourgeois society solemnly proclaimed 'the freedom of the individual,' a new slavery of the working classes resulted from this principle."

Much in this anthology is surprising, some of it is moving, and all of it is valuable. If you have ever been stirred by *The Internationale*, this book is for you. Yet, aside from those with a strong commitment to either Marxism or anarchism, and those for whom the history of the working class is deeply important, this book will be useful to anyone with an interest in the actual practice of politics, and especially the relationship between grassroots activism on the one hand and visionary leadership on the other.

© 2014 George C. Comninel
York University, Toronto

Index

For Product Safety Concerns and Information please contact our
EU representative GPSR@taylorandfrancis.com Taylor & Francis
Verlag GmbH, Kaufingerstraße 24, 80331 München, Germany.